28

Famous Myths and Legends

Young Reader's Library

Famous Myths and Legends

Edited by Thomas J. Shahan

Originally published as *The Book of Famous Myths and Legends*

DERRYDALE BOOKS
NEW YORK

This 1991 edition is published by Derrydale Books, distributed by
Outlet Book Company, Inc., a Random House Company, 225 Park Avenue
South, New York, New York 10003.

Printed and bound in the United States of America

Library of Congress Cataloging-in-Publication Data

Book of famous myths and legends.
    Famous myths and legends / edited by Thomas J. Shahan.
       p.   cm.—(Young reader's library)
    Reprint. Originally published: A book of famous myths and legends.
  Boston : Hall and Locke, 1902. (Young folk's library)
    Summary: A collection of thirty-six tales of gods, heroes, and monsters,
  retold from famous myths and legends of the world.
    ISBN 0-517-03762-9
    1. Mythology—Juvenile literature.   2. Legends—Juvenile literature.
  [1. Mythology.] I. Shahan, Thomas J. (Thomas Joseph), 1857-1932. II. Title.
III. Series.
BL311.B66   1991
398.2—dc20   90-14025
                                         CIP
                                         AC

8 7 6 5 4 3 2 1

CONTENTS

PAGE

FOREWORD vii

THE OLDEST STORIES OF THE WORLD ix
BY T. J. SHAHAN.

THE GOLDEN TOUCH 1
BY NATHANIEL HAWTHORNE.

THE PARADISE OF CHILDREN 23
BY NATHANIEL HAWTHORNE.

THE THREE GOLDEN APPLES 44
BY NATHANIEL HAWTHORNE.

THE MIRACULOUS PITCHER 69
BY NATHANIEL HAWTHORNE.

THE ARGONAUTS.
BY CHARLES KINGSLEY.
    I. HOW THE CENTAUR TRAINED THE HEROES 93
    II. HOW JASON LOST HIS SANDAL 103
    III. HOW THEY BUILT THE SHIP 113
    IV. HOW THE ARGONAUTS SAILED 118
    V. IN THE UNKNOWN SEA 144
    VI. THE END OF THE HEROES 170

THE ODYSSEY; OR, THE ADVENTURES OF ULYSSES.
BY ALFRED J. CHURCH.
    I. THE CYCLOPS 174
    II. ÆOLUS—CIRCE 186
    III. THE REGIONS OF THE DEAD, SCYLLA, AND CALYPSO . . 194
    IV. TELEMACHUS AND PENELOPE 201
    V. NESTOR AND MENELAUS 207
    VI. ULYSSES ON HIS RAFT 217
    VII. NAUSICAA AND ALCINOUS 223
    VIII. ULYSSES AND THE SWINEHERD 234
    IX. THE RETURN OF TELEMACHUS 241
    X. ULYSSES IN HIS HOME 247
    XI. THE TRIAL OF THE BOW 256
    XII. THE SLAYING OF THE SUITORS 262

vi Contents

PAGE

KING ARTHUR AND THE KNIGHTS OF THE ROUND TABLE.

    I. SIR GARETH'S TRIAL 268
    II. GARETH AND LYNETTE 278
    III. LAUNCELOT AND ELAINE 288
    IV. GERAINT AND ENID 293
    V. DEATH OF KING ARTHUR 304

CHILDE HORN 314

THE STORY OF BEOWULF.

    I. GRENDEL THE MONSTER 335
    II. THE WATER–WITCH 341
    III. THE DRAGON'S HOARD 346

RIP VAN WINKLE 350
    BY WASHINGTON IRVING.

SELECTIONS FROM OSSIAN.

    CATH–LODA, A TALE OF THE TIMES OF OLD 372
    THE WAR OF INIS–THONA 377
    CARTHON; A POEM 383
    A WAR TALE 387

FOREWORD

The Young Reader's Library offers reprint editions of selected volumes from a classic series of children's books originally published at the turn of the century.

Famous Myths and Legends presents thirty-six tales of the great gods and heroes, retold from the famous myths and legends of the world and suitable for reading out loud or alone.

Here are such classic stories as Pandora's box, the legend of King Midas and the golden touch, Odysseus and the Cyclops, and Jason and the golden fleece—as well as selected tales of King Arthur and the knights of the Round Table, Beowolf, and the legend of Rip Van Winkle.

These timeless and immortal tales are always delightful and enchanting, yet they are also an important element of our cultural heritage. *Famous Myths and Legends* offers an easy-to-read, illustrated introduction to some of the greatest stories of all time—filled with hours of entertainment for all generations.

LOIS HILL

New York
1991

THE

OLDEST STORIES OF THE WORLD

BY

T. J. SHAHAN.

———

AGES ago, when the world was young, people did not know as much of nature and its secrets as we do now. Moreover, they did not have the art of writing, or if known to them, it was used only by a few, and its value for handing down the facts of history was not clearly understood. Thus, two great fields of knowledge, the world of nature and the world of history, were known only in a dim and vague way. Yet men and women were even then anxious to find out the causes of what they saw about them in nature, as well as to know whence and how they came to their native lands, through what journeys and labors, who were their ancient leaders in war, the builders of their cities, the founders of their laws and customs, and the like.

These are some of the causes of the growth of what we call Myths and Legends. Myths are attempts of early man to explain the great wonders of our daily life — the blue heavens above us, the light and the darkness, the bright fire, the swift wind, the rolling waters, the clouds, and the earth, and the dark world of things that lie beneath its green breast. Myths are only the ideas of men about the causes of those natural things which do not now seem wonders to us. There are yet many secrets in nature that escape the skill of all teachers. How many must there have been when the first man and woman looked out on the marvels of land and sea, heaven and earth, day and night, the seasons and their changes!

Myths have always been told among men. The most lovely and humane are those of the Greek people; for instance, the Myth of Psyche, which is all about the human soul. From the Greeks, by many ways, most of our Myths have come down to us. But mankind makes up these Myths forever; even to-day we find such "stories" in all parts of the world. The Red Men had and have yet many Myths. So, too, have the Bushmen and the natives of the South Sea Islands. In the pretty stories that the Micmacs of Nova Scotia tell about their god and good friend, Glooscap, we can see how peoples of a simple mind, with a weak training, could invent tales that do not differ from the best Greek stories, except in their ruder language and coarser form. It is as if we looked at the raw wool being fed to the loom and then saw the finished fabric in all its beauty.

If Myths are so old, how have they come down to us, and how have they gotten into the forms we now see? Many learned men have written on this subject, but they do not agree. Some think that Myths are twisted fragments of divine truths that the Creator first made known to mankind. Others believe that they are owing to the decay, the wear and tear of an ancient tongue once spoken in the far East, by the men from whom most of us in this land descend. Still others maintain that all Myths are the product of a low state of the savage mind, and that this is seen in certain bad and cruel traits that yet cling even to the finest of them. How closely akin are the chief Myths of the world may be seen from the stories that were made up very early about fire, its uses and dangers. Thus, it is the same idea which is the core of the stories about Agni, the God of Fire in India, and Vesta, the Goddess of the Common Hearth at Rome; about Vulcan, the Roman God of Ironsmiths, and the Greek Prometheus (or Forethought) who stole fire from heaven for the good of mankind.

Legends, on the other hand, deal with real actions of men and women. They always have some grains of truth in them, some facts that have become twisted in the mind of the story-teller; for legends are only "stories" told by some person for his own pleasure and that of others, or because it was his office to talk or sing about the past when his friends and neighbors met in order to provide for the common weal, or to worship God, or the powers that they loved or feared as their Gods.

Legends are like the vines and tendrils that grow up about a tree. These sometimes hide its strength and cause its death, but they also lend to it a great and varied charm of color and outline. So Legends sometimes take the place of the real facts of history, but usually only add to them some touch of pathos or tender human interest. To-day trained judgment has pruned away many old Legends from the great trunk of history. In this cleansing process, however, we have learned that Legends, like Myths, have their uses; that they are often symbols of deep truths that were once known to all, but in time became changed into new shapes, often through ignorance and bad passions of the heart and mind.

Myths and Legends grow up sometimes on the same spot, and about the same names. Thus the Romance of King Arthur may be a great Myth told about the Sun, and as true as the story of the Four and Twenty Blackbirds. Its many Legends may be no more worthy of belief than the tales about Jack the Giant Killer, or the Twelve Labors of Hercules. The bards and the minstrels of the Middle Ages through whom come down many such old stories, were not very choice in their treatment of them. They were more anxious to please and surprise than to narrate true history. We must be cautious, therefore, in dealing with old Myths and Legends; they are the stories of peoples and races less refined than we are; but in all these stories they have left some traces of their thoughts, their hopes, their fancies, their faiths and even their sorrows of mind and body.

The study of the old beliefs, old customs, old memories that have thus floated down among the simple, remote and unlearned peoples of the world reveals much history that would else be unknown — the history of the mind of man and its inner secret workings. In certain early stages of human society the great forces of nature seemed to unlearned men like real persons, with a will and a mind. They could hear, reason, show kindness or do much evil, it was thought. So, too, the world of animals seemed endowed with human sense and gifts. The trees and rivers had their sprites, or " spirits," that dwelled also in the lakes and mountains. In the legends of the saints many pretty stories are told of the elves, dragons or "worms," and serpents that long ago seemed to haunt all the lonely springs and the wild fens, all the hill-caves, the forest glens, and the sedgy marshes. By a careful study of these Myths and Legends we learn no little about the first far-away homes, faith, habits, the customs of war and peace, the common daily life, of the old peoples from whom most of us draw our descent.

Without some knowledge of Myths and Legends we

shall not enjoy keenly the beauties of our own tongue. As the English language is soaked with the spirit and temper of the Bible because of the countless words and phrases borrowed from it, so it is filled with other words and phrases borrowed from the Myths and Legends of many peoples. To be a perfect scholar in all that pertains to the English language requires a knowledge of such Myths and Legends as are most famous. Thus, the great poet Milton cannot be truly our delight unless we know something of the many old "stories" that he has worked into his great poems, always with a meaning. This is, to say the least, equally true of Shakespeare, whose plays abound with Myths and Legends that he has painted in such perfect words that they will never die while the poet's book is read.

Many ancient Myths had deep moral meanings. The dangers of Scylla and Charybdis, the evil tempting of the Sirens, the pleasures of the island of Calypso, the fire stolen from the gods by Prometheus, the Titans stricken by lightning, the story of Dionysos or Bacchus, the Blessed Fields, the Happy Islands, the Dark Under-World, had once a real moral warning attached to them. In the same way the stories of Tannhäuser, of Gudrun, Roland, Olger the Dane, Havelok, and many stories of the Arthur-Romance, like the tale of Guenevere and Launcelot, had a moral purpose in them; so that the hearer might shape his conduct according to the lesson told or sung in the tale.

Much knowledge of nature was conveyed to young and old by means of Myths and Legends. Thus the Norse peoples tell the story of Big Bird Dan, a boat that goes of itself, if you only say "Boat, boat, go on." It is the same story that the Greek minstrels sang more than three thousand years ago about the wonderful ships of the good king Alcinous. In the Odyssey of Homer it is told how they could speak and hear, and went their way without any human help. In both stories are meant the self-moving clouds that go always straight to their mark across the blue seas of heaven. Similarly, the movements and aspects of the Sun were given each some striking name, that expressed the endless uses and charms of the orb of day. His conflict with darkness and cold explains many of the fabulous conflicts of bright heroes with dark demons and monsters, ending in the rescue of some lovely maiden. Sometimes such Myths remained tame and uncouth; sometimes they are "touched by the highest human genius," and are thenceforth counted among the rarest gems of the human mind. But always they acted as a helpful schooling for whole peoples and races, and epochs of time, when such ways of forming the mind were the only ones known, or at least, were the most popular.

Thomas J. Shahan

THE GOLDEN TOUCH

By NATHANIEL HAWTHORNE.

ONCE upon a time, there lived a very rich man, and a king besides, whose name was Midas; and he had a little daughter, whom nobody but myself ever heard of, and whose name I either never knew, or have entirely forgotten. So, because I love odd names for little girls, I choose to call her Marygold. This King Midas was fonder of gold than of anything else in the world. He valued his royal crown chiefly because it was composed of that precious metal. If he loved anything better, or half so well, it was the one little maiden who played so merrily around her father's footstool. But the more Midas loved his daughter, the more did he desire and seek for wealth. He thought, foolish man! that the best thing he could possibly do for this dear child would be to bequeath her the immensest pile of yellow, glistening coin, that had ever been heaped together since the world was made. Thus, he gave all his thoughts and all his time to this one purpose. If ever he happened to gaze for an in-

1

stant at the gold-tinted clouds of sunset, he wished that they were real gold, and that they could be squeezed safely into his strong box. When little Marygold ran to meet him, with a bunch of buttercups and dande- lions, he used to say, "Poh, poh, child! If these flowers were as golden as they look, they would be worth the plucking!"

And yet, in his earlier days, before he was so en- tirely possessed of this insane desire for riches, King Midas had shown a great taste for flowers. He had planted a garden, in which grew the biggest and beau- tifullest and sweetest roses that any mortal ever saw or smelt. These roses were still growing in the garden, as large, as lovely, and as fragrant, as when Midas used to pass whole hours in gazing at them, and inhaling their perfume. But now, if he looked at them at all, it was only to calculate how much the garden would be worth if each of the innumerable rose-petals were a thin plate of gold. And though he once was fond of music (in spite of an idle story about his ears, which were said to resemble those of an ass), the only music for poor Midas, now, was the chink of one coin against another.

At length (as people always grow more and more foolish, unless they take care to grow wiser and wiser), Midas had got to be so exceedingly unreasonable, that he could scarcely bear to see or touch any object that was not gold. He made it his custom, therefore, to pass a large portion of every day in a dark and dreary apartment, under ground, at the basement of his palace. It was here that he kept his wealth. To this dismal hole — for it was little better than a dungeon — Midas betook himself, whenever he wanted to be particularly happy. Here, after carefully locking the door, he would take a bag of gold coin, or a gold cup as big as a wash-bowl, or a heavy golden bar, or a peck-measure of gold dust, and bring them from the obscure corners of the room into the one bright and narrow sunbeam that fell from the dungeon-like window. He valued the sunbeam for no other reason but that his treasure would not shine without its help. And then would he reckon over the coins in the bag; toss up the bar, and catch it as it came down; sift the gold-dust through his fingers; look at the funny image of his own face, as reflected in the burnished circumference of the cup; and whisper to himself, "O Midas, rich King Midas, what a happy man art thou!" But it was laughable to see how the image of his face kept grinning at him, out of the polished surface of the cup. It seemed to be aware of his foolish behavior, and to have a naughty inclination to make fun of him.

Midas called himself a happy man, but felt that he was not yet quite so happy as he might be. The very tiptop of enjoyment would never be reached, unless the whole world were to become his treasure-room, and be filled with yellow metal which should be all his own.

Now, I need hardly remind such wise little people as you are, that in the old, old times, when King Midas was alive, a great many things came to pass, which we should consider wonderful if they were to happen in our own day and country. And, on the other hand, a great many things take place nowadays, which seem not only wonderful to us, but at which the people of old times would have stared their eyes out. On the whole, I regard our own times as the strangest of the two ; but, however that may be, I must go on with my story.

Midas was enjoying himself in his treasure-room, one day, as usual, when he perceived a shadow fall over the heaps of gold; and, looking suddenly up, what should he behold but the figure of a stranger, standing in the bright and narrow sunbeam ! It was a young man, with a cheerful and ruddy face. Whether it was that the imagination of King Midas threw a yellow tinge over everything, or whatever the cause might be, he could not help fancying that the smile with which the stranger regarded him had a kind of golden radiance in it. Certainly, although his figure intercepted the sunshine, there was now a brighter gleam upon all the piled-up treasures than before. Even the remotest corners had their share of it, and were lighted up, when the stranger smiled, as with tips of flame and sparkles of fire.

As Midas knew that he had carefully turned the key in the lock, and that no mortal strength could possibly break into his treasure-room, he, of course, concluded that his visitor must be something more than mortal. It is no matter about telling you who he was. In those days, when the earth was comparatively a new affair, it was supposed to be often the resort of beings endowed with supernatural power, and who used to interest themselves in the joys and sorrows of men, women, and children, half playfully and half seriously. Midas had met such beings before now, and was not sorry to meet one of them again. The stranger's aspect, indeed, was so good-humored and kindly, if not beneficent, that it would have been unreasonable to suspect him of intending any mischief. It was far more probable that he came to do Midas a favor. And what could that favor be, unless to multiply his heaps of treasure?

The stranger gazed about the room; and when his lustrous smile had glistened upon all the golden objects that were there, he turned again to Midas.

"You are a wealthy man, friend Midas!" he observed. "I doubt whether any other four walls on earth contain so much gold as you have contrived to pile up in this room."

"I have done pretty well, — pretty well," answered Midas, in a discontented tone. "But, after all, it is but a trifle, when you consider that it has taken me my whole life to get it together. If one could live a thousand years, he might have time to grow rich!"

"What!" exclaimed the stranger. "Then you are not satisfied?"

Midas shook his head.

"And pray what would satisfy you?" asked the stranger. "Merely for the curiosity of the thing, I should be glad to know."

Midas paused and meditated. He felt a presentiment that this stranger, with such a golden lustre in his good-humored smile, had come hither with both the power and the purpose of gratifying his utmost wishes. Now, therefore, was the fortunate moment, when he had but to speak, and obtain whatever possible, or seemingly impossible thing, it might come into his head to ask. So he thought, and thought, and thought, and heaped up one golden mountain upon another, in his imagination, without being able to imagine them big enough. At last, a bright idea occurred to King Midas. It seemed really as bright as the glistening metal which he loved so much.

Raising his head, he looked the lustrous stranger in the face.

"Well, Midas," observed his visitor, "I see that you have at length hit upon something that will satisfy you. Tell me your wish."

"It is only this," replied Midas. "I am weary of collecting my treasures with so much trouble, and beholding the heap so diminutive, after I have done my best. I wish everything that I touch to be changed to gold!"

The stranger's smile grew so very broad, that it seemed to fill the room like an outburst of the sun, gleaming into the shadowy dell, where the yellow autumnal leaves — for so looked the lumps and particles of gold — lie strewn in the glow of light.

"The Golden Touch!" exclaimed he. "You certainly deserve credit, friend Midas, for striking out so brilliant a conception. But are you quite sure that this will satisfy you?"

"How could it fail?" said Midas.

"And will you never regret the possession of it?"

"What could induce me?" asked Midas. "I ask nothing else, to render me perfectly happy."

"Be it as you wish, then," replied the stranger, waving his hand in token of farewell. "To-morrow, at sunrise, you will find yourself gifted with the Golden Touch."

The figure of the stranger then became exceedingly

bright, and Midas involuntarily closed his eyes. On opening them again, he beheld only one yellow sunbeam in the room, and, all around him, the glistening of the metal which he had spent his life in hoarding up.

Whether Midas slept as usual that night, the story does not say. Asleep or awake, however, his mind was probably in the state of a child's, to whom a beautiful new plaything has been promised in the morning. At any rate, day had hardly peeped over the hills, when King Midas was broad awake, and, stretching his arms out of bed, began to touch the objects that were within reach. He was anxious to prove whether the Golden Touch had really come, according to the stranger's promise. So he laid his finger on a chair by the bedside, and on various other things, but was grievously disappointed to perceive that they remained of exactly the same substance as before. Indeed, he felt very much afraid that he had only dreamed about the lustrous stranger, or else that the latter had been making game of him. And what a miserable affair would it be, if, after all his hopes, Midas must content himself with what little gold he could scrape together by ordinary means, instead of creating it by a touch!

All this while, it was only the gray of the morning, with but a streak of brightness along the edge of the sky, where Midas could not see it. He lay in a very disconsolate mood, regretting the downfall of his hopes, and kept growing sadder and sadder, until the earliest sunbeam shone through the window, and gilded the ceiling over his head. It seemed to Midas that this bright yellow sunbeam was reflected in rather a singu-

lar way on the white covering of the bed. Looking
more closely, what was his astonishment and delight,
when he found that this linen fabric had been transmuted to what seemed a woven texture of the purest
and brightest gold! The Golden Touch had come to
him with the first sunbeam!

Midas started up, in a kind of joyful frenzy, and
ran about the room, grasping at everything that
happened to be in his way. He seized one of the bed-
posts, and it became immediately a fluted golden pillar.
He pulled aside a window-curtain, in order to admit a
clear spectacle of the wonders which he was performing; and the tassel grew heavy in his hand, — a mass
of gold. He took up a book from the table. At his first
touch it assumed the appearance of such a splendidly
bound and gilt-edged volume as one often meets with,
nowadays; but, on running his fingers through the
leaves, behold! it was a bundle of thin golden plates,
in which all the wisdom of the book had grown illegi-
ble. He hurriedly put on his clothes, and was enrap-
tured to see himself in a magnificent suit of gold cloth,
which retained its flexibility and softness, although it
burdened him a little with its weight. He drew out
his handkerchief, which little Marygold had hemmed
for him. That was likewise gold, with the dear child's
neat and pretty stitches running all along the border,
in gold thread!

Somehow or other, this last transformation did not
quite please King Midas. He would rather that his
little daughter's handiwork should have remained just
the same as when she climbed his knee and put it into
his hand.

But it was not worth while to vex himself about a trifle. Midas now took his spectacles from his pocket, and put them on his nose, in order that he might see more distinctly what he was about. In those days, spectacles for common people had not been invented, but were already worn by kings; else, how could Midas have had any? to his great perplexity, however, excellent as the glasses were, he discovered that he could not possibly see through them. But this was the most natural thing in the world; for, on taking them off, the transparent crystals turned out to be plates of yellow metal, and, of course, were worthless as spectacles, though valuable as gold. It struck Midas as rather inconvenient, that, with all his wealth, he could never again be rich enough to own a pair of serviceable spectacles.

"It is no great matter, nevertheless," said he to himself, very philosophically. "We cannot expect any great good, without its being accompanied with some small inconvenience. The Golden Touch is worth the sacrifice of a pair of spectacles, at least, if not of one's very eyesight. My own eyes will serve for ordinary purposes, and little Marygold will soon be old enough to read to me."

Wise King Midas was so exalted by his good fortune, that the palace seemed not sufficiently spacious to contain him. He therefore went down-stairs, and smiled, on observing that the balustrade of the staircase became a bar of burnished gold, as his hand passed over it, in his descent. He lifted the door-latch (it was brass only a moment ago, but golden when his fingers quitted it) and emerged into the gar-

den. Here, as it happened, he found a great number
of beautiful roses in full bloom, and others in all the
stages of lovely bud and blossom. Very delicious was
their fragrance in the morning breeze. Their delicate
blush was one of the fairest sights in the world; so
gentle, so modest, and so full of sweet tranquillity, did
these roses seem to be.

But Midas knew a way to make them far more
precious, according to his way of thinking, than roses
had ever been before. So he took great pains in going
from bush to bush, and exercised his magic touch most
indefatigably; until every individual flower and bud,
and even the worms at the heart of some of them, were
changed to gold. By the time this good work was
completed, King Midas was summoned to breakfast;
and as the morning air had given him an excellent appetite, he made haste back to the palace.

What was usually a king's breakfast in the days of
Midas, I really do not know, and cannot stop now to
investigate. To the best of my belief, however, on this
particular morning, the breakfast consisted of hot
cakes, some nice little brook-trout, roasted potatoes,
fresh boiled eggs, and coffee, for King Midas himself,
and a bowl of bread and milk for his daughter Marygold. At all events, this is a breakfast fit to set before
a king; and, whether he had it or not, King Midas
could not have had a better.

Little Marygold had not yet made her appearance.
Her father ordered her to be called, and, seating himself at table, awaited the child's coming, in order to
begin his own breakfast. To do Midas justice he

really loved his daughter, and loved her so much the more this morning on account of the good fortune which had befallen him. It was not a great while before he heard her coming along the passageway crying bitterly. This circumstance surprised him, because Marygold was one of the cheerfulest little people whom you would see in a summer's day, and hardly shed a thimbleful of tears in a twelvemonth. When Midas heard her sobs, he determined to put little Marygold into better spirits, by an agreeable surprise; so, leaning across the table, he touched his daughter's bowl (which was a China one, with pretty figures all around it), and transmuted it to gleaming gold.

Meanwhile, Marygold slowly and disconsolately opened the door, and showed herself with her apron at her eyes, still sobbing as if her heart would break.

"How now, my little lady!" cried Midas. "Pray what is the matter with you, this bright morning?"

Marygold, without taking the apron from her eyes, held out her hand, in which was one of the roses which Midas had so recently transmuted.

"Beautiful!" exclaimed her father. "And what is there in this magnificent golden rose to make you cry?"

"Ah, dear father!" answered the child, as well as her sobs would let her; "it is not beautiful, but the ugliest flower that ever grew! As soon as I was dressed I ran into the garden to gather some roses for you; because I know you like them, and like them the better when gathered by your little daughter. But, oh dear, dear me! What do you think has happened? Such a misfortune! All the beautiful roses, that smelled so

sweetly and had so many lovely blushes, are blighted
and spoilt! They are grown quite yellow, as you see
this one, and have no longer any fragrance! What
can have been the matter with them?"

"Poh, my dear little girl, — pray don't cry about
it!" said Midas, who was ashamed to confess that he
himself had wrought the change which so greatly
afflicted her. "Sit down and eat your bread and
milk!" You will find it easy enough to exchange a
golden rose like that (which will last hundreds of
years) for an ordinary one which would wither in a
day."

"I don't care for such roses as this!" cried Marygold,
tossing it contemptuously away. "It has no smell, and
the hard petals prick my nose!"

The child now sat down to table, but was so oc-
cupied with her grief for the blighted roses that she
did not even notice the wonderful transmutation of her
China bowl. Perhaps this was all the better; for
Marygold was accustomed to take pleasure in looking
at the queer figures, and strange trees and houses, that
were painted on the circumference of the bowl; and
these ornaments were now entirely lost in the yellow
hue of the metal.

Midas, meanwhile, had poured out a cup of coffee,
and, as a matter of course, the coffee-pot, whatever
metal it may have been when he took it up, was gold
when he set it down. He thought to himself, that it
was rather an extravagant style of splendor, in a king
of his simple habits, to breakfast off a service of gold,
and began to be puzzled with the difficulty of keeping
his treasures safe. The cupboard and the kitchen

would no longer be a secure place of deposit for articles so valuable as golden bowls and coffee-pots.

Amid these thoughts, he lifted a spoonful of coffee to his lips, and, sipping it, was astonished to perceive that, the instant his lips touched the liquid, it became molten gold, and, the next moment, hardened into a lump!

"Ha!" exclaimed Midas, rather aghast.

"What is the matter, father?" asked little Marygold, gazing at him, with the tears still standing in her eyes.

"Nothing, child, nothing!" said Midas. "Eat your milk, before it gets quite cold."

He took one of the nice little trouts on his plate, and, by way of experiment, touched its tail with his finger. To his horror, it was immediately transmuted from an admirably fried brook-trout into a goldfish, though not one of those gold-fishes which people often keep in glass globes, as ornaments for the parlor. No; but it was really a metallic fish, and looked as if it had been very cunningly made by the nicest goldsmith in the world. Its little bones were now golden wires; its fins and tail were thin plates of gold; and there were the marks of the fork in it, and all the delicate, frothy appearance of a nicely fried fish, exactly imitated in metal. A very pretty piece of work, as you may suppose; only King Midas, just at that moment, would much rather have had a real trout in his dish than this elaborate and valuable imitation of one.

"I don't quite see," thought he to himself, "how I am to get any breakfast!"

He took one of the smoking-hot cakes, and had

scarcely broken it, when, to his cruel mortification, though, a moment before, it had been of the whitest wheat, it assumed the yellow hue of Indian meal. To say the truth, if it had really been a hot Indian cake, Midas would have prized it a good deal more than he now did, when its solidity and increased weight made him too bitterly sensible that it was gold. Almost in despair, he helped himself to a boiled egg, which immediately underwent a change similar to those of the trout and the cake. The egg, indeed, might have been mistaken for one of those which the famous goose, in the story-book, was in the habit of laying; but King Midas was the only goose that had had anything to do with the matter.

"Well, this is a quandary!" thought he, leaning back in his chair, and looking quite enviously at little Marygold, who was now eating her bread and milk with great satisfaction. "Such a costly breakfast before me, and nothing that can be eaten!"

Hoping that, by dint of great despatch, he might avoid what he now felt to be a considerable inconvenience, King Midas next snatched a hot potato, and attempted to cram it into his mouth, and swallow it in a hurry. But the Golden Touch was too nimble for him. He found his mouth full, not of mealy potato, but of solid metal, which so burnt his tongue that he roared aloud, and, jumping up from the table, began to dance and stamp about the room, both with pain and affright.

"Father, dear father!" cried little Marygold, who was a very affectionate child, "pray what is the matter? Have you burnt your mouth?"

"Ah, dear child," groaned Midas, dolefully, "I don't know what is to become of your poor father!"

And, truly, my dear little folks, did you ever hear of such a pitiable case in all your lives? Here was literally the richest breakfast that could be set before a king, and its very richness made it absolutely good for nothing. The poorest laborer, sitting down to his crust of bread and cup of water, was far better off than King Midas, whose delicate food was really worth its weight in gold. And what was to be done? Already, at breakfast, Midas was excessively hungry. Would he be less so by dinner-time? And how ravenous would be his appetite for supper, which must undoubtedly consist of the same sort of indigestible dishes as those now before him! How many days, think you, would he survive a continuance of this rich fare?

These reflections so troubled wise King Midas, that he began to doubt whether, after all, riches are the one desirable thing in the world, or even the most desirable. But this was only a passing thought. So fascinated was Midas with the glitter of the yellow metal, that he would still have refused to give up the Golden Touch for so paltry a consideration as a breakfast. Just imagine what a price for one meal's victuals! It would have been the same as paying millions and millions of money (and as many millions more as would take forever to reckon up) for some fried trout, an egg, a potato, a hot cake, and a cup of coffee!

"It would be quite too dear," thought Midas.

Nevertheless, so great was his hunger, and the perplexity of his situation, that he again groaned aloud,

and very grievously too.   Our pretty Marygold could
endure it no longer.   She sat, a moment, gazing at her
father, and trying, with all the might of her little wits,
to find out what was the matter with him.   Then, with
a sweet and sorrowful impulse to comfort him, she
started from her chair, and, running to Midas, threw
her arms affectionately about his knees.   He bent down
and kissed her.   He felt that his little daughter's love
was worth a thousand times more than he had gained
by the Golden Touch.

"My precious, precious Marygold!" cried he.

But Marygold made no answer.

Alas, what had he done?   How fatal was the gift
which the stranger bestowed!   The moment the lips of
Midas touched Marygold's forehead, a change had taken
place.   Her sweet, rosy face, so full of affection as it
had been, assumed a glittering yellow color, with yellow
tear-drops congealing on her cheeks.   Her beautiful
brown ringlets took the same tint.   Her soft and tender
little form grew hard and inflexible within her father's
encircling arms.   Oh, terrible misfortune!   The victim of his insatiable desire for wealth, little Marygold, was a human child no longer, but a golden
statue!

Yes, there she was, with the questioning look of
love, grief, and pity, hardened into her face.   It was
the prettiest and most woful sight that ever mortal
saw.   All the features and tokens of Marygold were
there; even the beloved little dimple remained in her
golden chin.   But, the more perfect was the resem-
blance, the greater was the father's agony at beholding
this golden image, which was all that was left him of a

daughter. It had been a favorite phrase of Midas whenever he felt particularly fond of the child, to say that she was worth her weight in gold. And now the phrase had become literally true. And now, at last, when it was too late, he felt how infinitely a warm and tender heart, that loved him, exceeded in value all the wealth that could be piled up betwixt the earth and sky!

It would be too sad a story, if I were to tell you how Midas, in the fulness of all his gratified desires, began to wring his hands and bemoan himself; and how he could neither bear to look at Marygold, nor yet to look away from her. Except when his eyes were fixed on the image, he could not possibly believe that she was changed to gold. But, stealing another glance, there was the precious little figure, with a yellow tear-drop on its yellow cheek, and a look so piteous and tender, that it seemed as if that very expression must needs soften the gold, and make it flesh again. This, however, could not be. So Midas had only to wring his hands, and to wish that he were the poorest man in the wide world, if the loss of all his wealth might bring back the faintest rose-color to his dear child's face.

While he was in this tumult of despair, he suddenly beheld a stranger standing near the door. Midas bent down his head, without speaking; for he recognized the same figure which had appeared to him, the day before, in the treasure-room, and had bestowed on him this disastrous faculty of the Golden Touch. The stranger's countenance still wore a smile, which seemed to shed a yellow lustre all about the room, and gleamed on little Marygold's image, and on the other objects that had been transmuted by the touch of Midas.

" Well, friend Midas," said the stranger, " pray how do you succeed with the Golden Touch ? "

Midas shook his head.

" I am very miserable," said he.

" Very miserable, indeed ? " exclaimed the stranger. " And how happens that ? Have I not faithfully kept my promise with you ? Have you not everything that your heart desired ? "

" Gold is not everything," answered Midas. " And I have lost all that my heart really cared for."

" Ah ! So you have made a discovery, since yesterday ? " observed the stranger. " Let us see, then. Which of these two things do you think is really worth the most, — the gift of the Golden Touch, or one cup of clear cold water ? "

" O blessed water ! " exclaimed Midas. " It will never moisten my parched throat again ! "

" The Golden Touch," continued the stranger, " or a crust of bread ? "

" A piece of bread," answered Midas, " is worth all the gold on earth ! "

" The Golden Touch," asked the stranger, " or your own little Marygold, warm, soft, and loving as she was an hour ago ? "

" O my child, my dear child ! " cried poor Midas, wringing his hands. " I would not have given that one small dimple in her chin for the power of changing this whole big earth into a solid lump of gold ! "

" You are wiser than you were, King Midas ! " said

the stranger, looking seriously at him. "Your own heart, I perceive, has not been entirely changed from flesh to gold. Were it so, your case would indeed be desperate. But you appear to be still capable of understanding that the commonest things, such as lie within everybody's grasp, are more valuable than the riches which so many mortals sigh and struggle after. Tell me, now, do you sincerely desire to rid yourself of this Golden Touch?"

"It is hateful to me!" replied Midas.

A fly settled on his nose, but immediately fell to the floor; for it, too, had become gold. Midas shuddered.

"Go, then," said the stranger, "and plunge into the river that glides past the bottom of your garden. Take likewise a vase of the same water, and sprinkle it over any object that you may desire to change back again from gold into its former substance. If you do this in earnestness and sincerity, it may possibly repair the mischief which your avarice has occasioned."

King Midas bowed low; and when he lifted his head, the lustrous stranger had vanished.

You will easily believe that Midas lost no time in snatching up a great earthen pitcher (but, alas me! it was no longer earthen after he touched it), and hastening to the riverside. As he scampered along, and forced his way through the shrubbery, it was positively marvellous to see how the foliage turned yellow behind him, as if the autumn had been there, and nowhere else. On reaching the river's brink, he plunged headlong in without waiting so much as to pull off his shoes.

" Poof! poof! poof!" snorted King Midas, as his head emerged out of the water. " Well; this is really a refreshing bath, and I think it must have quite washed away the Golden Touch. And now for filling my pitcher!"

As he dipped the pitcher into the water, it gladdened his very heart to see it change from gold into the same good, honest earthen vessel which it had been before he touched it. He was conscious, also, of a change within himself. A cold, hard, and heavy weight seemed to have gone out of his bosom. No doubt, his heart had been gradually losing its human substance, and transmuting itself into insensible metal, but had now softened back again into flesh. Perceiving a violet, that grew on the bank of the river, Midas touched it with his finger, and was overjoyed to find that the delicate flower retained its purple hue, instead of undergoing a yellow blight. The curse of the Golden Touch had, therefore, really been removed from him.

King Midas hastened back to the palace; and, I suppose, the servants knew not what to make of it when they saw their royal master so carefully bringing home an earthen pitcher of water. But that water, which was to undo all the mischief that his folly had wrought, was more precious to Midas than an ocean of molten gold could have been. The first thing he did, as you need hardly be told, was to sprinkle it by handfuls over the golden figure of little Marygold.

No sooner did it fall on her than you would have laughed to see how the rosy color came back to the dear child's cheek! and how she began to sneeze and sputter! — and how astonished she was to find herself dripping wet, and her father still throwing more water over her!

"Pray, do not, dear father!" cried she. "See how you have wet my nice frock, which I put on only this morning!"

For Marygold did not know that she had been a little golden statue; nor could she remember anything that had happened since the moment when she ran with outstretched arms to comfort poor King Midas.

Her father did not think it necessary to tell his beloved child how very foolish he had been, but contented himself with showing how much wiser he had now grown. For this purpose, he led little Marygold into the garden, where he sprinkled all the remainder of the water over the rose-bushes, and with such good effect that above five thousand roses recovered their beautiful bloom. There were two circumstances, however, which, as long as he lived, used to put King Midas in mind of the Golden Touch. One was, that the sands of the river sparkled like gold; the other, that little Marygold's hair had now a golden tinge, which he had never observed in it before she had been transmuted by the effect of his kiss. This change of hue was really an improvement, and made Marygold's hair richer than in her babyhood.

When King Midas had grown quite an old man, and used to trot Marygold's children on his knee, he was fond of telling them this marvellous story, pretty much as I have now told it to you. And then would he stroke their glossy ringlets, and tell them that their hair, likewise, had a rich shade of gold, which they had inherited from their mother.

" And to tell you the truth, my precious little folks,"
quoth King Midas, diligently trotting the children all
the while, ever since that morning, " I have hated the
very sight of all other gold, save this ! "

THE PARADISE OF CHILDREN

By NATHANIEL HAWTHORNE.

LONG, long ago, when this old world was in its tender infancy, there was a child, named Epimetheus, who never had either father or mother; and, that he might not be lonely, another child, fatherless and motherless like himself, was sent from a far country, to live with him, and be his playfellow and helpmate. Her name was Pandora.

The first thing that Pandora saw, when she entered the cottage where Epimetheus dwelt, was a great box. And almost the first question which she put to him, after crossing the threshold, was this,—

"Epimetheus, what have you in that box?"

"My dear little Pandora," answered Epimetheus, "that is a secret, and you must be kind enough not to ask any questions about it. The box was left here to be kept safely, and I do not myself know what it contains."

"But who gave it to you?" asked Pandora. "And where did it come from?"

"That is a secret, too," replied Epimetheus.

"How provoking!" exclaimed Pandora, pouting her lip. "I wish the great ugly box were out of the way!"

"Oh come, don't think of it any more," cried Epimetheus. "Let us run out of doors, and have some nice play with the other children."

It is thousands of years since Epimetheus and Pandora were alive; and the world, nowadays, is a very different sort of thing from what it was in their time. Then, everybody was a child. There needed no fathers and mothers to take care of the children; because there was no danger, nor trouble of any kind, and no clothes to be mended, and there was always plenty to eat and drink. Whenever a child wanted his dinner, he found it growing on a tree; and, if he looked at the tree in the morning, he could see the expanding blossom of that night's supper; or, at eventide, he saw the tender bud of to-morrow's breakfast. It was a very pleasant life indeed. No labor to be done, no tasks to be studied; nothing but sports and dances, and sweet voices of children talking, or carolling like birds, or gushing out in merry laughter, throughout the livelong day.

What was most wonderful of all, the children never quarrelled among themselves; neither had they any crying fits; nor, since time first began, had a single one of these little mortals ever gone apart into a corner, and sulked. Oh, what a good time was that to be alive in! The truth is, those ugly little winged monsters, called Troubles, which are now almost as numerous as mosquitoes, had never yet been seen on the earth. It is probable that the very greatest disquietude which a child had ever experienced was Pandora's vexation at not being able to discover the secret of the mysterious box.

This was at first only the faint shadow of a Trouble; but, every day, it grew more and more substantial, until, before a great while, the cottage of Epimetheus and Pandora was less sunshiny than those of the other children.

"Whence can the box have come?" Pandora continually kept saying to herself and to Epimetheus. "And what in the world can be inside of it?"

"Always talking about this box!" said Epimetheus, at last; for he had grown extremely tired of the subject. "I wish, dear Pandora, you would try to talk of something else. Come, let us go and gather some ripe figs, and eat them under the trees, for our supper. And I know a vine that has the sweetest and juiciest grapes you ever tasted."

"Always talking about grapes and figs!" cried Pandora, pettishly.

"Well, then," said Epimetheus, who was a very good-tempered child, like a multitude of children in those days, "let us run out and have a merry time with our playmates."

"I am tired of merry times, and don't care if I never have any more!" answered our pettish little Pandora. "And, besides, I never do have any. This ugly box! I am so taken up with thinking about it all the time. I insist upon your telling me what is inside of it."

"As I have already said, fifty times over, I do not know!" replied Epimetheus, getting a little vexed. "How, then, can I tell you what is inside?"

"You might open it," said Pandora, looking sideways at Epimetheus, "and then we could see for ourselves."

"Pandora, what are you thinking of?" exclaimed Epimetheus.

And his face expressed so much horror at the idea of looking into a box, which had been confided to him on the condition of his never opening it, that Pandora thought it best not to suggest it any more. Still, however, she could not help thinking and talking about the box.

"At least," said she, "you can tell me how it came here."

"It was left at the door," replied Epimetheus, "just before you came, by a person who looked very smiling and intelligent, and who could hardly forbear laughing as he put it down. He was dressed in an odd kind of a cloak, and had on a cap that seemed to be made partly of feathers, so that it looked almost as if it had wings."

"What sort of a staff had he?" asked Pandora.

"Oh, the most curious staff you ever saw!" cried Epimetheus. "It was like two serpents twisting around a stick, and was carved so naturally that I, at first, thought the serpents were alive."

"I know him," said Pandora, thoughtfully. "Nobody else has such a staff. It was Quicksilver; and he brought me hither, as well as the box. No doubt he intended it for me; and, most probably, it contains pretty dresses for me to wear, or toys for you and me to play with, or something very nice for us both to eat!"

"Perhaps so," answered Epimetheus, turning away. "But until Quicksilver comes back and tells us so, we have neither of us any right to lift the lid of the box."

"What a dull boy he is!" muttered Pandora, as Epimetheus left the cottage. "I do wish he had a little more enterprise!"

For the first time since her arrival, Epimetheus had gone out without asking Pandora to accompany him. He went to gather figs and grapes by himself, or to seek whatever amusement he could find, in other society than his little playfellow's. He was tired to death of hearing about the box, and heartily wished that Quicksilver, or whatever was the messenger's name, had left it at some other child's door, where Pandora would never have set eyes on it. So perseveringly as she did babble about this one thing! The box, the box, and nothing but the box! It seemed as if the box were bewitched, and as if the cottage were not big enough to hold it, without Pandora's continually stumbling over it, and making Epimetheus stumble over it likewise, and bruising all four of their shins.

Well, it was really hard that poor Epimetheus should have a box in his ears from morning till night; especially as the little people of the earth were so unaccustomed to vexations, in those happy days, that they knew not how to deal with them. Thus, a small vexation made as much disturbance then as a far bigger one would in our own times.

After Epimetheus was gone, Pandora stood gazing at the box. She had called it ugly, above a hundred times; but, in spite of all that she had said against it, it was positively a very handsome article of furniture, and would have been quite an ornament to any room in which it should be placed. It was made of a beautiful kind of wood, with dark and rich veins spreading

over its surface, which was so highly polished that
little Pandora could see her face in it. As the child
had no other looking-glass, it is odd that she did not
value the box, merely on this account.

The edges and corners of the box were carved with
most wonderful skill. Around the margin there were
figures of graceful men and women, and the prettiest
children ever seen, reclining or sporting amid a pro-
fusion of flowers and foliage ; and these various objects
were so exquisitely represented, and were wrought
together in such harmony, that flowers, foliage, and
human beings seemed to combine into a wreath of
mingled beauty. But here and there, peeping forth
from behind the carved foliage, Pandora once or twice
fancied that she saw a face not so lovely, or something
or other that was disagreeable, and which stole the
beauty out of all the rest. Nevertheless, on looking
more closely, and touching the spot with her finger, she
could discover nothing of the kind. Some face, that
was really beautiful, had been made to look ugly by her
catching a sideway glimpse at it.

The most beautiful face of all was done in what is
called high relief, in the centre of the lid. There was
nothing else, save the dark, smooth richness of the
polished wood, and this one face in the centre, with a
garland of flowers about its brow. Pandora had looked
at this face a great many times, and imagined that the
mouth could smile if it liked, or be grave when it chose,
the same as any living mouth. The features, indeed,
all wore a very lively and rather mischievous expression, which looked almost as if it needs must burst out
of the carved lips, and utter itself in words.

Had the mouth spoken, it would probably have been something like this : ·

" Do not be afraid, Pandora ! What harm can there be in opening the box ? Never mind that poor, simple Epimetheus ! You are wiser than he, and have ten times as much spirit. Open the box, and see if you do not find something very pretty ! "

The box, I had almost forgotten to say, was fastened ; not by a lock, nor by any other such contrivance, but by a very intricate knot of gold cord. There appeared to be no end to this knot, and no beginning. Never was a knot so cunningly twisted, nor with so many ins and outs, which roguishly defied the skilfullest fingers to disentangle them. And yet, by the very difficulty that there was in it, Pandora was the more tempted to examine the knot, and just see how it was made. Two or three times, already, she had stooped over the box, and taken the knot between her thumb and forefinger, but without positively trying to undo it.

" I really believe," said she to herself, " that I begin to see how it was done. Nay, perhaps I could tie it up again, after undoing it. There would be no harm in that, surely. Even Epimetheus would not blame me for that. I need not open the box, and should not, of course, without the foolish boy's consent, even if the knot were untied."

It might have been better for Pandora if she had had a little work to do, or anything to employ her mind upon, so as not to be so constantly thinking of this one subject. But children led so easy a life, before any Troubles came into the world, that they had really a

great deal too much leisure.   They could not be forever
playing at hide-and-seek among the flower-shrubs, or at
blind-man's-buff with garlands over their eyes, or at
whatever other games had been found out, while Mother
Earth was in her babyhood.   When life is all sport, toil
is the real play.   There was absolutely nothing to do.
A little sweeping and dusting about the cottage, I suppose, and the gathering of fresh flowers (which were
only too abundant everywhere), and arranging them in
vases, — and poor little Pandora's day's work was over.
And then, for the rest of the day, there was the box.

After all, I am not quite sure that the box was not
a blessing to her in its way.   It supplied her with such
a variety of ideas to think of, and to talk about, whenever she had anybody to listen!   When she was in
good-humor, she could admire the bright polish of its
sides, and the rich border of beautiful faces and foliage
that ran all around it.   Or, if she chanced to be ill-
tempered, she could give it a push, or kick it with her
naughty little foot.   And many a kick did the box —
(but it was a mischievous box, as we shall see, and
deserved all it got) — many a kick did it receive.   But,
certain it is, if it had not been for the box, our active-
minded little Pandora would not have known half so
well how to spend her time as she now did.

For it was really an endless employment to guess
what was inside.   What could it be, indeed?   Just
imagine, my little hearers, how busy your wits would
be, if there were a great box in the house, which, as
you might have reason to suppose, contained something
new and pretty for your Christmas or New Year's
gifts.   Do you think that you should be less curious

than Pandora? If you were left alone with the box, might you not feel a little tempted to lift the lid? But you would not do it. Oh, fie! No, no! Only, if you thought there were toys in it, it would be so very hard to let slip an opportunity of taking just one peep! I know not whether Pandora expected any toys; for none had yet begun to be made, probably, in those days, when the world itself was one great plaything for the children that dwelt upon it. But Pandora was convinced that there was something very beautiful and valuable in the box; and therefore she felt just as anxious to take a peep as any of these little girls, here around me, would have felt. And, possibly, a little more so; but of that I am not quite so certain.

On this particular day, however, which we have so long been talking about, her curiosity grew so much greater than it usually was, that, at last, she approached the box. She was more than half determined to open it, if she could. Ah, naughty Pandora!

First, however, she tried to lift it. It was heavy; quite too heavy for the slender strength of a child, like Pandora. She raised one end of the box a few inches from the floor, and let it fall again, with a pretty loud thump. A moment afterwards, she almost fancied that she heard something stir inside of the box. She applied her ear as closely as possible, and listened. Positively, there did seem to be a kind of stifled murmur, within! Or was it merely the singing in Pandora's ears? Or could it be the beating of her heart? The child could not quite satisfy herself whether she had heard anything or no. But, at all events, her curiosity was stronger than ever.

As she drew back her head, her eyes fell upon the knot of gold cord.

"It must have been a very ingenious person who tied this knot," said Pandora to herself. "But I think I could untie it nevertheless. I am resolved, at least, to find the two ends of the cord."

So she took the golden knot in her fingers, and pried into its intricacies as sharply as she could. Almost without intending it, or quite knowing what she was about, she was soon busily engaged in attempting to undo it. Meanwhile, the bright sunshine came through the open window; as did likewise the merry voices of the children, playing at a distance, and perhaps the voice of Epimetheus among them. Pandora stopped to listen. What a beautiful day it was! Would it not be wiser, if she were to let the troublesome knot alone, and think no more about the box, but run and join her little playfellows, and be happy?

All this time, however, her fingers were half unconsciously busy with the knot; and happening to glance at the flower-wreathed face on the lid of the enchanted box, she seemed to perceive it slyly grinning at her.

"That face looks very mischievous," thought Pandora. "I wonder whether it smiles because I am doing wrong! I have the greatest mind in the world to run away!"

But just then, by the merest accident, she gave the knot a kind of a twist, which produced a wonderful result. The gold cord untwined itself, as if by magic, and left the box without a fastening.

"This is the strangest thing I ever knew!" said Pandora. "What will Epimetheus say? And how can I possibly tie it up again?"

She made one or two attempts to restore the knot, but soon found it quite beyond her skill. It had disentangled itself so suddenly that she could not in the least remember how the strings had been doubled into one another; and when she tried to recollect the shape and appearance of the knot, it seemed to have gone entirely out of her mind. Nothing was to be done, therefore, but to let the box remain as it was until Epimetheus should come in.

"But," said Pandora, "when he finds the knot untied, he will know that I have done it. How shall I make him believe that I have not looked into the box?"

And then the thought came into her naughty little heart, that since she would be suspected of having looked into the box, she might just as well do so at once. Oh, very naughty and very foolish Pandora! You should have thought only of doing what was right, and of leaving undone what was wrong, and not of what your playfellow Epimetheus would have said or believed. And so perhaps she might, if the enchanted face on the lid of the box had not looked so bewitchingly persuasive at her, and if she had not seemed to hear, more distinctly than before, the murmur of small voices within. She could not tell whether it was fancy or no; but there was quite a little tumult of whispers in her ear, — or else it was her curiosity that whispered, —

"Let us out, dear Pandora, — pray let us out! We will be such nice pretty playfellows for you! Only let us out!"

"What can it be?" thought Pandora. "Is there something alive in the box? Well!—yes!—I am resolved to take just one peep! Only one peep; and then the lid shall be shut down as safely as ever! There cannot possibly be any harm in just one little peep!"

But it is now time for us to see what Epimetheus was doing.

This was the first time, since his little playmate had come to dwell with him, that he had attempted to enjoy any pleasure in which she did not partake. But nothing went right; nor was he nearly so happy as on other days. He could not find a sweet grape or a ripe fig (if Epimetheus had a fault, it was a little too much fondness for figs); or, if ripe at all, they were over-ripe, and so sweet as to be cloying. There was no mirth in his heart, such as usually made his voice gush out, of its own accord, and swell the merriment of his companions. In short, he grew so uneasy and discontented, that the other children could not imagine what was the matter with Epimetheus. Neither did he himself know what ailed him, any better than they did. For you must recollect that, at the time we are speaking of, it was everybody's nature, and constant habit, to be happy. The world had not yet learned to be otherwise. Not a single soul or body, since these children were first sent to enjoy themselves on the beautiful earth, had ever been sick or out of sorts.

At length, discovering that, somehow or other, he put a stop to all the play, Epimetheus judged it best to go back to Pandora, who was in a humor better suited to his own. But, with a hope of giving her pleasure, he gathered some flowers, and made them into a wreath, which he meant to put upon her head. The flowers were very lovely, — roses, and lilies, and orange-blossoms, and a great many more, which left the trail of fragrance behind, as Epimetheus carried them along; and the wreath was put together with as much skill as could reasonably be expected of a boy. The fingers of little girls, it has always appeared to me, are the fittest to twine flower-wreaths; but boys could do it, in those days, rather better than they can now.

And here I must mention that a great black cloud had been gathering in the sky, for some time past, although it had not yet overspread the sun. But, just as Epimetheus reached the cottage door, this cloud began to intercept the sunshine, and thus to make a sudden and sad obscurity.

He entered softly; for he meant, if possible, to steal behind Pandora, and fling the wreath of flowers over her head, before she should be aware of his approach. But, as it happened, there was no need of his treading so very lightly. He might have trod as heavily as he pleased, — as heavily as a grown man, — as heavily, I was going to say, as an elephant, — without much probability of Pandora's hearing his footsteps. She was too intent upon her purpose. At the moment of his entering the cottage, the naughty child had put her hand to the lid, and was on the point of opening the mysterious box. Epimetheus beheld her. If he had cried out, Pandora would probably have withdrawn her hand, and the fatal mystery of the box might never have been known.

But Epimetheus himself, although he said very little about it, had his own share of curiosity to know what was inside. Perceiving that Pandora was resolved to find out the secret, he determined that his playfellow should not be the only wise person in the cottage. And if there were anything pretty or valuable in the box, he meant to take half of it to himself. Thus, after all his sage speeches to Pandora about restraining her curiosity, Epimetheus turned out to be quite as foolish, and nearly as much in fault, as she. So, whenever we blame Pandora for what happened, we must not forget to shake our heads at Epimetheus likewise.

As Pandora raised the lid, the cottage grew very dark and dismal; for the black cloud had now swept quite over the sun, and seemed to have buried it alive. There had, for a little while past, been a low growling and muttering which all at once broke into a heavy peal of thunder. But Pandora, heeding nothing of all this, lifted the lid nearly upright, and looked inside. It seemed as if a sudden swarm of winged creatures brushed past her, taking flight out of the box, while, at the same instant, she heard the voice of Epimetheus, with a lamentable tone, as if he were in pain.

"Oh, I am stung!" cried he. "I am stung! Naughty Pandora! why have you opened this wicked box?"

Pandora let fall the lid, and, starting up, looked about her, to see what had befallen Epimetheus. The thunder-cloud had so darkened the room that she could not very clearly discern what was in it. But she heard a disagreeable buzzing, as if a great many huge flies, or gigantic mosquitoes, or those insects which we call dor-

bugs, and pinching-dogs, were darting about. And, as
her eyes grew more accustomed to the imperfect light,
she saw a crowd of ugly little shapes, with bats' wings,
looking abominably spiteful, and armed with terribly
long stings in their tails. It was one of these that had
stung Epimetheus. Nor was it a great while before
Pandora herself began to scream, in no less pain and
affright than her playfellow, and making a vast deal
more hubbub about it. An odious little monster had
settled on her forehead, and would have stung her I
know not how deeply, if Epimetheus had not run and
brushed it away.

Now, if you wish to know what these ugly things
might be, which had made their escape out of the box,
I must tell you that they were the whole family of
earthly Troubles. There were evil Passions; there
were a great many species of Cares; there were more
than a hundred and fifty Sorrows; there were Diseases,
in a vast number of miserable and painful shapes; there
were more kinds of Naughtiness than it would be of
any use to talk about. In short, everything that has
since afflicted the souls and bodies of mankind had been
shut up in the mysterious box, and given to Epimetheus
and Pandora to be kept safely, in order that the happy
children of the world might never be molested by them.
Had they been faithful to their trust, all would have
gone well. No grown person would ever have been sad,
nor any child have had cause to shed a single tear, from
that hour until this moment.

But — and you may see by this how a wrong act of
any one mortal is a calamity to the whole world — by
Pandora's lifting the lid of that miserable box, and by

the fault of Epimetheus, too, in not preventing her, these Troubles have obtained a foothold among us, and do not seem very likely to be driven away in a hurry. For it was impossible, as you will easily guess, that the two children should keep the ugly swarm in their own little cottage. On the contrary, the first thing that they did was to fling open the doors and windows, in hopes of getting rid of them; and, sure enough, away flew the winged Troubles all abroad, and so pestered and tormented the small people, everywhere about, that none of them so much as smiled for many days afterwards. And, what was very singular, all the flowers and dewy blossoms on earth, not one of which had hitherto faded, now began to droop and shed their leaves, after a day or two. The children, moreover, who before seemed immortal in their childhood, now grew older, day by day, and came soon to be youths and maidens, and men and women by and by, and aged people, before they dreamed of such a thing.

Meanwhile, the naughty Pandora, and hardly less naughty Epimetheus, remained in their cottage. Both of them had been grievously stung, and were in a good deal of pain, which seemed the more intolerable to them, because it was the very first pain that had ever been felt since the world began. Of course, they were entirely unaccustomed to it, and could have no idea what it meant. Besides all this, they were in exceeding bad humor, both with themselves and with one another. In order to indulge it to the utmost, Epimetheus sat down sullenly in a corner with his back towards Pandora; while Pandora flung herself upon the floor and rested her head on the fatal and abominable box. She was crying bitterly, and sobbing as if her heart would break.

Suddenly there was a gentle little tap on the inside of the lid.

" What can that be ? " cried Pandora, lifting her head.

But either Epimetheus had not heard the tap, or was too much out of humor to notice it. At any rate, he made no answer.

" You are very unkind," said Pandora, sobbing anew, " not to speak to me ! "

Again the tap ! It sounded like the tiny knuckles of a fairy's hand, knocking lightly and playfully on the inside of the box.

" Who are you ? " asked Pandora, with a little of her former curiosity. " Who are you inside of this naughty box ? "

A sweet little voice spoke from within, —

" Only lift the lid, and you shall see."

" No, no," answered Pandora, again beginning to sob, " I have had enough of lifting the lid ! You are inside of the box, naughty creature, and there you shall stay ! There are plenty of your ugly brothers and sisters already flying about the world. You need never think that I shall be so foolish as to let you out ! "

She looked towards Epimetheus, as she spoke, perhaps expecting that he would commend her for her wisdom. But the sullen boy only muttered that she was wise a little too late.

" Ah," said the sweet little voice again, " you had much better let me out. I am not like those naughty

creatures that have stings in their tails. They are no
brothers and sisters of mine, as you would see at once,
if you were only to get a glimpse of me. Come, come,
my pretty Pandora! I am sure you will let me
out!"

And, indeed, there was a kind of cheerful witchery
in the tone, that made it almost impossible to refuse
anything which this little voice asked. Pandora's heart
had insensibly grown lighter, at every word that came
from within the box. Epimetheus, too, though still in
the corner, had turned half round, and seemed to be in
rather better spirits than before.

"My dear Epimetheus," cried Pandora, "have you
heard this little voice?"

"Yes, to be sure I have," answered he, but in no
very good-humor as yet. "And what of it?"

"Shall I lift the lid again?" asked Pandora.

"Just as you please," said Epimetheus. "You have
done so much mischief already, that perhaps you may
as well do a little more. One other Trouble, in such a
swarm as you have set adrift about the world, can
make no very great difference."

"You might speak a little more kindly!" murmured
Pandora, wiping her eyes.

"Ah, naughty boy!" cried the little voice within the
box, in an arch and laughing tone. "He knows he is
longing to see me. Come, my dear Pandora, lift up
the lid. I am in a great hurry to comfort you. Only
let me have some fresh air, and you shall soon see that
matters are not quite so dismal as you think them!"

"Epimetheus," exclaimed Pandora, "come what may,
I am resolved to open the box!"

"And, as the lid seems very heavy," cried Epimetheus, running across the room, " I will help you!"

So, with one consent, the two children again lifted the lid. Out flew a sunny and smiling little personage, and hovered about the room, throwing a light wherever she went. Have you never made the sunshine dance into dark corners, by reflecting it from a bit of looking-glass? Well, so looked the winged cheerfulness of this fairy-like stranger, amid the gloom of the cottage. She flew to Epimetheus, and laid the least touch of her finger on the inflamed spot where the Trouble had stung him, and immediately the anguish of it was gone. Then she kissed Pandora on the forehead, and her hurt was cured likewise.

After performing these good offices, the bright stranger fluttered sportively over the children's heads, and looked so sweetly at them, that they both began to think it not so very much amiss to have opened the box, since, otherwise, their cheery guest must have been kept a prisoner among those naughty imps with stings in their tails.

" Pray, who are you, beautiful creature?" inquired Pandora.

" I am to be called Hope!" answered the sunshiny figure. " And because I am such a cheery little body, I was packed into the box, to make amends to the human race for that swarm of ugly Troubles, which was destined to be let loose among them. Never fear! we shall do pretty well in spite of them all."

" Your wings are colored like the rainbow!" exclaimed Pandora. " How very beautiful!"

" Yes, they are like the rainbow," said Hope, " because, glad as my nature is, I am partly made of tears as well as smiles."

"And will you stay with us," asked Epimetheus, "forever and ever?"

"As long as you need me," said Hope, with her pleasant smile, — "and that will be as long as you live in the world, — I promise never to desert you. There may come times and seasons, now and then, when you will think that I have utterly vanished. But again, and again, and again, when perhaps you least dream of it, you shall see the glimmer of my wings on the ceiling of your cottage. Yes, my dear children, and I know something very good and beautiful that is to be given you hereafter!"

"Oh tell us," they exclaimed, — "tell us what it is!"

"Do not ask me," replied Hope, putting her finger on her rosy mouth. "But do not despair, even if it should never happen while you live on this earth. Trust in my promise, for it is true."

"We do trust you!" cried Epimetheus and Pandora, both in one breath.

And so they did; and not only they, but so has everybody trusted Hope, that has since been alive. And to tell you the truth, I cannot help being glad — (though, to be sure, it was an uncommonly naughty thing for her to do) — but I cannot help being glad that our foolish Pandora peeked into the box. No doubt — no doubt — the Troubles are still flying about the world, and have increased in multitude, rather than lessened, and are a very ugly set of imps, and carry most venomous stings in their tails. I have felt them already, and expect to feel them more, as I grow older.

But then that lovely and lightsome little figure of Hope! What in the world could we do without her? Hope spiritualizes the earth; Hope makes it always new; and, even in the earth's best and brightest aspect, Hope shows it to be only the shadow of an infinite bliss hereafter!

THE THREE GOLDEN APPLES

By NATHANIEL HAWTHORNE.

DID you ever hear of the golden apples, that grew in the garden of the Hesperides? Ah, those were such apples as would bring a great price, by the bushel, if any of them could be found growing in the orchards of nowadays! But there is not, I suppose, a graft of that wonderful fruit on a single tree in the wide world. Not so much as a seed of those apples exists any longer.

And, even in the old, old, half-forgotten times, before the garden of the Hesperides was overrun with weeds, a great many people doubted whether there could be real trees that bore apples of solid gold upon their branches. All had heard of them, but nobody remembered to have seen any. Children, nevertheless, used to listen, open-mouthed, to stories of the golden apple-tree, and resolved to discover it, when they should be big enough. Adventurous young men, who desired to do a braver thing than any of their fellows, set out in quest of this fruit. Many of them returned no more; none of them brought back the apples. No wonder that they found it impossible to gather them! It is said that there was a dragon beneath the tree, with a hundred terrible heads, fifty of which were always on the watch, while the other fifty slept.

In my opinion it was hardly worth running so much risk for the sake of a solid golden apple. Had the apples been sweet, mellow, and juicy, indeed that would be another matter. There might then have been some sense in trying to get at them, in spite of the hundred-headed dragon.

But, as I have already told you, it was quite a common thing with young persons, when tired of too much peace and rest, to go in search of the garden of the Hesperides. And once the adventure was undertaken by a hero who had enjoyed very little peace or rest since he came into the world. At the time of which I am going to speak, he was wandering through the pleasant land of Italy, with a mighty club in his hand, and a bow and quiver slung across his shoulders. He was wrapt in the skin of the biggest and fiercest lion that ever had been seen, and which he himself had killed; and though, on the whole, he was kind and generous and noble, there was a good deal of the lion's fierceness in his heart. As he went on his way, he continually inquired whether that were the right road to the famous garden. But none of the country people knew anything about the matter, and many looked as if they would have laughed at the question, if the stranger had not carried so very big a club.

So he journeyed on and on, still making the same inquiry, until, at last, he came to the brink of a river where some beautiful young women sat twining wreaths of flowers.

"Can you tell me, pretty maidens," asked the stranger, "whether this is the right way to the garden of the Hesperides?"

The young women had been having a fine time together, weaving the flowers into wreaths, and crowning one another's heads. And there seemed to be a kind of magic in the touch of their fingers, that made the flowers more fresh and dewy, and of brighter hues, and sweeter fragrance, while they played with them, than even when they had been growing on their native stems. But, on hearing the stranger's question, they dropped all their flowers on the grass, and gazed at him with astonishment.

"The garden of the Hesperides!" cried one. "We thought mortals had been weary of seeking it, after so many disappointments. And pray, adventurous traveller, what do you want there?"

"A certain king, who is my cousin," replied he, "has ordered me to get him three of the golden apples."

"Most of the young men who go in quest of these apples," observed another of the damsels, "desire to obtain them for themselves, or to present them to some fair maiden whom they love. Do you, then, love this king, your cousin, so very much?"

"Perhaps not," replied the stranger, sighing. "He has often been severe and cruel to me. But it is my destiny to obey him."

"And do you know," asked the damsel who had first spoken, "that a terrible dragon, with a hundred heads, keeps watch under the golden apple-tree?"

"I know it well," answered the stranger, calmly. "But, from my cradle upwards, it has been my business, and almost my pastime, to deal with serpents and dragons."

The young women looked at his massive club, and at

the shaggy lion's skin which he wore, and likewise at his heroic limbs and figure; and they whispered to each other that the stranger appeared to be one who might reasonably expect to perform deeds far beyond the might of other men. But, then, the dragon with a hundred heads! What mortal, even if he possessed a hundred lives, could hope to escape the fangs of such a monster! So kind-hearted were the maidens, that they could not bear to see this brave and handsome traveller attempt what was so very dangerous, and devote himself most probably, to become a meal for the dragon's hundred ravenous mouths.

"Go back," cried they all, — " go back to your own home! Your mother, beholding you safe and sound, will shed tears of joy; and what can she do more, should you win ever so great a victory? No matter for the golden apples! No matter for the king, your cruel cousin! We do not wish the dragon with the hundred heads to eat you up!"

The stranger seemed to grow impatient at these remonstrances. He carelessly lifted his mighty club, and let it fall upon a rock that lay half buried in the earth, near by. With the force of that idle blow, the great rock was shattered all to pieces. It cost the stranger no more effort to achieve this feat of a giant's strength than for one of the young maidens to touch her sister's rosy cheek with a flower.

" Do you not believe," said he, looking at the damsels with a smile, " that such a blow would have crushed one of the dragon's hundred heads?"

Then he sat down on the grass, and told them the story of his life, or as much of it as he could remember,

from the day when he was first cradled in a warrior's
brazen shield. While he lay there, two immense serpents came gliding over the floor, and opened their hideous jaws to devour him; and he, a baby of a few
months old, had griped one of the fierce snakes in each
of his little fists, and strangled them to death. When
he was but a stripling, he had killed a huge lion, almost
as big as the one whose vast and shaggy hide he now
wore upon his shoulders. The next thing that he had
done was to fight a battle with an ugly sort of monster,
called a hydra, which had no less than nine heads, and
exceedingly sharp teeth in every one.

"But the dragon of the Hesperides, you know,"
observed one of the damsels, "has a hundred heads!"

"Nevertheless," replied the stranger, "I would rather
fight two such dragons than a single hydra. For, as
fast as I cut off a head, two others grew in its place;
and, besides, there was one of the heads that could not
possibly be killed, but kept biting as fiercely as ever,
long after it was cut off. So I was forced to bury it
under a stone, where it is doubtless alive to this very
day. But the hydra's body, and its eight other heads,
will never do any further mischief."

The damsels, judging that the story was likely to
last a good while, had been preparing a repast of bread
and grapes, that the stranger might refresh himself in
the intervals of his talk. They took pleasure in helping him to this simple food; and, now and then, one of
them would put a sweet grape between her rosy lips,
lest it should make him bashful to eat alone.

The traveller proceeded to tell how he had chased a

very swift stag, for a twelvemonth together, without ever stopping to take breath, and had at last caught it by the antlers, and carried it home alive. And he had fought with a very odd race of people, half horses and half men, and had put them all to death, from a sense of duty, in order that their ugly figures might never be seen any more. Besides all this, he took to himself great credit for having cleaned out a stable.

"Do you call that a wonderful exploit?" asked one of the young maidens, with a smile. "Any clown in the country has done as much!"

"Had it been an ordinary stable," replied the stranger, "I should not have mentioned it. But this was so gigantic a task that it would have taken me all my life to perform it, if I had not luckily thought of turning the channel of a river through the stable-door. That did the business in a very short time!"

Seeing how earnestly his fair auditors listened, he next told them how he had shot some monstrous birds, and had caught a wild bull alive and let him go again, and had tamed a number of very wild horses, and had conquered Hippolyta, the warlike queen of the Amazons. He mentioned, likewise, that he had taken off Hippolyta's enchanted girdle, and had given it to the daughter of his cousin, the king.

"Was it the girdle of Venus," inquired the prettiest of the damsels, "which makes women beautiful?"

"No," answered the stranger. "It had formerly been the sword-belt of Mars; and it can only make the wearer valiant and courageous."

"An old sword-belt!" cried the damsel, tossing her head. "Then I should not care about having it!"

"You are right," said the stranger.

Going on with his wonderful narrative, he informed the maidens that as strange an adventure as ever happened was when he fought with Geryon, the six-legged man. This was a very odd and frightful sort of figure, as you may well believe. Any person, looking at his tracks in the sand or snow, would suppose that three sociable companions had been walking along together. On hearing his footsteps at a little distance, it was no more than reasonable to judge that several people must be coming. But it was only the strange man Geryon clattering onward, with his six legs!

Six legs, and one gigantic body! Certainly, he must have been a very queer monster to look at; and, my stars, what a waste of shoe-leather!

When the stranger had finished the story of his adventures, he looked around at the attentive faces of the maidens.

"Perhaps you may have heard of me before," said he modestly. "My name is Hercules!"

"We had already guessed it," replied the maidens; "for your wonderful deeds are known all over the world. We do not think it strange, any longer, that you should set out in quest of the golden apples of the Hesperides. Come, sisters, let us crown the hero with flowers!"

Then they flung beautiful wreaths over his stately head and mighty shoulders, so that the lion's skin was almost entirely covered with roses. They took possession of his ponderous club, and so entwined it about with the brightest, softest, and most fragrant blossoms, that not a finger's breadth of its oaken substance could be seen. It looked all like a huge bunch of flowers. Lastly, they joined hands, and danced around him, chanting words which became poetry of their own accord, and grew into a choral song, in honor of the illustrious Hercules.

And Hercules was rejoiced, as any other hero would have been, to know that these fair young girls had heard of the valiant deeds which it had cost him so much toil and danger to achieve. But, still, he was not satisfied. He could not think that what he had already done was worthy of so much honor, while there remained any bold or difficult adventure to be undertaken.

"Dear maidens," said he, when they paused to take breath, "now that you know my name, will you not tell me how I am to reach the garden of the Hesperides?"

"Ah! must you go so soon?" they exclaimed. "you — that have performed so many wonders, and spent such a toilsome life — cannot you content yourself to repose a little while on the margin of this peaceful river?"

Hercules shook his head.

"I must depart now," said he.

"We will then give you the best directions we can," replied the damsels. "You must go to the seashore, and find out the Old One, and compel him to inform you where the golden apples are to be found."

"The Old One!" repeated Hercules, laughing at this odd name. "And, pray, who may the Old One be?"

"Why, the Old Man of the Sea, to be sure!" answered one of the damsels. "He has fifty daughters, whom some people call very beautiful; but we do not

think it proper to be acquainted with them because
they have sea-green hair, and taper away like fishes.
You must talk with this Old Man of the Sea. He is a
sea-faring person, and knows all about the garden of
the Hesperides; for it is situated in an island which he
is often in the habit of visiting."

Hercules then asked whereabouts the Old One was
most likely to be met with. When the damsels had
informed him, he thanked them for all their kindness,
— for the bread and grapes with which they had fed
him, the lovely flowers with which they had crowned
him, and the songs and dances wherewith they had
done him honor, — and he thanked them, most of all,
for telling him the right way, — and immediately set
forth upon his journey.

But before he was out of hearing, one of the maidens
called after him.

"Keep fast hold of the Old One, when you catch
him!" cried she, smiling, and lifting her finger to
make the caution more impressive. "Do not be astonished at anything that may happen. Only hold him
fast, and he will tell you what you wish to know."

Hercules again thanked her and pursued his way,
while the maidens resumed their pleasant labor of
making flower-wreaths. They talked about the hero,
long after he was gone.

"We will crown him with the loveliest of our garlands," said they, "when he returns hither with the
three golden apples, after slaying the dragon with a
hundred heads."

Meanwhile, Hercules travelled constantly onward,
over hill and dale, and through the solitary woods.

Sometimes he swung his club aloft, and splintered a mighty oak with a downright blow. His mind was so full of the giants and monsters with whom it was the business of his life to fight, that perhaps he mistook the great tree for a giant or a monster. And so eager was Hercules to achieve what he had undertaken, that he almost regretted to have spent so much time with the damsels, wasting idle breath upon the story of his adventures. But thus it always is with persons who are destined to perform great things. What they have already done seems less than nothing. What they have taken in hand to do seems worth toil, danger, and life itself.

Persons who happened to be passing through the forest must have been affrighted to see him smite the trees with his great club. With but a single blow, the trunk was riven as by the stroke of lightning, and the broad boughs came rustling and crashing down.

Hastening forward, without ever pausing or looking behind, he by and by heard the sea roaring at a distance. At this sound, he increased his speed, and soon came to a beach, where the great surf-waves tumbled themselves upon the hard sand, in a long line of snowy foam. At one end of the beach, however, there was a pleasant spot, where some green shrubbery clambered up a cliff, making its rocky face look soft and beautiful. A carpet of verdant grass, largely intermixed with sweet-smelling clover, covered the narrow space between the bottom of the cliff and the sea. And what should Hercules espy there, but an old man, fast asleep!

But was it really and truly an old man? Certainly, at first sight, it looked very like one; but, on closer inspection, it rather seemed to be some kind of a creature that lived in the sea. For, on his legs and arms there were scales, such as fishes have; he was web-footed and web-fingered, after the fashion of a duck; and his long beard, being of a greenish tinge, had more the appearance of a tuft of sea-weed than of an ordinary beard. Have you never seen a stick of timber, that has been long tossed about by the waves, and has got all overgrown with barnacles, and, at last drifting ashore, seems to have been thrown up from the very deepest bottom of the sea? Well, the old man would have put you in mind of just such a wave-tost spar! But Hercules, the instant he set eyes on this strange figure, was convinced that it could be no other than the Old One, who was to direct him on his way.

Yes, it was the self-same Old Man of the Sea whom the hospitable maidens had talked to him about. Thanking his stars for the lucky accident of finding the old fellow asleep, Hercules stole on tiptoe towards him, and caught him by the arm and leg.

"Tell me," cried he, before the Old One was well awake, "which is the way to the garden of the Hesperides?"

As you may easily imagine, the Old Man of the Sea awoke in a fright. But his astonishment could hardly have been greater than was that of Hercules, the next moment. For, all of a sudden, the Old One seemed to disappear out of his grasp, and he found himself holding a stag by the fore and hind leg! But still he kept fast hold. Then the stag disappeared, and in its stead there was a sea-bird, fluttering and screaming, while Hercules clutched it by the wing and claw! But the bird could not get away. Immediately afterwards, there was an ugly three-headed dog, which growled and barked at Hercules, and snapped fiercely at the hands by which he held him! But Hercules would not let him go. In another minute, instead of the three-headed dog, what should appear but Geryon, the six-legged man-monster, kicking at Hercules with five of his legs, in order to get the remaining one at liberty! But Hercules held on. By and by, no Geryon was there, but a huge snake, like one of those which Hercules had strangled in his babyhood, only a hundred times as big; and it twisted and twined about the hero's neck and body, and threw its tail high into the air, and opened its deadly jaws as if to devour him outright; so that it was really a very terrible spectacle! But Hercules was no whit disheartened, and squeezed the great snake so tightly that he soon began to hiss with pain.

You must understand that the Old Man of the Sea, though he generally looked so much like the wave-beaten figure-head of a vessel, had the power of assuming any shape he pleased. When he found himself so roughly seized by Hercules, he had been in hopes of putting him into such surprise and terror, by these magical transformations, that the hero would be glad to let him go. If Hercules had relaxed his grasp, the Old One would certainly have plunged down to the very bottom of the sea, whence he would not soon have given himself the trouble of coming up, in order to answer any impertinent questions. Ninety-nine people out of a hundred,

I suppose, would have been frightened out of their wits by the very first of his ugly shapes, and would have taken to their heels at once. For, one of the hardest things in this world is, to see the difference between real dangers and imaginary ones.

But, as Hercules held on so stubbornly, and only squeezed the Old One so much the tighter at every change of shape, and really put him to no small torture, he finally thought it best to reappear in his own figure. So there he was again, a fishy, scaly, web-footed sort of personage, with something like a tuft of sea-weed at his chin.

"Pray, what do you want with me?" cried the Old One, as soon as he could take breath; for it is quite a tiresome affair to go through so many false shapes. "Why do you squeeze me so hard? Let me go, this moment, or I shall begin to consider you an extremely uncivil person!"

"My name is Hercules!" roared the mighty stranger. "And you will never get out of my clutch, until you tell me the nearest way to the garden of the Hesperides!"

When the old fellow heard who it was that had caught him, he saw, with half an eye, that it would be necessary to tell him everything that he wanted to know. The Old One was an inhabitant of the sea, you must recollect, and roamed about everywhere, like other sea-faring people. Of course, he had often heard of the fame of Hercules, and of the wonderful things that he was constantly performing, in various parts of the earth, and how determined he always was to accomplish whatever he undertook. He therefore made no more attempts to escape, but told the hero how to find the garden of the Hesperides, and likewise warned him of many difficulties which must be overcome, before he could arrive thither.

"You must go on, thus and thus," said the Old Man of the Sea, after taking the points of the compass, " till you come in sight of a very tall giant, who holds the sky on his shoulders. And the giant, if he happens to be in the humor, will tell you exactly where the garden of the Hesperides lies."

" And if the giant happens not to be in the humor," remarked Hercules, balancing his club on the tip of his finger, " perhaps I shall find means to persuade him ! "

Thanking the Old Man of the Sea, and begging his pardon for having squeezed him so roughly, the hero resumed his journey. He met with a great many strange adventures, which would be well worth your hearing, if I had leisure to narrate them as minutely as they deserve.

It was in this journey, if I mistake not, that he encountered a prodigious giant, who was so wonderfully contrived by nature, that, every time he touched the earth, he became ten times as strong as ever he had been before. His name was Antæus. You may see, plainly enough, that it was a very difficult business to fight with such a fellow; for, as often as he got a knock-down blow, up he started again, stronger, fiercer, and abler to use his weapons, than if his enemy had let him alone. Thus, the harder Hercules pounded the giant with his club, the further he seemed from winning the victory. I have sometimes argued with such people, but never fought with one. The only way in which Hercules found it possible to finish the battle, was by lifting Antæus off his feet into the air, and squeezing, and squeezing, and squeezing him, until, finally, the strength was quite squeezed out of his enormous body.

When this affair was finished, Hercules continued his travels, and went to the land of Egypt, where he was taken prisoner, and would have been put to death, if he had not slain the king of the country, and made his escape. Passing through the deserts of Africa, and going as fast as he could, he arrived at last on the shore of the great ocean. And here, unless he could walk on the crests of the billows, it seemed as if his journey must needs be at the end.

Nothing was before him, save the foaming, dashing, measureless ocean. But, suddenly, as he looked towards the horizon, he saw something, a great way off, which he had not seen the moment before. It gleamed very brightly, almost as you may have beheld the round, golden disk of the sun, when it rises or sets over the edge of the world. It evidently drew nearer; for, at every instant, this wonderful object became larger and more lustrous. At length, it had come so nigh that Hercules discovered it to be an immense cup or bowl, made either of gold or burnished brass. How it had got afloat upon the sea is more than I can tell you. There it was, at all events, rolling on the tumultuous billows, which tossed it up and down, and heaved their foamy tops against its sides, but without ever throwing their spray over the brim.

"I have seen many giants, in my time," thought Hercules, "but never one that would need to drink his wine out of a cup like this!"

And, true enough, what a cup it must have been! It was as large — as large — but, in short, I am afraid to say how immeasurably large it was. To speak within bounds, it was ten times larger than a great mill-wheel; and, all of metal as it was, it floated over the heaving surges more lightly than an acorn-cup adown the brook. The waves tumbled it onward, until it grazed against the shore, within a short distance of the spot where Hercules was standing.

As soon as this happened, he knew what was to be done; for he had not gone through so many remarkable adventures without learning pretty well how to conduct himself, whenever anything came to pass a little out of the common rule. It was just as clear as daylight that this marvellous cup had been sent adrift by some unseen power, and guided hitherward, in order to carry Hercules across the sea, on his way to the garden of the Hesperides. Accordingly, without a moment's delay, he clambered over the brim, and slid down on the inside, where, spreading out his lion's skin, he proceeded to take a little repose. He had scarcely rested, until now, since he bade farewell to the damsels on the margin of the river. The waves dashed, with a pleasant and ringing sound, against the circumference of the hollow cup; it rocked lightly to and fro, and the motion was so soothing that it speedily rocked Hercules into an agreeable slumber.

His nap had probably lasted a good while, when the cup chanced to graze against a rock, and, in consequence, immediately resounded and reverberated through its golden or brazen substance, a hundred

times as loudly as ever you heard a church-bell. The
noise awoke Hercules, who instantly started up and
gazed around him, wondering whereabouts he was.
He was not long in discovering that the cup had floated
across a great part of the sea, and was approaching the
shore of what seemed to be an island. And, on that
island, what do you think he saw?

No; you will never guess it, not if you were to try
fifty thousand times! It positively appears to me that
this was the most marvellous spectacle that had ever
been seen by Hercules, in the whole course of his
wonderful travels and adventures. It was a greater
marvel than the hydra with nine heads, which kept
growing twice as fast as they were cut off; greater
than the six-legged man-monster; greater than Antæus;
greater than anything that was ever beheld by anybody,
before or since the days of Hercules, or than anything
that remains to be beheld, by travellers in all time to
come. It was a giant!

But such an intolerable big giant! A giant as tall as
a mountain; so vast a giant, that the clouds rested
about his midst, like a girdle, and hung like a hoary
beard from his chin, and flitted before his huge eyes, so
that he could neither see Hercules nor the golden cup
in which he was voyaging. And, most wonderful of
all, the giant held up his great hands and appeared
to support the sky, which, so far as Hercules could
discern through the clouds, was resting upon his head!
This does really seem almost too much to believe.

Meanwhile, the bright cup continued to float onward,
and finally touched the strand. Just then a breeze
wafted away the clouds from before the giant's visage,

and Hercules beheld it, with all its enormous features; eyes each of them as big as yonder lake, a nose a mile long, and a mouth of the same width. It was a countenance terrible from its enormity of size, but disconsolate and weary, even as you may see the faces of many people, nowadays, who are compelled to sustain burdens above their strength. What the sky was to the giant, such are the cares of earth to those who let themselves be weighed down by them. And whenever men undertake what is beyond the just measure of their abilities, they encounter precisely such a doom as had befallen this poor giant.

Poor fellow! He had evidently stood there a long while. An ancient forest had been growing and decaying around his feet; and oak-trees, of six or seven centuries old, had sprung from the acorn, and forced themselves between his toes.

The giant now looked down from the far height of his great eyes, and, perceiving Hercules, roared out, in a voice that resembled thunder, proceeding out of the cloud that had just flitted away from his face.

"Who are you, down at my feet there? And whence do you come, in that little cup?"

"I am Hercules!" thundered back the hero, in a voice pretty nearly or quite as loud as the giant's own. "And I am seeking for the garden of the Hesperides!"

"Ho! ho! ho!" roared the giant, in a fit of immense laughter. "That is a wise adventure, truly!"

"And why not?" cried Hercules, getting a little angry at the giant's mirth. "Do you think I am afraid of the dragon with a hundred heads?"

Just at this time, while they were talking together,

some black clouds gathered about the giant's middle, and burst into a tremendous storm of thunder and lightning, causing such a pother that Hercules found it impossible to distinguish a word. Only the giant's immeasurable legs were to be seen, standing up into the obscurity of the tempest; and, now and then, a momentary glimpse of his whole figure, mantled in a volume of mist. He seemed to be speaking, most of the time; but his big, deep, rough voice chimed in with the reverberations of the thunder-claps, and rolled away over the hills, like them. Thus, by talking out of season, the foolish giant expended an incalculable quantity of breath, to no purpose; for the thunder spoke quite as intelligibly as he.

At last, the storm swept over, as suddenly as it had come. And there again was the clear sky, and the weary giant holding it up, and the pleasant sunshine beaming over his vast height, and illuminating it against the background of the sullen thunder-clouds. So far above the shower had been his head, that not a hair of it was moistened by the rain-drops!

When the giant could see Hercules still standing on the sea-shore, he roared out to him anew.

"I am Atlas, the mightiest giant in the world! And I hold the sky upon my head!"

"So I see," answered Hercules. "But, can you show me the way to the garden of the Hesperides?"

"What do you want there?" asked the giant.

"I want three of the golden apples," shouted Hercules, "for my cousin, the king."

"There is nobody but myself," quoth the giant, "that can go to the garden of the Hesperides, and gather the golden apples. If it were not for this little business of holding up the sky, I would make half a dozen steps across the sea, and get them for you."

"You are very kind," replied Hercules. "And cannot you rest the sky upon a mountain?"

"None of them are quite high enough," said Atlas, shaking his head. "But, if you were to take your stand on the summit of that nearest one, your head would be pretty nearly on a level with mine. You seem to be a fellow of some strength. What if you should take my burden on your shoulders, while I do your errand for you?"

Hercules, as you must be careful to remember, was a remarkably strong man; and though it certainly requires a great deal of muscular power to uphold the sky, yet, if any mortal could be supposed capable of such an exploit, he was the one. Nevertheless, it seemed so difficult an undertaking, that, for the first time in his life, he hesitated.

"Is the sky very heavy?" he inquired.

"Why, not particularly so, at first," answered the giant, shrugging his shoulders. "But it gets to be a little burdensome, after a thousand years!"

"And how long a time," asked the hero, "will it take you to get the golden apples?"

"Oh! that will be done in a few moments," cried Atlas. "I shall take ten or fifteen miles at a stride, and be at the garden and back again before your shoulders begin to ache."

"Well, then," answered Hercules, "I will climb the mountain behind you there, and relieve you of your burden."

The truth is, Hercules had a kind heart of his own, and considered that he should be doing the giant a favor, by allowing him this opportunity for a ramble. And, besides, he thought that it would be still more for his own glory, if he could boast of upholding the sky, than merely to do so ordinary a thing as to conquer a dragon with a hundred heads. Accordingly, without more words, the sky was shifted from the shoulders of Atlas, and placed upon those of Hercules.

When this was safely accomplished, the first thing that the giant did was to stretch himself; and you may imagine what a prodigious spectacle he was then. Next, he slowly lifted one of his feet out of the forest that had grown up around it; then, the other. Then, all at once, he began to caper, and leap, and dance, for joy at his freedom; flinging himself nobody knows how high into the air, and floundering down again with a shock that made the earth tremble. Then he laughed —Ho! ho! ho!—with a thunderous roar that was echoed from the mountains, far and near, as if they and the giant had been so many rejoicing brothers. When his joy had a little subsided, he stepped into the sea; ten miles at the first stride, which brought him midleg deep; and ten miles at the second, when the water came just above his knees; and ten miles more at the third, by which he was immersed nearly to his waist. This was the greatest depth of the sea.

Hercules watched the giant, as he still went onward; for it was really a wonderful sight, this immense human form, more than thirty miles off, half hidden in the ocean, but with his upper half as tall, and misty, and

blue, as a distant mountain. At last the gigantic shape
faded entirely out of view. And now Hercules began
to consider what he should do, in case Atlas should be
drowned in the sea, or if he were to be stung to death
by the dragon with the hundred heads, which guarded
the golden apples of the Hesperides. If any such misfortune were to happen, how could he ever get rid of
the sky? And, by the by, its weight began already to
be a little irksome to his head and shoulders.

"I really pity the poor giant," thought Hercules.
"If it wearies me so much in ten minutes, how must it
have wearied him in a thousand years?"

O my sweet little people, you have no idea what a
weight there was in that same blue sky, which looks so
soft and aerial above our heads! And there, too, was
the bluster of the wind, and the chill and watery clouds,
and the blazing sun, all taking their turns to make
Hercules uncomfortable! He began to be afraid that
the giant would never come back. He gazed wistfully
at the world beneath him, and acknowledged to himself
that it was a far happier kind of life to be a shepherd
at the foot of a mountain, than to stand on its dizzy
summit, and bear up the firmament with his might and
main. For, of course, as you will easily understand,
Hercules had an immense responsibility on his mind,
as well as a weight on his head and shoulders. Why,
if he did not stand perfectly still, and keep the sky
immovable, the sun would perhaps be put ajar! Or,
after nightfall, a great many of the stars might be
loosened from their places, and shower down, like fiery
rain, upon the people's heads! And how ashamed
would the hero be, if, owing to his unsteadiness beneath

its weight, the sky should crack, and show a great fissure quite across it!

I know not how long it was before, to his unspeakable joy, he beheld the huge shape of the giant, like a cloud, on the far-off edge of the sea. At his nearer approach, Atlas held up his hand, in which Hercules could perceive three magnificent golden apples, as big as pumpkins, all hanging from one branch.

"I am glad to see you again," shouted Hercules, when the giant was within hearing. "So you have got the golden apples?"

"Certainly, certainly," answered Atlas; "and very fair apples they are. I took the finest that grew on the tree, I assure you. Ah! it is a beautiful spot, that garden of the Hesperides. Yes; and the dragon with a hundred heads is a sight worth any man's seeing. After all, you had better have gone for the apples yourself."

"No matter," replied Hercules. "You have had a pleasant ramble, and have done the business as well as I could. I heartily thank you for your trouble. And now, as I have a long way to go, and am rather in haste, — and as the king, my cousin, is anxious to receive the golden apples, — will you be kind enough to take the sky off my shoulders again?"

"Why, as to that," said the giant, chucking the golden apples into the air twenty miles high, or thereabouts, and catching them as they came down, — "as to that, my good friend, I consider you a little unreasonable. Cannot I carry the golden apples to the king, your cousin, much quicker than you could? As his majesty is in such a hurry to get them, I promise you

to take my longest strides.. And, besides, I have no
fancy for burdening myself with the sky, just now."

Here Hercules grew impatient, and gave a great
shrug of his shoulders. It being now twilight, you
might have seen two or three stars tumble out of their
places. Everybody on earth looked upward in affright,
thinking that the sky might be going to fall next.

"Oh, that will never do!" cried Giant Atlas, with
a great roar of laughter. "I have not let fall so many
stars within the last five centuries. By the time you
have stood there as long as I did, you will begin to
learn patience!"

"What!" shouted Hercules, very wrathfully, "do
you intend to make me bear this burden forever?"

"We will see about that, one of these days," answered the giant. "At all events, you ought not to
complain, if you have to bear it the next hundred
years, or perhaps the next thousand. I bore it a good
while longer, in spite of the back-ache. Well, then,
after a thousand years, if I happen to feel in the mood,
we may possibly shift about again. You are certainly
a very strong man, and can never have a better opportunity to prove it. Posterity will talk of you, I warrant it!"

"Pish! a fig for its talk!" cried Hercules, with
another hitch of his shoulders. "Just take the sky
upon your head one instant, will you? I want to
make a cushion of my lion's skin, for the weight to
rest upon. It really chafes me, and will cause unne-
cessary inconvenience in so many centuries as I am to
stand here."

"That's no more than fair, and I'll do it!" quoth

the giant; for he had no unkind feeling towards Hercules, and was merely acting with a too selfish consideration of his own ease. " For just five minutes, then, I'll take back the sky. Only for five minutes, recollect! I have no idea of spending another thousand years as I spent the last. Variety is the spice of life, say I."

Ah, the thick-witted old rogue of a giant! He threw down the golden apples, and received back the sky, from the head and shoulders of Hercules, upon his own, where it rightly belonged. And Hercules picked up the three golden apples, that were as big or bigger than pumpkins, and straightway set out on his journey homeward, without paying the slightest heed to the thundering tones of the giant, who bellowed after him to come back. Another forest sprang up around his feet, and grew ancient there; and again might be seen oak-trees, of six or seven centuries old, that had waxed thus aged betwixt his enormous toes.

And there stands the giant to this day; or, at any rate, there stands a mountain as tall as he, and which bears his name; and when the thunder rumbles about its summit, we may imagine it to be the voice of Giant Atlas bellowing after Hercules!

THE MIRACULOUS PITCHER

By NATHANIEL HAWTHORNE.

ONE evening, in times long ago, old Philemon and his old wife Baucis sat at their cottage-door, enjoying the calm and beautiful sunset. They had already eaten their frugal supper, and intended now to spend a quiet hour or two before bedtime. So they talked together about their garden, and their cow, and their bees, and their grapevine, which clambered over the cottage-wall, and on which the grapes were beginning to turn purple. But the rude shouts of children, and the fierce barking of dogs, in the village near at hand, grew louder and louder, until, at last, it was hardly possible for Baucis and Philemon to hear each other speak.

"Ah, wife," cried Philemon, "I fear some poor traveller is seeking hospitality among our neighbors yonder, and, instead of giving him food and lodging, they have set their dogs at him, as their custom is!"

"Well-a-day!" answered old Baucis, "I do wish our neighbors felt a little more kindness for their fellow-creatures. And only think of bringing up their children in this naughty way, and patting them on the head when they fling stones at strangers!"

" Those children will never come to any good," said
Philemon, shaking his white head. " To tell you the
truth, wife, I should not wonder if some terrible thing
were to happen to all the people in the village, unless
they mend their manners.   But, as for you and me, as
long as Providence affords us a crust of bread, let us
be ready to give half to any poor homeless stranger,
that may come along and need it."

" That's right, husband ! " said Baucis. " So we
will ! "

These old folks, you must know, were quite poor,
and had to work pretty hard for a living. Old Philemon toiled diligently in his garden, while Baucis was
always busy with her distaff, or making a little butter
and cheese with their cow's milk, or doing one thing
and another about the cottage. Their food was seldom
anything but bread, milk, and vegetables, with sometimes a portion of honey from their beehive, and now
and then a bunch of grapes, that had ripened against
the cottage-wall. But they were two of the kindest
old people in the world, and would cheerfully have
gone without their dinners, any day, rather than refuse
a slice of their brown loaf, a cup of new milk, and a
spoonful of honey, to the weary traveller who might
pause before their door. They felt as if such guests
had a sort of holiness, and that they ought, therefore,
to treat them better and more bountifully than their
own selves.

Their cottage stood on a rising ground, at some
short distance from a village, which lay in a hollow
valley, that was about half a mile in breadth. This
valley, in past ages, when the world was new, had prob-

ably been the bed of a lake. There, fishes had glided
to and fro in the depths, and water-weeds had grown
along the margin, and trees and hills had seen their
reflected images in the broad and peaceful mirror.
But, as the waters subsided, men had cultivated the
soil, and built houses on it, so that it was now a fertile
spot, and bore no traces of the ancient lake, except a
very small brook, which meandered through the midst
of the village, and supplied the inhabitants with water.
The valley had been dry land so long, that oaks had
sprung up, and grown great and high, and perished
with old age, and been succeeded by others, as tall and
stately as the first. Never was there a prettier or
more fruitful valley. The very sight of the plenty
around them should have made the inhabitants kind
and gentle, and ready to show their gratitude to
Providence by doing good to their fellow-creatures.

But, we are sorry to say, the people of this lovely
village were not worthy to dwell in a spot on which
Heaven had smiled so beneficently. They were a very
selfish and hard-hearted people, and had no pity for the
poor, nor sympathy with the homeless. They would
only have laughed, had anybody told them that human
beings owe a debt of love to one another, because there
is no other method of paying the debt of love and care
which all of us owe to Providence. You will hardly
believe what I am going to tell you. These naughty
people taught their children to be no better than themselves, and used to clap their hands, by way of encouragement, when they saw the little boys and girls run
after some poor stranger, shouting at his heels, and
pelting him with stones. They kept large and fierce

dogs, and whenever a traveller ventured to show himself in the village street, this pack of disagreeable curs scampered to meet him, barking, snarling, and showing their teeth. Then they would seize him by his leg, or by his clothes, just as it happened; and if he were ragged when he came, he was generally a pitiable object before he had time to run away. This was a very terrible thing to poor travellers, as you may suppose, especially when they chanced to be sick, or feeble, or lame, or old. Such persons (if they once knew how badly these unkind people, and their unkind children and curs, were in the habit of behaving) would go miles and miles out of their way, rather than try to pass through the village again.

What made the matter seem worse, if possible, was that when rich persons came in their chariots, or riding on beautiful horses, with their servants in rich liveries attending on them, nobody could be more civil and obsequious than the inhabitants of the village. They would take off their hats, and make the humblest bows you ever saw. If the children were rude, they were pretty certain to get their ears boxed; and as for the dogs, if a single cur in the pack presumed to yelp, his master instantly beat him with a club, and tied him up without any supper. This would have been all very well, only it proved that the villagers cared much about the money that a stranger had in his pocket, and nothing whatever for the human soul, which lives equally in the beggar and the prince.

So now you can understand why old Philemon spoke so sorrowfully, when he heard the shouts of the children and the barking of the dogs, at the farther extremity of the village street. There was a confused din, which lasted a good while, and seemed to pass quite through the breadth of the valley.

"I never heard the dogs so loud!" observed the good old man.

"Nor the children so rude!" answered his good old wife.

They sat shaking their heads, one to another, while the noise came nearer and nearer; until, at the foot of the little eminence on which their cottage stood, they saw two travellers approaching on foot. Close behind them came the fierce dogs, snarling at their very heels. A little farther off, ran a crowd of children, who sent up shrill cries, and flung stones at the two strangers, with all their might. Once or twice, the younger of the two men (he was a slender and very active figure) turned about and drove back the dogs with a staff which he carried in his hand. His companion, who was a very tall person, walked calmly along, as if disdaining to notice either the naughty children, or the pack of curs, whose manners the children seemed to imitate.

Both of the travellers were very humbly clad, and looked as if they might not have money enough in their pockets to pay for a night's lodging. And this, I am afraid, was the reason why the villagers had allowed their children and dogs to treat them so rudely.

"Come, wife," said Philemon to Baucis, "let us go and meet these poor people. No doubt, they feel almost too heavy-hearted to climb the hill."

"Go you and meet them," answered Baucis, "while I make haste within doors, and see whether we can get

them anything for supper. A comfortable bowl of
bread and milk would do wonders towards raising their
spirits."

Accordingly, she hastened into the cottage. Philemon, on his part, went forward, and extended his hand
with so hospitable an aspect that there was no need
of saying what nevertheless he did say, in the heartiest
tone imaginable, —

"Welcome, strangers! welcome!"

"Thank you!" replied the younger of the two, in a
lively kind of way, notwithstanding his weariness and
trouble. "This is quite another greeting than we have
met with yonder in the village. Pray, why do you live
in such a bad neighborhood?"

"Ah!" observed old Philemon, with a quiet and
benign smile, "Providence put me here, I hope, among
other reasons, in order that I may make you what
amends I can for the inhospitality of my neighbors."

"Well said, old father!" cried the traveller, laughing; "and, if the truth must be told, my companion
and myself need some amends. Those children (the
little rascals!) have bespattered us finely with their
mud-balls; and one of the curs has torn my cloak,
which was ragged enough already. But I took him
across the muzzle with my staff; and I think you may
have heard him yelp, even thus far off."

Philemon was glad to see him in such good spirits;
nor, indeed, would you have fancied, by the traveller's
look and manner, that he was weary with a long day's
journey, besides being disheartened by rough treatment
at the end of it. He was dressed in rather an odd way,
with a sort of cap on his head, the brim of which stuck

out over both ears. Though it was a summer evening, he wore a cloak, which he kept wrapt closely about him, perhaps because his undergarments were shabby. Philemon perceived, too, that he had on a singular pair of shoes; but, as it was now growing dusk, and as the old man's eyesight was none the sharpest, he could not precisely tell in what the strangeness consisted. One thing, certainly, seemed queer. The traveller was so wonderfully light and active, that it appeared as if his feet sometimes rose from the ground of their own accord, or could only be kept down by an effort.

"I used to be light-footed, in my youth," said Philemon to the traveller. "But I always found my feet grow heavier towards nightfall."

"There is nothing like a good staff to help one along," answered the stranger; "and I happen to have an excellent one, as you see."

This staff, in fact, was the oddest-looking staff that Philemon had ever beheld. It was made of olive-wood, and had something like a little pair of wings near the top. Two snakes, carved in the wood, were represented as twining themselves about the staff, and were so very skilfully executed that old Philemon (whose eyes, you know, were getting rather dim) almost thought them alive, and that he could see them wriggling and twisting.

"A curious piece of work, sure enough!" said he. "A staff with wings! It would be an excellent kind of stick for a little boy to ride astride of!"

By this time, Philemon and his two guests had reached the cottage-door.

"Friends," said the old man, "sit down and rest

yourselves here on this bench. My good wife Baucis has gone to see what you can have for supper. We are poor folks; but you shall be welcome to whatever we have in the cupboard."

The younger stranger threw himself carelessly on the bench, letting his staff fall, as he did so. And here happened something rather marvellous, though trifling enough, too. The staff seemed to get up from the ground of its own accord, and, spreading its little pair of wings, it half hopped, half flew, and leaned itself against the wall of the cottage. There it stood quite still, except that the snakes continued to wriggle. But, in my private opinion, old Philemon's eyesight had been playing him tricks again.

Before he could ask any questions, the elder stranger drew his attention from the wonderful staff, by speaking to him.

"Was there not," asked the stranger, in a remarkably deep tone of voice, "a lake, in very ancient times, covering the spot where now stands yonder village?"

"Not in my day, friend," answered Philemon; "and yet I am an old man, as you see. There were always the fields and meadows, just as they are now, and the old trees, and the little stream murmuring through the midst of the valley. My father, nor his father before him, ever saw it otherwise, so far as I know; and doubtless it will still be the same, when old Philemon shall be gone and forgotten."

"That is more than can be safely foretold," observed the stranger; and there was something very stern in his deep voice. He shook his head, too, so that his dark and heavy curls were shaken with the movement.

"Since the inhabitants of yonder village have forgotten the affections and sympathies of their nature, it were better that the lake should be rippling over their dwellings again!"

The traveller looked so stern, that Philemon was really almost frightened; the more so, that, at his frown, the twilight seemed suddenly to grow darker, and that, when he shook his head, there was a roll as of thunder in the air.

But, in a moment afterwards, the stranger's face became so kindly and mild, that the old man quite forgot his terror. Nevertheless, he could not help feeling that this elder traveller must be no ordinary personage, although he happened now to be attired so humbly and to be journeying on foot. Not that Philemon fancied him a prince in disguise, or any character of that sort; but rather some exceedingly wise man, who went about the world in this poor garb, despising wealth and all worldly objects, and seeking everywhere to add a mite to his wisdom. This idea appeared the more probable, because, when Philemon raised his eyes to the stranger's face, he seemed to see more thought there, in one look, than he could have studied out in a lifetime.

While Baucis was getting the supper, the travellers both began to talk very sociably with Philemon. The younger, indeed, was extremely loquacious, and made such shrewd and witty remarks, that the good old man continually burst out a-laughing, and pronounced him the merriest fellow whom he had seen for many a day. "Pray, my young friend," said he, as they grew familiar together, "what may I call your name?"

" Why, I am very nimble, as you see," answered the traveller. " So, if you call me Quicksilver, the name will fit tolerably well."

"Quicksilver? Quicksilver?" repeated Philemon, looking in the traveller's face, to see if he were making fun of him. " It is a very odd name! And your companion there? Has he as strange a one?"

" You must ask the thunder to tell it you! " replied Quicksilver, putting on a mysterious look. " No other voice is loud enough."

This remark, whether it were serious or in jest, might have caused Philemon to conceive a very great awe of the elder stranger, if, on venturing to gaze at him, he had not beheld so much beneficence in his visage. But, undoubtedly, here was the grandest figure that ever sat so humbly beside a cottage-door. When the stranger conversed, it was with gravity, and in such a way that Philemon felt irresistibly moved to tell him everything which he had most at heart. This is always the feeling that people have, when they meet with any one wise enough to comprehend all their good and evil, and to despise not a tittle of it.

But Philemon, simple and kind-hearted old man that he was, had not many secrets to disclose. He talked, however, quite garrulously, about the events of his past life, in the whole course of which he had never been a score of miles from this very spot. His wife Baucis and himself had dwelt in the cottage from their youth upward, earning their bread by honest labor, always poor, but still contented. He told what excellent butter and cheese Baucis made, and how nice were the vegetables which he raised in his garden. He said, too, that,

because they loved one another so very much, it was
the wish of both that death might not separate them,
but they should die, as they had lived, together.

As the stranger listened, a smile beamed over his
countenance, and made its expression as sweet as it was
grand.

" You are a good old man," said he to Philemon,
" and you have a good old wife to be your helpmeet.
It is fit that your wish be granted."

And it seemed to Philemon, just then, as if the sunset clouds threw up a bright flash from the west, and
kindled a sudden light in the sky.

Baucis had now got supper ready, and, coming to the
door, began to make apologies for the poor fare which
she was forced to set before her guests.

" Had we known you were coming," said she, " my
good man and myself would have gone without a morsel, rather than you should lack a better supper.   But
I took the most part of to-day's milk to make cheese ;
and our last loaf is already half eaten.   Ah me! I
never feel the sorrow of being poor, save when a poor
traveller knocks at our door."

"All will be very well; do not trouble yourself, my
good dame," replied the elder stranger kindly.   "An
honest, hearty welcome to a guest works miracles with
the fare, and is capable of turning the coarsest food to
nectar and ambrosia."

" A welcome you shall have," cried Baucis, " and
likewise a little honey that we happen to have left, and
a bunch of purple grapes besides."

" Why, Mother Baucis, it is a feast!" exclaimed
Quicksilver, laughing, "an absolute feast! and you

shall see how bravely I will play my part at it! I think I never felt hungrier in my life."

"Mercy on us!" whispered Baucis to her husband. "If the young man has such a terrible appetite, I am afraid there will not be half enough supper!"

They all went into the cottage.

And now, my little auditors, shall I tell you something that will make you open your eyes very wide? It is really one of the oddest circumstances in the whole story. Quicksilver's staff, you recollect, had set itself up against the wall of the cottage. Well; when its master entered the door, leaving this wonderful staff behind, what should it do but immediately spread its little wings, and go hopping and fluttering up the door steps! Tap, tap, went the staff, on the kitchen floor; nor did it rest until it had stood itself on end, with the greatest gravity and decorum, beside Quicksilver's chair. Old Philemon, however, as well as his wife, was so taken up in attending to their guests, that no notice was given to what the staff had been about.

As Baucis had said, there was but a scanty supper for two hungry travellers. In the middle of the table was the remnant of a brown loaf, with a piece of cheese on one side of it, and a dish of honeycomb on the other. There was a pretty good bunch of grapes for each of the guests. A moderately sized earthen pitcher, nearly full of milk, stood at a corner of the board; and when Baucis had filled two bowls, and set them before the strangers, only a little milk remained in the bottom of the pitcher. Alas! it is a very sad business, when a bountiful heart finds itself pinched and squeezed among narrow circumstances.

Poor Baucis kept wishing that she might starve for a week to come, if it were possible, by so doing, to provide these hungry folks a more plentiful supper.

And, since the supper was so exceedingly small, she could not help wishing that their appetites had not been quite so large. Why, at their very first sitting down, the travellers both drank off all the milk in their two bowls, at a draught.

"A little more milk, kind Mother Baucis, if you please," said Quicksilver. "The day has been hot, and I am very much athirst."

"Now, my dear people," answered Baucis, in great confusion, "I am so sorry and ashamed! But the truth is, there is hardly a drop more milk in the pitcher. O husband! husband! why didn't we go without our supper?"

"Why, it appears to me," cried Quicksilver, starting up from table and taking the pitcher by the handle, "it really appears to me that matters are not quite so bad as you represent them. Here is certainly more milk in the pitcher."

So saying, and to the vast astonishment of Baucis, he proceeded to fill, not only his own bowl, but his companion's likewise, from the pitcher, that was supposed to be almost empty. The good woman could scarcely believe her eyes. She had certainly poured out nearly all the milk, and had peeped in afterwards, and seen the bottom of the pitcher, as she set it down upon the table.

"But I am old," thought Baucis to herself, "and apt to be forgetful. I suppose I must have made a mistake. At all events the pitcher cannot help being empty now, after filling the bowl twice over."

"What excellent milk!" observed Quicksilver, after quaffing the contents of the second bowl. "Excuse me, my kind hostess, but I must really ask you for a little more."

Now Baucis had seen, as plainly as she could see anything, that Quicksilver had turned the pitcher upside down, and consequently had poured out every drop of milk, in filling the last bowl. Of course, there could not possibly be any left. However, in order to let him know precisely how the case was, she lifted the pitcher, and made a gesture as if pouring milk into Quicksilver's bowl, but without the remotest idea that any milk would stream forth. What was her surprise, therefore, when such an abundant cascade fell bubbling into the bowl, that it was immediately filled to the brim, and overflowed upon the table! The two snakes that were twisted about Quicksilver's staff (but neither Baucis nor Philemon happened to observe this circumstance) stretched out their heads, and began to lap up the spilt milk.

And then what a delicious fragrance the milk had! It seemed as if Philemon's only cow must have pastured, that day, on the richest herbage that could be found anywhere in the world. I only wish that each of you, my beloved little souls, could have a bowl of such nice milk, at supper-time!

"And now a slice of your brown loaf, Mother Baucis," said Quicksilver, "and a little of that honey."

Baucis cut him a slice accordingly; and though the loaf, when she and her husband ate of it, had been rather too dry and crusty to be palatable, it was now as light and moist as if but a few hours out of the oven.

Tasting a crumb, which had fallen on the table, she found it more delicious than bread ever was before, and could hardly believe that it was a loaf of her own kneading and baking. Yet, what other loaf could it possibly be?

But, oh the honey! I may just as well let it alone, without trying to describe how exquisitely it smelt and looked. Its color was that of the purest and most transparent gold; and it had the odor of a thousand flowers; but of such flowers as never grew in an earthly garden, and to seek which the bees must have flown high above the clouds. The wonder is, that, after alighting on a flower-bed of so delicious fragrance and immortal bloom, they should have been content to fly down again to their hive in Philemon's garden. Never was such honey tasted, seen, or smelt. The perfume floated around the kitchen, and made it so delightful, that, had you closed your eyes, you would instantly have forgotten the low ceiling and smoky walls, and have fancied yourself in an arbor, with celestial honeysuckles creeping over it.

Although good Mother Baucis was a simple old dame, she could not but think that there was something rather out of the common way, in all that had been going on. So, after helping the guests to bread and honey, and laying a bunch of grapes by each of their plates, she sat down by Philemon, and told him what she had seen, in a whisper.

"Did you ever hear the like?" asked she.

"No, I never did," answered Philemon, with a smile. "And I rather think, my dear old wife, you have been

walking about in a sort of a dream. If I had poured
out the milk, I should have seen through the business
at once. There happened to be a little more in the
pitcher than you thought, — that is all."

"Ah, husband," said Baucis, "say what you will,
these are very uncommon people."

"Well, well," replied Philemon, still smiling, "perhaps they are. They certainly do look as if they had
seen better days; and I am heartily glad to see them
making so comfortable a supper."

Each of the guests had now taken his bunch of
grapes upon his plate. Baucis (who rubbed her eyes,
in order to see the more clearly) was of opinion that
the clusters had grown larger and richer, and that each
separate grape seemed to be on the point of bursting
with ripe juice. It was entirely a mystery to her how
such grapes could ever have been produced from the
old stunted vine that climbed against the cottage-wall.

"Very admirable grapes these!" observed Quicksilver, as he swallowed one after another, without
apparently diminishing his cluster. "Pray, my good
host, whence did you gather them?"

"From my own vine," answered Philemon. "You
may see one of its branches twisting across the window,
yonder. But wife and I never thought the grapes very
fine ones."

"I never tasted better," said the guest. "Another
cup of this delicious milk, if you please, and I shall
then have supped better than a prince."

This time, old Philemon bestirred himself, and took
up the pitcher; for he was curious to discover whether
there was any reality in the marvels which Baucis had

whispered to him. He knew that his good old wife was incapable of falsehood, and that she was seldom mistaken in what she supposed to be true; but this was so very singular a case, that he wanted to see into it with his own eyes. On taking up the pitcher, therefore, he slyly peeped into it, and was fully satisfied that it contained not so much as a single drop. All at once, however, he beheld a little white fountain, which gushed up from the bottom of the pitcher, and speedily filled it to the brim with foaming and deliciously fragrant milk. It was lucky that Philemon, in his surprise, did not drop the miraculous pitcher from his hand.

" Who are ye, wonder-working strangers ! " cried he, even more bewildered than his wife had been.

" Your guests, my good Philemon, and your friends," replied the elder traveller, in his mild, deep voice, that had something at once sweet and awe-inspiring in it. " Give me likewise a cup of the milk; and may your pitcher never be empty for kind Baucis and yourself, any more than for the needy wayfarer ! "

The supper being now over, the strangers requested to be shown to their place of repose. The old people would gladly have talked to them a little longer, and have expressed the wonder which they felt, and their delight at finding the poor and meagre supper prove so much better and more abundant than they hoped. But the elder traveller had inspired them with such reverence, that they dared not ask him any questic is. And when Philemon drew Quicksilver aside, and inquired how under the sun a fountain of milk could have got into an old earthen pitcher, this latter personage pointed to his staff.

"There is the whole mystery of the affair," quoth Quicksilver; "and if you can make it out, I'll thank you to let me know. I can't tell what to make of my staff. It is always playing such odd tricks as this; sometimes getting me a supper, and, quite as often stealing it away. If I had any faith in such nonsense, I should say the stick was bewitched!"

He said no more, but looked so slyly in their faces, that they rather fancied he was laughing at them. The magic staff went hopping at his heels, as Quicksilver quitted the room. When left alone, the good old couple spent some little time in conversation about the events of the evening, and then lay down on the floor, and fell fast asleep. They had given up their sleeping-room to the guests, and had no other bed for themselves, save these planks, which I wish had been as soft as their own hearts.

The old man and his wife were stirring, betimes, in the morning, and the strangers likewise arose with the sun, and made their preparations to depart. Philemon hospitably entreated them to remain a little longer, until Baucis could milk the cow, and bake a cake upon the hearth, and, perhaps, find them a few fresh eggs, for breakfast. The guests, however, seemed to think it better to accomplish a good part of their journey before the heat of the day should come on. They, therefore, persisted in setting out immediately, but asked Philemon and Baucis to walk forth with them a short distance, and show them the road which they were to take.

So they all four issued from the cottage, chatting together like old friends. It was very remarkable, indeed, how familiar the old couple insensibly grew with the elder traveller, and how their good and simple spirits melted into his, even as two drops of water would melt into the illimitable ocean. And as for Quicksilver, with his keen, quick, laughing wits, he appeared to discover every little thought that but peeped into their minds, before they suspected it themselves. They sometimes wished, it is true, that he had not been quite so quick-witted, and also that he would fling away his staff, which looked so mysteriously mischievous, with the snakes always writhing about it. But then, again, Quicksilver showed himself so very good-humored, that they would have been rejoiced to keep him in their cottage, staff, snakes, and all, every day, and the whole day long.

"Ah me! Well-a-day!" exclaimed Philemon, when they had walked a little way from their door. "If our neighbors only knew what a blessed thing it is to show hospitality to strangers, they would tie up all their dogs, and never allow their children to fling another stone."

"It is a sin and shame for them to behave so, — that it is!" cried good old Baucis, vehemently. "And I mean to go this very day, and tell some of them what naughty people they are!"

"I fear," remarked Quicksilver, slyly smiling, "that you will find none of them at home."

The elder traveller's brow, just then, assumed such a grave, stern, and awful grandeur, yet serene withal, that neither Baucis nor Philemon dared to speak a word. They gazed reverently into his face, as if they had been gazing at the sky.

"When men do not feel towards the humblest stran-

ger as if he were a brother," said the traveller, in tones
so deep that they sounded like those of an organ, " they
are unworthy to exist on earth, which was created as
the abode of a great human brotherhood ! "

" And, by the by, my dear old people," cried Quicksilver, with the liveliest look of fun and mischief in his
eyes, " where is this same village that you talk about?
On which side of us does it lie ?   Methinks I do not see
it hereabouts."

Philemon and his wife turned towards the valley,
where, at sunset, only the day before, they had seen the
meadows, the houses, the gardens, the clumps of trees,
the wide, green-margined street, with children playing in it, and all the tokens of business, enjoyment,
and prosperity.   But what was their astonishment!
There was no longer any appearance of a village.
Even the fertile vale, in the hollow of which it lay,
had ceased to have existence.   In its stead, they beheld
the broad, blue surface of a lake, which filled the great
basin of the valley from brim to brim, and reflected the
surrounding hills in its bosom with as tranquil an
image as if it had been there ever since the creation of
the world.   For an instant, the lake remained perfectly
smooth.   Then, a little breeze sprang up, and caused
the water to dance, glitter, and sparkle in the early
sunbeams, and to dash, with a pleasant rippling murmur, against the hither shore.

The lake seemed so strangely familiar, that the old
couple were greatly perplexed, and felt as if they could
only have been dreaming about a village having lain
there.   But, the next moment, they remembered the

vanished dwellings, and the faces and characters of the inhabitants, far too distinctly for a dream. The village had been there yesterday, and now was gone!

"Alas!" cried these kind-hearted old people, "what has become of our poor neighbors?"

"They exist no longer as men and women," said the elder traveller, in his grand and deep voice, while a roll of thunder seemed to echo it at a distance. "There was neither use nor beauty in such a life as theirs; for they never softened or sweetened the hard lot of mortality by the exercise of kindly affections between man and man. They retained no image of the better life in their bosoms; therefore, the lake, that was of old, has spread itself forth again, to reflect the sky!"

"And as for those foolish people," said Quicksilver, with his mischievous smile, "they are all transformed to fishes. They needed but little change, for they were already a scaly set of rascals, and the coldest-blooded beings in existence. So, kind Mother Baucis, whenever you or your husband has an appetite for a dish of broiled trout, he can throw in a line, and pull out half a dozen of your old neighbors!"

"Ah," cried Baucis, shuddering, "I would not, for the world, put one of them on the gridiron!"

"No," added Philemon, making a wry face, "we could never relish them!"

"As for you, good Philemon," continued the elder traveller, — "and you, kind Baucis, — you, with your scanty means, have mingled so much heartfelt hospitality with your entertainment of the homeless stranger, that the milk became an inexhaustible fount of nectar, and the brown loaf and the honey were ambrosia. Thus, the divinities have feasted at your board, off the same viands that supply their banquets on Olympus. You have done well, my dear old friends. Wherefore, request whatever favor you have most at heart, and it is granted."

Philemon and Baucis looked at one another, and then, — I know not which of the two it was who spoke, but that one uttered the desire of both their hearts.

"Let us live together, while we live, and leave the world at the same instant, when we die! For we have always loved one another!"

"Be it so!" replied the stranger, with majestic kindness. "Now look toward your cottage!"

They did so. But what was their surprise on beholding a tall edifice of white marble, with a wide-open portal, occupying the spot where their humble residence had so lately stood!

"There is your home," said the stranger, beneficently smiling on them both. "Exercise your hospitality in yonder palace as freely as in the poor hovel to which you welcomed us last evening."

The old folks fell on their knees to thank him; but, behold! neither he nor Quicksilver was there.

So Philemon and Baucis took up their residence in the marble palace, and spent their time, with vast satisfaction to themselves, in making everybody jolly and comfortable who happened to pass that way. The milk-pitcher, I must not forget to say, retained its marvellous quality of being never empty, when it was desirable to have it full. Whenever an honest, good-humored, and free-hearted guest took a draught from this pitcher, he invariably found it the sweetest and most invigorating fluid that ever ran down his throat. But, if a cross and disagreeable curmudgeon happened to sip, he was pretty certain to twist his visage into a hard knot, and pronounce it a pitcher of sour milk!

Thus the old couple lived in their palace a great, great while, and grew older and older, and very old indeed. At length, however, there came a summer morning when Philemon and Baucis failed to make their appearance, as on other mornings, with one hospitable smile overspreading both their pleasant faces, to invite the guests of over-night to breakfast. The guests searched everywhere, from top to bottom of the spacious palace, and all to no purpose. But, after a great deal of perplexity, they espied, in front of the portal, two venerable trees, which nobody could remember to have seen there the day before. Yet there they stood, with their roots fastened deep into the soil, and a huge breadth of foliage overshadowing the whole front of the edifice. One was an oak, and the other a linden-tree. Their boughs — it was strange and beautiful to see — were intertwined together, and embraced one another, so that each tree seemed to live in the other tree's bosom much more than in its own.

While the guests were marvelling how these trees, that must have required at least a century to grow, could have come to be so tall and venerable in a single night, a breeze sprang up, and set their intermingled boughs astir. And then there was a deep, broad murmur in the air, as if the two mysterious trees were speaking.

"I am old Philemon!" murmured the oak.

"I am old Baucis!" murmured the linden-tree.

But, as the breeze grew stronger, the trees both spoke at once, — "Philemon! Baucis! Baucis! Philemon!" — as if one were both and both were one, and talking together in the depths of their mutual heart. It was plain enough to perceive that the good old couple had renewed their age, and were now to spend a quiet and delightful hundred years or so, Philemon as an oak, and Baucis as a linden-tree. And oh, what a hospitable shade did they fling around them! Whenever a wayfarer paused beneath it, he heard a pleasant whisper of the leaves above his head, and wondered how the sound should so much resemble words like these: —

"Welcome, welcome, dear traveller, welcome!"

And some kind soul, that knew what would have pleased old Baucis and old Philemon best, built a circular seat around both their trunks, where, for a great while afterwards, the weary, and the hungry, and the thirsty used to repose themselves, and quaff milk abundantly out of the miraculous pitcher.

And I wish, for all our sakes, that we had the pitcher here now!

THE ARGONAUTS

By CHARLES KINGSLEY.

PART I.

HOW THE CENTAUR TRAINED THE HEROES ON PELION.

I HAVE a tale to tell of heroes who sailed away into a distant land to win themselves renown forever, in the adventure of the Golden Fleece.

Whither they sailed, my children, I cannot clearly tell. It all happened long ago; so long that it has all grown dim, like a dream which you dreamed last year. And why they went I cannot tell; some say that it was to win gold. It may be so; but the noblest deeds which have been done on earth, have not been done for gold. It was not for the sake of gold that the Lord came down and died, and the Apostles went out to preach the good news in all lands. The Spartans looked for no reward in money when they fought and died at Thermopylæ; and Socrates the wise asked no pay from his countrymen, but lived poor and barefoot all his days, only caring to make good men. And there are heroes in our days also, who do noble deeds, but not for gold. Our

93

discoverers did not go to make themselves rich, when they sailed out one after another into the dreary frozen seas; nor did the ladies, who went out from home to drudge in the hospitals of the East, making themselves poor, that they might be rich in noble works. And young men, too, whom you know, children, and some of them of your own kin, did they say to themselves, "How much money shall I earn?" when they went out to the war, leaving wealth, and comfort, and a pleasant home, and all that money can give, to face hunger and thirst, and wounds and death, that they might fight for their country and their Queen? No, children, there is a better thing on earth than wealth, a better thing than life itself; and that is, to have done something before you die, for which good men may honor you, and God your Father smile upon your work.

Therefore we will believe — why should we not?— of these same Argonauts of old, that they too were noble men, who planned and did a noble deed; and that therefore their fame has lived, and been told in story and in song, mixed up, no doubt, with dreams and fables, and yet true and right at heart. So we will honor these old Argonauts, and listen to their story as it stands; and we will try to be like them, each of us in our place; for each of us has a Golden Fleece to seek, and a wild sea to sail over, ere we reach it, and dragons to fight ere it be ours.

And what was that first Golden Fleece? I do not know, nor care. The old Hellenes said that it hung in Colchis, which we call the Circassian coast, nailed to a beech-tree in the War-god's wood; and that it was the fleece of the wondrous ram, who bore Phrixus and Helle across the Euxine sea. For Phrixus and Helle were the children of the cloud-nymph, and of Athamas the Minuan king. And when a famine came upon the land, their cruel step-mother, Ino, wished to kill them, that her own children might reign, and said that they must be sacrificed on an altar, to turn away the anger of the gods. So the poor children were brought to the altar, and the priest stood ready with his knife, when out of the clouds came the Golden Ram, and took them on his back, and vanished. Then madness came upon that foolish king Athamas, and ruin upon Ino and her children. For Athamas killed one of them in his fury, and Ino fled from him with the other in her arms, and leaped from a cliff into the sea, and was changed into a dolphin, such as you have seen, which wanders over the waves forever sighing, with its little one clasped to its breast.

But the people drove out King Athamas, because he had killed his child; and he roamed about in his misery, till he came to the Oracle in Delphi. And the Oracle told him that he must wander for his sin, till the wild beasts should feast him as their guest. So he went on in hunger and sorrow for many a weary day, till he saw a pack of wolves. The wolves were tearing a sheep; but when they saw Athamas they fled, and left the sheep for him, and he ate of it; and then he knew that the oracle was fulfilled at last. So he wandered no more; but settled, and built a town, and became a king again.

But the ram carried the two children far away over land and sea, till he came to the Thracian Chersonese, and there Helle fell into the sea. So those narrow straits are called "Hellespont," after her; and they bear that name until this day.

Then the ram flew on with Phrixus to the northeast across the sea which we call the Black Sea now; but the Hellenes called it Euxine. And at last, they say, he stopped at Colchis, on the steep Circassian coast; and there Phrixus married Chalciope, the daughter of Aietes the king; and offered the ram in sacrifice; and Aietes nailed the ram's fleece to a beech, in the grove of Ares the War-god.

And after awhile Phrixus died, and was buried, but his spirit had no rest; for he was buried far from his native land, and the pleasant hills of Hellas. So he came in dreams to the heroes of the Minuai, and called sadly by their beds, — "Come and set my spirit free, that I may go home to my fathers and to my kinsfolk, and the pleasant Minuan land."

And they asked — "How shall we set your spirit free?"

"You must sail over the sea to Colchis, and bring home the Golden Fleece; and then my spirit will come back with it, and I shall sleep with my fathers and have rest."

He came thus, and called to them often: but when they woke they looked at each other, and said — "Who dare sail to Colchis, or bring home the Golden Fleece?" And in all the country none was brave enough to try it; for the man and the time were not come.

Phrixus had a cousin called Æson, who was king in Iolcos by the sea. There he ruled over the rich Minuan heroes, as Athamas his uncle ruled in Bœotia; and like

Athamas, he was an unhappy man. For he had a step-brother named Pelias, of whom some said that he was a nymph's son, and there were dark and sad tales about his birth. When he was a babe he was cast out on the mountains, and a wild mare came by and kicked him. But a shepherd passing found the baby, with its face all blackened by the blow; and took him home, and called him Pelias, because his face was bruised and black. And he grew up fierce and lawless, and did many a fearful deed; and at last he drove out Æson his step-brother, and then his own brother Neleus, and took the kingdom to himself, and ruled over the rich Minuan heroes, in Iolcos by the sea.

And Æson, when he was driven out, went sadly away out of the town, leading his little son by the hand; and he said to himself, "I must hide the child in the mountains; or Pelias will surely kill him, because he is the heir."

So he went up from the sea across the valley, through the vineyards and the olive groves, and across the torrent of Anauros, toward Pelion the ancient mountain, whose brows are white with snow.

He went up and up into the mountain, over marsh, and crag, and down, till the boy was tired and foot-sore, and Æson had to bear him in his arms, till he came to the mouth of a lonely cave, at the foot of a mighty cliff.

Above the cliff the snow wreaths hung, dripping and cracking in the sun: but at its foot around the cave's mouth grew all fair flowers and herbs, as if in a garden, ranged in order, each sort by itself. There they grew gayly in the sunshine, and the spray of the torrent from above; while from the cave came the sound of music, and a man's voice singing to the harp.

Then Æson put down the lad, and whispered, —

" Fear not, but go in, and whomsoever you shall find, lay your hands upon his knees, and say, ' In the name of Zeus the father of gods and men, I am your guest from this day forth.' "

Then the lad went in without trembling, for he too was a hero's son: but when he was within, he stopped in wonder, to listen to that magic song.

And there he saw the singer lying, upon bear-skins and fragrant boughs; Cheiron, the ancient Centaur, the wisest of all things beneath the sky. Down to the waist he was a man; but below he was a noble horse; his white hair rolled down over his broad shoulders, and his white beard over his broad brown chest; and his eyes were wise and mild, and his forehead like a mountain-wall.

And in his hands he held a harp of gold, and struck it with a golden key; and as he struck, he sang till his eyes glittered, and filled all the cave with light.

And he sang of the birth of Time, and of the heavens and the dancing stars; and of the ocean, and the ether, and the fire, and the shaping of the wondrous earth. And he sang of the treasures of the hills, and the hidden jewels of the mine, and the veins of fire and metal, and the virtues of all healing herbs, and of the speech of birds, and of prophecy, and of hidden things to come.

Then he sang of health, and strength, and manhood, and a valiant heart, and of music, and hunting, and wrestling, and all the games which heroes love; and of travel, and wars, and sieges, and a noble death in fight; and then he sang of peace and plenty, and of equal justice in the land; and as he sang, the boy listened wide-eyed, and forgot his errand in the song.

And at the last old Cheiron was silent, and called the lad with a soft voice.

And the lad ran trembling to him, and would have lain his hands upon his knees: but Cheiron smiled, and said, " Call hither your father Æson, for I know you, and all that has befallen, and saw you both afar in the valley, even before you left the town."

Then Æson came in sadly, and Cheiron asked him, " Why came you not yourself to me, Æson the Æolid ? "

And Æson said, —

" I thought, Cheiron will pity the lad if he sees him come alone; and I wished to try whether he was fearless, and dare venture like a hero's son. But now I entreat you by Father Zeus, let the boy be your guest till better times, and train him among the sons of the heroes, that he may avenge his father's house."

Then Cheiron smiled, and drew the lad to him, and laid his hand upon his golden locks, and said, " Are you afraid of my horse's hoofs, fair boy, or will you be my pupil from this day ? "

" I would gladly have horse's hoofs like you, if I could sing such songs as yours."

And Cheiron laughed, and said, " Sit here by me till sundown, when your playfellows will come home, and you shall learn like them to be a king, worthy to rule over gallant men."

Then he turned to Æson, and said, " Go back in

peace, and bend before the storm like a prudent man. This boy shall not cross the Anauros again, till he has become a glory to you and to the house of Æolus."

And Æson wept over his son and went away; but the boy did not weep, so full was his fancy of that strange cave, and the Centaur, and his song, and the play-fellows whom he was to see.

Then Cheiron put the lyre into his hands, and taught him how to play it, till the sun sank low behind the cliff, and a shout was heard outside.

And then in came the sons of the heroes, Æneas, and Heracles, and Peleus, and many another mighty name.

And great Cheiron leapt up joyfully, and his hoofs made the cave resound, as they shouted, "Come out, Father Cheiron; come out and see our game." And one cried, "I have killed two deer," and another, "I took a wild cat among the crags;" and Heracles dragged a wild goat after him by its horns, for he was as huge as a mountain crag; and Cæneus carried a bear-cub under each arm, and laughed when they scratched and bit; for neither tooth nor steel could wound him.

And Cheiron praised them all, each according to his deserts.

Only one walked apart and silent, Asclepius, the too-wise child, with his bosom full of herbs and flowers, and round his wrist a spotted snake; he came with down-cast eyes to Cheiron, and whispered how he had watched the snake cast his old skin, and grow young again before his eyes, and how he had gone down into a village in the vale, and cured a dying man with an herb which he had seen a sick goat eat.

And Cheiron smiled, and said, "To each Athene and

Apollo give some gift, and each is worthy in his place;
but to this child they have given an honor beyond all
honors, to cure while others kill."

Then the lads brought in wood, and split it, and
lighted a blazing fire; and others skinned the deer and
quartered them, and set them to roast before the fire;
and while the venison was cooking they bathed in the
snow torrent, and washed away the dust and sweat.

And then all ate till they could eat no more (for they
had tasted nothing since the dawn), and drank of the
clear spring water, for wine is not fit for growing lads.
And when the remnants were put away, they all lay
down upon the skins and leaves about the fire, and each
took the lyre in turn, and sang and played with all his
heart.

And after a while they all went out to a plot of
grass at the cave's mouth, and there they boxed, and
ran, and wrestled, and laughed till the stones fell from
the cliffs.

Then Cheiron took his lyre, and all the lads joined
hands; and as he played, they danced to his measure,
in and out, and round and round. There they danced
hand in hand, till the night fell over land and sea,
while the black glen shone with their broad white limbs,
and the gleam of their golden hair.

And the lad danced with them, delighted, and then
slept a wholesome sleep, upon fragrant leaves of bay,
and myrtle, and marjoram, and flowers of thyme; and
rose at the dawn, and bathed in the torrent, and became a schoolfellow to the heroes' sons, and forgot
Ioclos, and his father, and all his former life. But he
grew strong, and brave and cunning, upon the pleasant

downs of Pelion, in the keen hungry mountain air.
And he learnt to wrestle, and to box, and to hunt, and
to play upon the harp ; and next he learnt to ride, for
old Cheiron used to mount him on his back ; and he
learnt the virtues of all herbs, and how to cure all
wounds ; and Cheiron called him Jason the healer, and
that is his name until this day.

PART II.

HOW JASON LOST HIS SANDAL IN ANAUROS.

AND ten years came and went, and Jason was grown to be a mighty man. Some of his fellows were gone, and some were growing up by his side. Asclepius was gone into Peloponnese, to work his wondrous cures on men; and some say he used to raise the dead to life. And Heracles was gone to Thebes, to fulfil those famous labors which have become a proverb among men. And Peleus had married a sea-nymph, and his wedding is famous to this day. And Æneas was gone home to Troy, and many a noble tale you will read of him, and of all the other gallant heroes, the scholars of Cheiron the just. And it happened on a day that Jason stood on the mountain, and looked north and south and east and west; and Cheiron stood by him and watched him, for he knew that the time was come.

And Jason looked and saw the plains of Thessaly, where the Lapithai breed their horses; and the lake of Boibé, and the stream which runs northward to Peneus and Tempe; and he looked north, and saw the mountain wall which guards the Magnesian shore; Olympus, the seat of the Immortals, and Ossa, and Pelion, where he stood. Then he looked east and saw the bright blue sea, which stretched away forever toward the dawn. Then he looked south, and saw a pleasant land, with white-walled towns and farms, nestling along the shore of a land-locked bay, while the smoke rose blue among the trees; and he knew it for the bay of Pagasai, and the rich lowlands of Hæmonia, and Iolcos by the sea.

Then he sighed, and asked: "Is it true what the heroes tell me, that I am heir of that fair land?"

"And what good would it be to you, Jason, if you were heir of that fair land?"

"I would take it and keep it."

"A strong man has taken it and kept it long. Are you stronger than Pelias the terrible?"

"I can try my strength with his," said Jason. But Cheiron sighed and said : —

"You have many a danger to go through before you rule in Iolcos by the sea; many a danger, and many a woe; and strange troubles in strange lands, such as man never saw before."

"The happier I," said Jason, "to see what man never saw before."

And Cheiron sighed again, and said: "The eaglet must leave the nest when it is fledged. Will you go to Iolcos by the sea? Then promise me two things before you go."

Jason promised, and Cheiron answered: "Speak harshly to no soul whom you may meet, and stand by the word which you shall speak."

Jason wondered why Cheiron asked this of him; but he knew that the Centaur was a prophet, and saw things long before they came. So he promised, and leapt down the mountain, to take his fortune like a man.

He went down through the arbutus thickets, and across the downs of thyme, till he came to the vineyard walls, and the pomegranates and the olives in the glen; and among the olives roared Anauros, all foaming with a summer flood.

And on the bank of Anauros sat a woman, all wrinkled, gray, and old; her head shook palsied on her breast, and her hands shook palsied on her knees; and when she saw Jason, she spoke whining: "Who will carry me across the flood?"

Jason was bold and hasty, and was just going to leap into the flood; and yet he thought twice before he leapt, so loud roared the torrent down, all brown from the mountain rains, and silver-veined with melting snow; while underneath he could hear the boulders rumbling like the tramp of horsemen or the roll of wheels, as they ground along the narrow channel, and shook the rocks on which he stood.

But the old woman whined all the more: "I am weak and old, fair youth. For Hera's sake, carry me over the torrent."

And Jason was going to answer her scornfully, when Cheiron's words came to his mind.

So he said: "For Hera's sake, the Queen of the Immortals on Olympus, I will carry you over the torrent, unless we both are drowned midway."

Then the old dame leapt upon his back, as nimbly as a goat; and Jason staggered in, wondering; and the first step was up to his knees.

The first step was up to his knees, and the second

step was up to his waist; and the stones rolled about
his feet, and his feet slipped about the stones; so he
went on staggering and panting, while the old woman
cried from off his back: —

"Fool, you have wet my mantle! Do you make
game of poor old souls like me?"

Jason had half a mind to drop her, and let her get
through the torrent by herself; but Cheiron's words
were in his mind, and he said only: "Patience, mother;
the best horse may stumble some day."

At last he staggered to the shore, and set her down
upon the bank; and a strong man he needed to have
been, or that wild water he never would have crossed.

He lay panting awhile upon the bank, and then leapt
up to go upon his journey; but he cast one look at the
old woman, for he thought, "she should thank me once
at least."

And as he looked, she grew fairer than all women,
and taller than all men on earth; and her garments
shone like the summer sea, and her jewels like the stars
of heaven; and over her forehead was a veil, woven of
the golden clouds of sunset; and through the veil she
looked down on him, with great soft heifer's eyes; with
great eyes, mild and awful, which filled all the glen
with light.

And Jason fell upon his knees, and hid his face between his hands.

And she spoke — "I am the Queen of Olympus, Hera
the wife of Zeus. As thou hast done to me, so will I do
to thee. Call on me in the hour of need, and try if the
Immortals can forget."

And when Jason looked up, she rose from off the

earth, like a pillar of tall white cloud, and floated away across the mountain peaks, toward Olympus the holy hill.

Then a great fear fell on Jason; but after a while he grew light of heart; and he blessed old Cheiron, and said — "Surely the Centaur is a prophet, and guessed what would come to pass, when he bade me speak harshly to no soul whom I might meet."

Then he went down toward Iolcos, and as he walked, he found that he had lost one of his sandals in the flood.

And as he went through the streets, the people came out to look at him, so tall and fair was he; but some of the elders whispered together; and at last one of them stopped Jason, and called to him — "Fair lad, who are you, and whence come you; and what is your errand in the town?"

"My name, good father, is Jason, and I come from Pelion up above; and my errand is to Pelias your king; tell me then where his palace is."

But the old man started, and grew pale, and said, "Do you not know the oracle, my son, that you go so boldly through the town, with but one sandal on?"

"I am a stranger here, and know of no oracle; but what of my one sandal? I lost the other in Anauros, while I was struggling with the flood."

Then the old man looked back to his companions; and one sighed and another smiled; at last he said — "I will tell you, lest you rush upon your ruin unawares. The oracle in Delphi has said, that a man wearing one sandal should take the kingdom from Pelias, and keep it for himself. Therefore beware how you go up to his palace, for he is the fiercest and most cunning of all kings."

Then Jason laughed a great laugh, like a war-horse in his pride — " Good news, good father, both for you and me.   For that very end I came into the town."

Then he strode on toward the palace of Pelias, while all the people wondered at his bearing.

And he stood in the doorway and cried, " Come out, come out, Pelias the valiant, and fight for your kingdom like a man."

Pelias came out wondering, and " Who are you, bold youth ? " he cried.

" I am Jason, the son of Æson, the heir of all this land."

Then Pelias lifted up his hands and eyes, and wept, or seemed to weep; and blessed the heavens which had brought his nephew to him, never to leave him more. " For," said he, " I have but three daughters, and no son to be my heir.   You shall be my heir then, and rule the kingdom after me, and marry whichsoever of my daughters you shall choose; though a sad kingdom you will find it, and whosoever rules it a miserable man.   But come in, come in, and feast."

So he drew Jason in, whether he would or not, and spoke to him so lovingly and feasted him so well, that Jason's anger passed; and after supper his three cousins came into the hall, and Jason thought that he should like well enough to have one of them for his wife.

But at last he said to Pelias, " Why do you look so sad, my uncle ?   And what did you mean just now, when you said that this was a doleful kingdom, and its ruler a miserable man ? "

Then Pelias sighed heavily again and again, and again, like a man who had to tell some dreadful story and was afraid to begin; but at last —

"For seven long years and more have I never known a quiet night; and no more will he who comes after me, till the Golden Fleece be brought home."

Then he told Jason the story of Phrixus, and of the Golden Fleece; and told him, too, which was a lie, that Phrixus's spirit tormented him, calling to him day and night. And his daughters came, and told the same tale, (for their father had taught them their parts,) and wept, and said, "Oh, who will bring home the Golden Fleece, that our uncle's spirit may have rest; and that we may have rest also, whom he never lets sleep in peace?"

Jason sat awhile, sad and silent; for he had often heard of that Golden Fleece; but he looked on it as a thing hopeless and impossible for any mortal man to win it.

But when Pelias saw him silent, he began to talk of other things, and courted Jason more and more, speaking to him as if he was certain to be his heir, and asking his advice about the kingdom; till Jason, who was young and simple, could not help saying to himself, "Surely he is not the dark man whom people call him. Yet why did he drive my father out?" And he asked Pelias boldly, "Men say that you are terrible, and a man of blood; but I find you a kind and hospitable man; and as you are to me, so will I be to you. Yet why did you drive my father out?"

Pelias smiled and sighed: "Men have slandered me in that, as in all things. Your father was growing old

and weary, and he gave the kingdom up to me of his
own will.   You shall see him to-morrow, and ask him;
and he will tell you the same."

Jason's heart leapt in him, when he heard that he
was to see his father; and he believed all that Pelias
said, forgetting that his father might not dare to tell
the truth.

"One thing more there is," said Pelias, "on which I
need your advice; for though you are young, I see in
you a wisdom beyond your years.   There is one neighbor of mine, whom I dread more than all men on
earth.   I am stronger than he now, and can command
him: but I know that if he stay among us, he will
work my ruin in the end.   Can you give me a plan,
Jason, by which I can rid myself of that man?"

After awhile, Jason answered, half laughing, "Were
I you, I would send him to fetch that same Golden
Fleece; for if he once set forth after it you would never
be troubled with him more."

And at that a bitter smile came across Pelias's lips,
and a flash of wicked joy into his eyes; and Jason saw
it and started; and over his mind came the warning
of the old man, and his own one sandal, and the oracle,
and he saw that he was taken in a trap.

But Pelias only answered gently, "My son, he shall
be sent forthwith."

"You mean me?" cried Jason, starting up, "because I came here with one sandal?"   And he lifted
his fist angrily, while Pelias stood up to him like a wolf
at bay; and whether of the two was the stronger and
the fiercer, it would be hard to tell.

But after a moment Pelias spoke gently — "Why

then so rash, my son? You, and not I, have said what is said; why blame me for what I have not done? Had you bid me love the man of whom I spoke, and make him my son-in-law and heir, I would have obeyed you; and what if I obey you now, and send the man to win himself immortal fame? I have not harmed you or him. One thing at least I know, that he will go, and that gladly: for he has a hero's heart within him; loving glory, and scorning to break the word which he has given."

Jason saw that he was entrapped: but his second promise to Cheiron came into his mind, and he thought, "What if the Centaur were a prophet in that also, and meant that I should win the fleece!" Then he cried aloud, —

"You have well spoken, cunning uncle of mine! I love glory, and I dare keep to my word. I will go and fetch this Golden Fleece. Promise me but this in return, and keep your word as I keep mine. Treat my father lovingly while I am gone, for the sake of the all-seeing Zeus; and give me up the kingdom for my own, on the day that I bring back the Golden Fleece."

Then Pelias looked at him and almost loved him, in the midst of all his hate; and said, "I promise, and I will perform. It will be no shame to give up my kingdom to the man who wins that fleece."

Then they swore a great oath between them; and afterwards both went in, and lay down to sleep.

But Jason could not sleep, for thinking of his mighty oath, and how he was to fulfil it, all alone, and without wealth or friends. So he tossed a long time upon his bed, and thought of this plan and of that; and some-

times Phrixus seemed to call him, in a thin voice, faint
and low, as if it came from far across the sea — "Let
me come home to my fathers and have rest." And
sometimes he seemed to see the eyes of Hera, and to
hear her words again,— "Call on me in the hour of
need, and see if the Immortals can forget."

And on the morrow he went to Pelias, and said,
"Give me a victim, that I may sacrifice to Hera." So
he went up, and offered his sacrifice; and as he stood
by the altar, Hera sent a thought into his mind; and
he went back to Pelias, and said —

"If you are indeed in earnest, give me two heralds,
that they may go round to all the princes of the
Minuai, who were pupils of the Centaur with me, that
we may fit out a ship together, and take what shall
befall."

At that Pelias praised his wisdom, and hastened to
send the heralds out; for he said in his heart, "Let all
the princes go with him, and like him, never return;
for so I shall be lord of all the Minuai, and the greatest
king in Hellas."

PART III.

HOW THEY BUILT THE SHIP ARGO IN IOLCOS.

SO the heralds went out, and cried to all the heroes of the Minuai, "Who dare come to the adventure of the golden fleece?"

And Hera stirred the hearts of all the princes, and they came from all their valleys to the yellow sands of Pagasai. And first came Heracles the mighty, with his lion's skin and club, and behind him Hylas his young squire, who bore his arrows and his bow; and Tiphys, the skilful steersman; and Butes, the fairest of all men; and Castor and Polydeuces the twins, the sons of the magic swan; and Caineus, the strongest of mortals, whom the Centaurs tried in vain to kill, and overwhelmed him with trunks of pine-trees, but even so he would not die; and thither came Zetes and Calais, the winged sons of the north wind; and Peleus, the father of Achilles, whose bride was silver-footed Thetis the goddess of the sea. And thither came Telamon and Oileus, the fathers of the two Aiantes, who fought upon the plains of Troy; and Mopsus, the wise soothsayer, who knew the speech of birds; and Idmon, to whom Phœbus gave a tongue to prophesy of things to come; and Ancaios, who could read the stars, and knew all the

circles of the heavens; and Argus, the famed ship-
builder, and many a hero more, in helmets of brass
and gold with tall dyed horse-hair crests, and embroidered shirts of linen beneath their coats of mail, and
greaves of polished tin to guard their knees in fight;
with each man his shield upon his shoulder, of many
a fold of tough bull's hide, and his sword of tempered
bronze in his silver-studded belt, and in his right hand
a pair of lances, of the heavy white ash-staves.

So they came down to Iolcos, and all the city came
out to meet them, and were never tired with looking at
their height, and their beauty, and their gallant bearing,
and the glitter of their inlaid arms.   And some said,
"Never was such a gathering of the heroes since the
Hellens conquered the land."   But the women sighed
over them, and whispered, "Alas! they are all going
to their death."

Then they felled the pines on Pelion, and shaped
them with the axe, and Argus taught them to build a
galley, the first long ship which ever sailed the seas.
They pierced her for fifty oars, an oar for each hero
of the crew, and pitched her with coal-black pitch, and
painted her bows with vermilion; and they named her
Argo after Argus, and worked at her all day long.
And at night Pelias feasted them like a king, and they
slept in his palace-porch.

But Jason went away to the northward, and into the
land of Thrace, till he found Orpheus, the prince of
minstrels, where he dwelt in his cave under Rhodope,
among the savage Cicon tribes.   And he asked him —
"Will you leave your mountains, Orpheus, my fellow-
scholar in old times, and cross Strymon once more with

me, to sail with the heroes of the Minuai, and bring
home the Golden Fleece, and charm for us all men and
all monsters with your magic harp and song?"

Then Orpheus sighed — "Have I not had enough of
toil and of weary wandering far and wide, since I lived
in Cheiron's cave, above Iolcos by the sea? In vain is
the skill and the voice which my goddess mother gave
me; in vain have I sung and labored; in vain I went
down to the dead, and charmed all the kings of Hades,
to win back Eurydice my bride. For I won her, my
beloved, and lost her again the same day, and wandered
away in my madness, even to Egypt and the Libyan sands,
and the isles of all the seas, driven on by the terrible
gadfly, while I charmed in vain the hearts of men, and
the savage forest beasts, and the trees, and the lifeless
stones, with my magic harp and song, giving rest, but
finding none. But at last Calliope, my mother, delivered me, and brought me home in peace; and I dwell
here in the cave alone, among the savage Cicon tribes,
softening their wild hearts with music and the gentle
laws of Zeus. And now I must go out again, to the
ends of all the earth, far away into the misty darkness,
to the last wave of the Eastern Sea. But what is
doomed must be, and a friend's demand obeyed; for
prayers are the daughters of Zeus, and who honors
them honors him."

Then Orphéus rose up sighing, and took his harp, and
went over Strymon. And he led Jason to the southwest, up the banks of Haliacmon and over the spurs of
Pindus, to Dodona the town of Zeus, where it stood
by the side of the sacred lake, and the fountain which
breathed out fire, in the darkness of the ancient oak-

wood, beneath the mountain of the hundred springs. And he led him to the holy oak, where the black dove settled in old times, and was changed into the priestess of Zeus, and gave oracles to all nations round. And he bade him cut down a bough, and sacrifice to Hera and to Zeus; and they took the bough and came to Iolcos, and nailed it to the beak-head of the ship.

And at last the ship was finished, and they tried to launch her down the beach; but she was too heavy for them to move her, and her keel sank deep in the sand. Then all the heroes looked at each other blushing; but Jason spoke, and said, " Let us ask the magic bough; perhaps it can help us in our need."

Then a voice came from the bough, and Jason heard the words it said, and bade Orpheus play upon the harp, while the heroes waited round, holding the pine-trunk rollers, to help her toward the sea.

Then Orpheus took his harp, and began his magic song: " How sweet it is to ride upon the surges, and to leap from wave to wave, while the wind sings cheerful in the cordage, and the oars flash fast among the foam! How sweet it is to roam across the ocean, and see new towns and wondrous lands, and to come home laden with treasure, and to win undying fame ! "

And the good ship Argo heard him, and longed to be away and out at sea ; till she stirred in every timber, and heaved from stem to stern, and leapt up from the sand upon the rollers, and plunged onward like a gallant horse; and the heroes fed her path with pine-trunks, till she rushed into the whispering sea.

Then they stored her well with food and water, and pulled the ladder up on board, and settled themselves

each man to his oar, and kept time to Orpheus's harp;
and away across the bay they rowed southward, while
the people lined the cliffs; and the women wept while
the men shouted, at the starting of that gallant crew.

PART IV.

HOW THE ARGONAUTS SAILED TO COLCHIS.

AND what happened next, my children, whether it be true or not, stands written in ancient songs, which you shall read for yourselves some day. And grand old songs they are, written in grand old rolling verse; and they call them the Songs of Orpheus, or the Orphics, to this day. And they tell how the heroes came to Aphetai, across the bay, and waited for the southwest wind, and chose themselves a captain from their crew: and how all called for Heracles, because he was the strongest and most huge; but Heracles refused, and called for Jason, because he was the wisest of them all. So Jason was chosen captain: and Orpheus heaped a pile of wood, and slew a bull, and offered it to Hera, and called all the heroes to stand round, each man's head crowned with olive, and to strike their swords into the bull. Then he filled a golden goblet with the bull's blood, and with wheaten flour, and honey, and wine, and the bitter salt sea-water, and bade the heroes taste. So each tasted the goblet, and passed it round, and vowed an awful vow: and they vowed before the sun, and the night, and the blue-haired sea who shakes the land, to stand by Jason faithfully, in the adventure of

the golden fleece; and whosoever shrank back, or dis-
obeyed, or turned traitor to his vow, then justice should
witness against him, and the Erinnues who track guilty
men.

Then Jason lighted the pile, and burnt the carcass of
the bull; and they went to their ship and sailed eastward, like men who have a work to do; and the place
from which they went was called Aphetai, the sailing-
place, from that day forth. Three thousand years and
more ago they sailed away, into the unknown Eastern
seas; and great nations have come and gone since then,
and many a storm has swept the earth; and many a
mighty armament, to which Argo would be but one small
boat, English and French, Turkish and Russian, have
sailed those waters since; yet the fame of that small
Argo lives forever, and her name has become a proverb
among men.

So they sailed past the Isle of Sciathos, with the Cape
of Sepius on their left, and turned to the northward
toward Pelion, up the long Magnesian shore. On their
right hand was the open sea, and on their left old
Pelion rose, while the clouds crawled round his dark
pine-forests, and his caps of summer snow. And their
hearts yearned for the dear old mountain, as they
thought of pleasant days gone by, and of the sports of
their boyhood, and their hunting, and their schooling in
the cave beneath the cliff. And at last Peleus spoke —
" Let us land here, friends, and climb the dear old hill
once more. We are going on a fearful journey: who
knows if we shall see Pelion again? Let us go up
to Cheiron our master, and ask his blessing ere we
start. And I have a boy, too, with him, whom he

trains as he trained me once, the son whom Thetis
brought me, the silver-footed lady of the sea, whom I
caught in the cave, and tamed her, though she changed
her shape seven times.   For she changed, as I held her,
into water, and to vapor, and to burning flame, and
to a rock, and to a black-maned lion, and to a tall and
stately tree.   But I held her and held her ever, till she
took her own shape again, and led her to my father's
house, and won her for my bride.   And all the rulers
of Olympus came to our wedding, and the heavens and
the earth rejoiced together, when an immortal wedded
mortal man.   And now let me see my son; for it is not
often I shall see him upon earth : famous he will be,
but short-lived, and die in the flower of youth."

So Tiphys, the helmsman, steered them to the shore
under the crags of Pelion; and they went up through
the dark pine-forests toward the Centaur's cave.

And they came into the misty hall, beneath the
snow-crowned crag; and saw the great Centaur lying
with his huge limbs spread upon the rock; and beside
him stood Achilles, the child whom no steel could
wound, and played upon his harp right sweetly, while
Cheiron watched and smiled.

Then Cheiron leapt up and welcomed them, and
kissed them every one, and set a feast before them, of
swine's flesh, and venison, and good wine; and young
Achilles served them, and carried the golden goblet
round.   And after supper all the heroes clapped their
hands, and called on Orpheus to sing; but he refused,
and said, " How can I, who am the younger, sing before
our ancient host ? "   So they called on Cheiron to sing,
and Achilles brought him his harp; and he began a

wondrous song; a famous story of old time, of the
fight between Centaurs and the Lapithai, which you
may still see carved in stone.   He sang how his
brothers came to ruin by their folly, when they were
mad with wine; and how they and the heroes fought,
with fists, and teeth, and the goblets from which they
drank; and how they tore up the pine-trees in their
fury, and hurled great crags of stone, while the mountains thundered with the battle, and the land was
wasted far and wide; till the Lapithai drove them
from their home in the rich Thessalian plains to the
lonely glens of Pindus, leaving Cheiron all alone.   And
the heroes praised his song right heartily; for some
of them had helped in that great fight.

Then Orpheus took the lyre, and sang of Chaos, and
the making of the wondrous World, and how all things
sprang from Love, who could not live alone in the
Abyss.   And as he sang, his voice rose from the cave,
above the crags, and through the tree-tops, and the
glens of oak and pine.   And the trees bowed their
heads when they heard it, and the gray rocks cracked
and rang, and the forest beasts crept near to listen,
and the birds forsook their nests and hovered round.
And old Cheiron clapt his hands together, and beat his
hoofs upon the ground, for wonder at that magic song.

Then Peleus kissed his boy, and wept over him, and
they went down to the ship; and Cheiron came down
with them, weeping, and kissed them one by one, and
blest them, and promised to them great renown.   And
the heroes wept when they left him, till their great
hearts could weep no more; for he was kind and just
and pious, and wiser than all beasts and men.   Then

he went up to a cliff, and prayed for them, that they might come home safe and well; while the heroes rowed away, and watched him standing on his cliff above the sea, with his great hands raised toward heaven, and his white locks waving in the wind; and they strained their eyes to watch him to the last, for they felt that they should look on him no more.

So they rowed on over the long swell of the sea, past Olympus, the seat of the immortals, and past the wooded bays of Athos, and Samothrace, the sacred isle; and they came past Lemnos to the Hellespont, and through the narrow strait of Abydos, and so on into the Propontis, which we call Marmora now. And there they met with Cyzicus, ruling in Asia over the Dolions, who, the songs say, was the son of Æneas, of whom you will hear many a tale some day. For Homer tells us how he fought at Troy; and Virgil how he sailed away and founded Rome; and men believed until late years that from him sprang our old British kings. Now Cyzicus, the songs say, welcomed the heroes; for his father had been one of Cheiron's scholars; so he welcomed them, and feasted them, and stored their ship with corn and wine, and cloaks and rugs, the songs say, and shirts, of which no doubt they stood in need.

But at night, while they lay sleeping, came down on them terrible men, who lived with the bears in the mountains, like Titans or giants in shape; for each of them had six arms, and they fought with young firs and pines. But Heracles killed them all before morn with his deadly poisoned arrows; but among them in the darkness, he slew Cyzicus the kindly prince.

Then they got to their ship and to their oars, and
Tiphys bade them cast off the hawsers, and go to sea.
But as he spoke a whirlwind came, and spun the Argo
round, and twisted the hawsers together, so that no
man could loose them. Then Tiphys dropped the
rudder from his hand, and cried, "This comes from the
Gods above." But Jason went forward, and asked
counsel of the magic bough.

Then the magic bough spoke and answered, — "This
is because you have slain Cyzicus your friend. You
must appease his soul, or you will never leave this
shore."

Jason went back sadly, and told the heroes what he
had heard. And they leapt on shore, and searched
till dawn; and at dawn they found the body, all rolled
in dust and blood, among the corpses of those monstrous
beasts. And they wept over their kind host, and laid
him on a fair bed, and heaped a huge mound over him,
and offered black sheep at his tomb, and Orpheus sang
a magic song to him, that his spirit might have rest.
And then they held games at the tomb, after the custom of those times, and Jason gave prizes to each win-
ner. To Ancæus he gave a golden cup, for he wrestled
best of all; and to Heracles a silver one, for he was the
strongest of all; and to Castor, who rode best, a golden
crest; and Polydeuces the boxer had a rich carpet, and
to Orpheus for his song, a sandal with golden wings.
But Jason himself was the best of all the archers, and
the Minuai crowned him with an olive crown; and so,
the songs say, the soul of the good Cyzicus was ap-
peased, and the heroes went on their way in peace.

But when Cyzicus's wife heard that he was dead,

she died likewise of grief; and her tears became a fountain of clear water, which flows the whole year round.

Then they rowed away, the songs say, along the Mysian shore, and past the mouth of Rhindacus, till they found a pleasant bay, sheltered by the long ridges of Arganthus, and by high walls of basalt rock. And there they ran the ship ashore upon the yellow sand, and furled the sail, and took the mast down, and lashed it in its crutch. And next they let down the ladder, and went ashore to sport and rest.

And there Heracles went away into the woods, bow in hand, to hunt wild deer; and Hylas the fair boy slipt away after him, and followed him by stealth, until he lost himself among the glens, and sat down weary to rest himself by the side of a lake; and there the water nymphs came up to look at him, and loved him, and carried him down under the lake to be their playfellow, forever happy and young. And Heracles sought for him in vain, shouting his name till all the mountains rang; but Hylas never heard him, far down under the sparkling lake. So while Heracles wandered searching for him, a fair breeze sprang up, and Heracles was nowhere to be found; and the Argo sailed away, and Heracles was left behind, and never saw the noble Phasian stream.

Then the Minuai came to a doleful land, where Amycus the giant ruled, and cared nothing for the laws of Zeus, but challenged all strangers to box with him, and those whom he conquered he slew. But Polydeuces the boxer struck him a harder blow than he ever felt before, and slew him; and the Minuai went on up the

Bosphorus, till they came to the city of Phineus, the fierce Bithynian king; for Zetes and Calais had Jason land there, because they had a work to do.

And they went up from the shore toward the city, through forests white with snow; and Phineus came out to meet them with a lean and woful face, and said, " Welcome, gallant heroes, to the land of bitter blasts, a land of cold and misery; yet I will feast you as best I can." And he led them in, and set meat before them; but before they could put their hands to their mouths, down came two fearful monsters, the like of whom man never saw; for they had the faces and the hair of fair maidens, but the wings and claws of hawks; and they snatched the meat from off the table, and flew shrieking out above the roofs.

Then Phineus beat his breast and cried, " These are the Harpies, whose names are the Whirlwind and the Swift, the daughters of Wonder and of the Amber-nymph, and they rob us night and day. They carried off the daughters of Pandareus, whom all the Gods had blest; for Aphrodite fed them on Olympus with honey and milk and wine; and Hera gave them beauty and wisdom, and Athene skill in all the arts; but when they came to their wedding, the Harpies snatched them both away, and gave them to be slaves to the Erinnues, and live in horror all their days. And now they haunt me, and my people, and the Bosphorus, with fearful storms; and sweep away our food from off our tables, so that we starve in spite of all our wealth."

Then up rose Zetes and Calais, the winged sons of the North-wind, and said, " Do you not know us, Phineus, and these wings which grow upon our backs?"

And Phineus hid his face in terror; but he answered not a word.

"Because you have been a traitor, Phineus, the Harpies haunt you night and day.   Where is Cleopatra our sister, your wife, whom you keep in prison? and where are her two children, whom you blinded in your rage, at the bidding of an evil woman, and cast them out upon the rocks?   Swear to us that you will right our sister, and cast out that wicked woman ; and then we will free you from your plague, and drive the whirl-wind maidens from the south: but if not, we will put out your eyes, as you put out the eyes of your own sons."

Then Phineus swore an oath to them, and drove out the wicked woman; and Jason took those two poor children, and cured their eyes with magic herbs.

But Zetes and Calais rose up sadly, and said, "Fare-well now, heroes all; farewell, our 'dear companions, with whom we played on Pelion in old times; for a fate is laid upon us, and our day is come at last, in which we may hunt the whirlwinds, over land and sea forever; and if we catch them they die, and if not, we die ourselves."

At that all the heroes wept: but the two young men sprang up, and aloft into the air after the Harpies, and the battle of the winds began.

The heroes trembled in silence as they heard the shrieking of the blasts; while the palace rocked and all the city, and great stones were torn from the crags, and the forest-pines were hurled eastward, north and south and east and west, and the Bosphorus boiled white with foam, and the clouds were dashed against the cliffs.

But at last the battle ended, and the Harpies fled screaming toward the south, and the sons of the North-wind rushed after them, and brought clear sunshine where they passed. For many a league they followed them, over all the isles of the Cyclades, and away to the southwest across Hellas, till they came to the Ionian . sea, and there they fell upon the Echinades, at the mouth of the Achelous; and those isles were called the Whirlwind Isles for many a hundred years. But what became of Zetes and Calais I know not; for the heroes never saw them again : and some say that Heracles met them, and quarrelled with them, and slew them with his arrows; and some say that they fell down from weariness and the heat of the summer sun, and that the Sun-god buried them among the Cyclades, in the pleasant Isle of Tenos; and for many hundred years their grave was shown there, and over it a pillar, which turned to every wind. But those dark storms and whirlwinds haunt the Bosphorus until this day.

But the Argonauts went eastward, and out into the open sea, which we now call the Black Sea, but it was called the Euxine then. No Hellen had ever crossed it, and all feared that dreadful sea, and its rocks, and shoals, and fogs, and bitter freezing storms; and they told strange stories of it, some false and some half true, how it stretched northward to the ends of the earth, and the sluggish Putrid Sea, and the everlasting night, and the regions of the dead. So the heroes trembled, for all their courage, as they came into that wild Black Sea, and saw it stretching out before them, without a shore, as far as eye could see.

And first Orpheus spoke, and warned them, — " We shall come now to the wandering blue rocks; my mother warned me of them, Calliope, the immortal muse."

And soon they saw the blue rocks shining, like spires and castles of gray glass, while an ice-cold wind blew from them, and chilled all the heroes' hearts. And as they neared, they could see them heaving, as they rolled upon the long sea-waves, crashing and grinding together, till the roar went up to heaven. The sea sprang up in spouts between them, and swept round them in white sheets of foam; but their heads swung nodding high in air, while the wind whistled shrill among the crags.

The heroes' hearts sank within them, and they lay upon their oars in fear; but Orpheus called to Tiphys the helmsman — " Between them we must pass; so look ahead for an opening, and be brave, for Hera is with us." But Tiphys the cunning helmsman stood silent, clenching his teeth, till he saw a heron come flying mast-high toward the rocks, and hover awhile before them, as if looking for a passage through. Then he cried, " Hera has sent us a pilot; let us follow the cunning bird."

Then the heron flapped to and fro a moment, till he saw a hidden gap, and into it he rushed like an arrow, while the heroes watched what would befall.

And the blue rocks clashed together as the bird fled swiftly through; but they struck but a feather from his tail, and then rebounded apart at the shock.

Then Tiphys cheered the heroes, and they shouted; and the oars bent like withes beneath their strokes, as they rushed between those toppling ice-crags, and the cold blue lips of death. And ere the rocks could meet again they had passed them, and were safe out in the open sea.

And after that they sailed on wearily along the Asian coast, by the Black Cape and Thyneis, where the hot stream of Thymbris falls into the sea, and Sangarius, whose waters float on the Euxine, till they came to Wolf the river, and to Wolf the kindly king. And there died two brave heroes, Idmon and Tiphys the wise helmsman; one died of an evil sickness, and one a wild boar slew. So the heroes heaped a mound above them, and set upon it an oar on high, and left them there to sleep together, on the far-off Lycian shore. But Idas killed the boar, and avenged Tiphys; and Ancaios took the rudder and was helmsman, and steered them on toward the east.

And they went on past Sinope, and many a mighty river's mouth, and past many a barbarous tribe, and the cities of the Amazons, the warlike women of the East, till all night they heard the clank of anvils and the roar of furnace-blasts, and the forge-fires shone like. sparks through the darkness, in the mountain glens aloft; for they were come to the shores of the Chalybes, the smiths who never tire, but serve Ares, the cruel War-god, forging weapons day and night.

And at day-dawn they looked eastward, and midway between the sea and the sky they saw white snow-peaks hanging, glittering sharp and bright above the clouds. And they knew that they were come to Caucasus, at the end of all the earth; Caucasus the highest of all mountains, the father of the rivers of the East. On his peak lies chained the Titan, while a vulture tears his heart; and at his feet are piled dark forests round the magic Colchian land.

And they rowed three days to the eastward, while Caucasus rose higher hour by hour, till they saw the dark stream of Phasis rushing headlong to the sea, and shining above the tree-tops, the golden roofs of king Aietes, the child of the sun.

Then out spoke Ancaios the helmsman, "We are come to our goal at last; for there are the roofs of Aietes, and the woods where all poisons grow; but who can tell us where among them is hid the golden fleece? Many a toil must we bear ere we find it, and bring it home to Greece."

But Jason cheered the heroes, for his heart was high and bold; and he said, "I will go alone up to Aietes, though he be the child of the sun, and win him with soft words. Better so than to go all together, and to come to blows at once." But the Minuai would not stay behind, so they rowed boldly up the stream.

And a dream came to Aietes, and filled his heart with fear. He thought he saw a shining star, which fell into his daughter's lap; and that Medeia his daughter took it gladly, and carried it to the river-side, and cast it in, and there the whirling river bore it down, and out into the Euxine Sea.

Then he leapt up in fear, and bade his servants bring his chariot, that he might go down to the river-side and appease the nymphs, and the heroes whose spirits haunt the bank. So he went down in his golden chariot, and his daughters by his side, Medeia the fair witch-maiden, and Chalciope, who had been Phrixus's wife, and behind him a crowd of servants and soldiers, for he was a rich and mighty prince.

And as he drove down by the reedy river, he saw Argo sliding up beneath the bank, and many a hero in her, like immortals for beauty and for strength, as their weapons glittered round them in the level morning sunlight, through the white mist of the stream. But Jason was the noblest of all; for Hera who loved him gave him beauty, and tallness, and terrible manhood.

And when they came near together and looked into each other's eyes, the heroes were awed before Aietes as he shone in his chariot, like his father the glorious Sun; for his robes were of rich gold tissue, and the rays of his diadem flashed fire; and in his hand he bore a jewelled sceptre, which glittered like the stars; and sternly he looked at them under his brows, and sternly he spoke and loud —

"Who are you, and what want you here, that you come to the shore of Cutaia? Do you take no account of my rule, nor of my people the Colchians who serve me, who never tired yet in the battle, and know well how to face an invader?"

And the heroes sat silent awhile before the face of that ancient king. But Hera the awful goddess put courage into Jason's heart, and he rose and shouted loudly in answer, "We are no pirates nor lawless men. We come not to plunder and to ravage, or carry away slaves from your land; but my uncle, the son of Poseidon, Pelias the Minuan king, he it is who has sent me on a quest to bring home the golden fleece. And these

too, my bold comrades, they are no nameless men; for
some are the sons of immortals, and some of heroes far
renowned. And we too never tire in battle, and know
well how to give blows and to take; yet we wish
to be guests at your table; it will be better so for
both."

Then Aietes's rage rushed up like a whirlwind, and
his eyes flashed fire as he heard; but he crushed his
anger down in his breast, and spoke mildly a cunning
speech, —

" If you will fight for the fleece with my Colchians,
then many a man must die. But do you indeed expect
to win from me the fleece in fight? So few you are,
that if you be worsted, I can load your ship with your
corpses. But if you will be ruled by me, you will find
it better far to choose the best man among you, and let
him fulfil the labors which I demand. Then I will
give him the golden fleece for a prize and a glory to
you all."

So saying, he turned his horses and drove back in
silence to the town. And the Minuai sat silent with
sorrow, and longed for Heracles and his strength; for
there was no facing the thousands of the Colchians, and
the fearful chance of war.

But Chalciope, Phrixus's widow, went weeping to the
town; for she remembered her Minuan husband, and all
the pleasures of her youth, while she watched the fair
faces of his kinsmen, and their long locks of golden
hair. And she whispered to Medeia her sister—"Why
should all these brave men die? why does not my father
give them up the fleece, that my husband's spirit may
have rest?"

And Medeia's heart pitied the heroes, and Jason most of all; and she answered, "Our father is stern and terrible, and who can win the golden fleece?" But Chalciope said, "These men are not like our men; there is nothing which they cannot dare nor do."

And Medeia thought of Jason and his brave countenance, and said, "If there was one among them who knew no fear, I could show him how to win the fleece."

So in the dusk of evening they went down to the river-side, Chalciope and Medeia the witch-maiden, and Argus, Phrixus's son. And Argus the boy crept forward, among the beds of reeds, till he came where the heroes were sleeping, on the thwarts of the ship, beneath the bank, while Jason kept ward on shore, and leant upon his lance full of thought. And the boy came to Jason, and said —

"I am the son of Phrixus, your cousin; and Chalciope my mother waits for you, to talk about the golden fleece."

Then Jason went boldly with the boy, and found the two princesses standing; and when Chalciope saw him she wept, and took his hands, and cried —

"O cousin of my beloved, go home before you die!"

"It would be base to go home now, fair princess, and to have sailed all these seas in vain." Then both the princesses besought him: but Jason said, "It is too late."

"But you know not," said Medeia, "what he must do who would win the fleece. He must tame the two brazen-footed bulls, who breathe devouring flame; and

with them he must plough ere nightfall four acres in
the field of Ares; and he must sow them with serpents'
teeth, of which each tooth springs up into an armed
man.   Then he must fight with all those warriors; and
little will it profit him to conquer them; for the fleece
is guarded by a serpent, more huge than any mountain
pine; and over his body you must step, if you would
reach the golden fleece."

Then Jason laughed bitterly.   "Unjustly is that
fleece kept here, and by an unjust and lawless king;
and unjustly shall I die in my youth, for I will attempt
it ere another sun be set."

Then Medeia trembled, and said, " No mortal man can
reach that fleece, unless I guide him through.   For round
it, beyond the river, is a wall full nine ells high, with
lofty towers and buttresses, and mighty gates of three-
fold brass; and over the gates the wall is arched, with
golden battlements above.   And over the gateway sits
Brimo, the wild witch-huntress of the woods, brandishing a pine-torch in her hands, while her mad hounds
howl around.   No man dare meet her or look on her,
but only I her priestess, and she watches far and wide
lest any stranger should come near."

" No wall so high but it may be climbed at last, and
no wood so thick but it may be crawled through; no
serpent so wary but he may be charmed, or witch-queen
so fierce but spells may soothe her; and I may yet
win the golden fleece, if a wise maiden help bold
men."

And he looked at Medeia cunningly, and held her with
his glittering eye, till she blushed and trembled, and
said —

" Who can face the fire of the bulls' breath, and fight
ten thousand armed men ? "

" He whom you help," said Jason, flattering her, " for
your fame is spread over all the earth. Are you not
the queen of all enchantresses, wiser even than your
sister Circe, in her fairy island in the West ? "

" Would that I were with my sister Circe in her fairy
island in the West, far away from sore temptation, and
thoughts which tear the heart ! But if it must be so —
for why should you die ? — I have an ointment here ;
I made it from the magic ice-flower which sprang from
Prometheus's wound, above the clouds on Caucasus, in
the dreary fields of snow. Anoint yourself with that,
and you shall have in you seven men's strength ; and
anoint your shield with it, and neither fire nor sword
can harm you. But what you begin you must end before sunset, for its virtue lasts only one day. And
anoint your helmet with it before you sow the serpents'
teeth ; and when the sons of earth spring up, cast your
helmet among their ranks, and the deadly crop of the
War-god's field will mow itself, and perish."

Then Jason fell on his knees before her, and thanked
her and kissed her hands ; and she gave him the vase
of ointment, and fled trembling through the reeds. And
Jason told his comrades what had happened, and showed
them the box of ointment ; and all rejoiced but Idas,
and he grew mad with envy.

And at sunrise Jason went and bathed, and anointed
himself from head to foot, and his shield, and his helmet, and his weapons, and bade his comrades try the
spell. So they tried to bend his lance, but it stood like
an iron bar ; and Idas in spite hewed at it with his

sword, but the blade flew to splinters in his face. Then
they hurled their lances at his shield, but the spear-
points turned like lead ; and Caineus tried to throw
him, but he never stirred a foot ; and Polydeuces struck
him first with his fist, a blow which would have killed
an ox ; but Jason only smiled, and the heroes danced
about him with delight ; and he leapt and ran, and
shouted, in the joy of that enormous strength, till the
sun rose, and it was time to go and to claim Aietes's
promise.

So he sent up Telamon and Aithalides to tell Aietes
that he was ready for the fight ; and they went up
among the marble walls, and beneath the roofs of gold,
and stood in Aietes's hall, while he grew pale with
rage.

" Fulfil your promise to us, child of the blazing sun.
Give us the serpents' teeth, and let loose the fiery bulls ;
for we have found a champion among us who can win
the golden fleece."

And Aietes bit his lips, for he fancied that they had
fled away by night ; but he could not go back from his
promise ; so he gave them the serpents' teeth.

Then he called for his chariot and his horses, and
sent heralds through all the town ; and all the people
went out with him to the dreadful War-god's field.

And there Aietes sat upon his throne, with his warriors on each hand, thousands and tens of thousands,
clothed from head to foot in steel-chain mail. And the
people and the women crowded to every window, and
bank, and wall ; while the Minuai stood together, a
mere handful in the midst of that great host.

And Chalciope was there and Argus, trembling, and

Medeia, wrapped closely in her veil; but Aietes did not know that she was muttering cunning spells between her lips.

Then Jason cried, "Fulfil your promise, and let your fiery bulls come forth."

Then Aietes bade open the gates, and the magic bulls leapt out. Their brazen hoofs rang upon the ground, and their nostrils sent out sheets of flame, as they rushed with lowered heads upon Jason; but he never flinched a step. The flame of their breath swept round him, but it singed not a hair of his head; and the bulls stopped short and trembled, when Medeia began her spell.

Then Jason sprang upon the nearest, and seized him by the horn; and up and down they wrestled, till the bull fell grovelling on his knees; for the heart of the brute died within him, and his mighty limbs were loosed, beneath the steadfast eye of that dark witch-maiden, and the magic whisper of her lips.

So both the bulls were tamed and yoked; and Jason bound them to the plough, and goaded them onward with his lance, till he had ploughed the sacred field.

And all the Minuai shouted; but Aietes bit his lips with rage; for the half of Jason's work was over, and the sun was yet high in heaven.

Then he took the serpents' teeth and sowed them, and waited what would befall. But Medeia looked at him and at his helmet, lest he should forget the lesson she had taught.

And every furrow heaved and bubbled, and out of every clod rose a man. Out of the earth they rose by thousands, each clad from head to foot in steel, and

drew their swords and rushed on Jason, where he stood
in the midst alone.

Then the Minuai grew pale with fear for him; but
Aietes laughed a bitter laugh. "See! if I had not
warriors enough already round me, I could call them
out of the bosom of the earth."

But Jason snatched off his helmet, and hurled it into
the thickest of the throng. And blind madness came
upon them, suspicion, hate, and fear; and one cried to
his fellow, "Thou didst strike me!" and another,
"Thou art Jason; thou shalt die!" So fury seized
those earth-born phantoms, and each turned his hand
against the rest; and they fought and were never
weary, till they all lay dead upon the ground. Then
the magic furrows opened, and the kind earth took
them home into her breast; and the grass grew up
all green again above them, and Jason's work was
done.

Then the Minuai rose and shouted, till Prometheus
heard them from his crag. And Jason cried — "Lead
me to the fleece this moment, before the sun goes
down."

But Aietes thought — "He has conquered the bulls;
and sown and reaped the deadly crop. Who is this
who is proof against all magic? He may kill the serpent yet." So he delayed, and sat taking counsel with
his princes, till the sun went down and all was dark.
Then he bade a herald cry, "Every man to his home
for to-night. To-morrow we will meet these heroes,
and speak about the golden fleece."

Then he turned and looked at Medeia: "This is
your doing, false witch-maid! You have helped these

yellow-haired strangers, and brought shame upon your father and yourself!"

Medeia shrank and trembled, and her face grew pale with fear; and Aietes knew that she was guilty, and whispered, "If they win the fleece, you die!"

But the Minuai marched toward their ship, growling like lions cheated of their prey; for they saw that Aietes meant to mock them, and to cheat them out of all their toil. And Oileus said, "Let us go to the grove together, and take the fleece by force."

And Idas the rash cried, "Let us draw lots who shall go in first; for while the dragon is devouring one, the rest can slay him, and carry off the fleece in peace." But Jason held them back, though he praised them; for he hoped for Medeia's help.

And after awhile Medeia came trembling, and wept a long while before she spoke. And at last, —

"My end is come, and I must die; for my father has found out that I have helped you. You he would kill if he dared; but he will not harm you, because you have been his guests. Go then, go, and remember poor Medeia when you are far away across the sea." But all the heroes cried —

"If you die, we die with you; for without you we cannot win the fleece, and home we will not go without it, but fall here fighting to the last man."

"You need not die," said Jason. "Flee home with us across the sea. Show us first how to win the fleece; for you can do it. Why else are you the priestess of the grove? Show us but how to win the fleece, and come with us, and you shall be my queen, and rule over the rich princes of the Minuai, in Iolcos by the sea."

And all the heroes pressed round, and vowed to her that she should be their queen.

Medeia wept, and shuddered, and hid her face in her hands; for her heart yearned after her sisters and her playfellows, and the home where she was brought up as a child.   But at last she looked up at Jason, and spoke between her sobs, —

"Must I leave my home and my people, to wander with strangers across the sea ?   The lot is cast, and I must endure it.   I will show you how to win the golden fleece.   Bring up your ship to the woodside, and moor her there against the bank, and let Jason come up at midnight, and one brave comrade with him, and meet me beneath the wall."

Then all the heroes cried together — "I will go!" "and I!" "and I!"   And Idas the rash grew mad with envy; for he longed to be foremost in all things. But Medeia calmed them, and said, "Orpheus shall go with Jason, and bring his magic harp; for I hear of him that he is the king of all minstrels, and can charm all things on earth."

And Orpheus laughed for joy, and clapped his hands, because the choice had fallen on him; for in those days poets and singers were as bold warriors as the best.

So at midnight they went up the bank, and found Medeia; and beside came Absyrtus her young brother, leading a yearling lamb.

Then Medeia brought them to a thicket, beside the War-god's gate; and there she bade Jason dig a ditch, and kill the lamb and leave it there, and strew on it magic herbs and honey from the honeycomb.

Then sprang up through the earth, with the red fire

flashing before her, Brimo the wild witch-huntress, while her mad hounds howled around. She had one head like a horse's, and another like a ravening hound's, and another like a hissing snake's, and a sword in either hand. And she leapt into the ditch with her hounds, and they ate and drank their fill, while Jason and Orpheus trembled, and Medeia hid her eyes. And at last the witch-queen vanished, and fled with her hounds into the woods; and the bars of the gates fell down, and the brazen doors flew wide, and Medeia and the heroes ran forward and hurried through the poison wood, among the dark stems of the mighty beeches, guided by the gleam of the golden fleece, until they saw it hanging on one vast tree in the midst. And Jason would have sprung to seize it: but Medeia held him back, and pointed shuddering to the tree-foot, where the mighty serpent lay, coiled in and out among the roots, with a body like a mountain-pine. His coils stretched many a fathom, spangled with bronze and gold; and half of him they could see, but no more; for the rest lay in the darkness far beyond.

And when he saw them coming, he lifted up his head, and watched them with his small bright eyes, and flashed his forked tongue, and roared like the fire among the woodlands, till the forest tossed and groaned. For his cry shook the trees from leaf to root, and swept over the long reaches of the river, and over Aietes's hall, and woke the sleepers in the city, till mothers clasped their children in their fear.

But Medeia called gently to him; and he stretched out his long spotted neck, and licked her hand, and looked up in her face, as if to ask for food. Then she made a sign to Orpheus, and he began his magic song.

And as he sung, the forest grew calm again, and the leaves on every tree hung still; and the serpent's head sank down, and his brazen coils grew limp, and his glittering eyes closed lazily, till he breathed as gently as a child, while Orpheus called to pleasant Slumber, who gives peace to men, and beasts, and waves.

Then Jason leapt forward warily, and stept across that mighty snake, and tore the fleece from off the tree-trunk; and the four rushed down the garden, to the bank where the Argo lay.

There was a silence for a moment, while Jason held the golden fleece on high. Then he cried — " Go now, good Argo, swift and steady, if ever you would see Pelion more."

And she went, as the heroes drove her, grim and silent all, with muffled oars, till the pine-wood bent like willow in their hands, and stout Arno groaned beneath their strokes.

On and on, beneath the dewy darkness, they fled swiftly down the swirling stream; underneath black walls, and temples, and the castles of the princes of the East; past sluice-mouths, and fragrant gardens, and groves of all strange fruits; past marshes where fat kine lay sleeping, and long beds of whispering reeds; till they heard the merry music of the surge upon the bar, as it tumbled in the moonlight all alone.

Into the surge they rushed, and Argo leapt the breakers like a horse; for she knew the time was come to show her mettle, and win honor for the heroes and herself.

Into the surge they rushed, and Argo leapt the breakers like a horse, till the heroes stopped all panting, each man upon his oar, as she slid into the still broad sea.

Then Orpheus took his harp and sang a pæan, till the heroes' hearts rose high again; and they rowed on stoutly and steadfastly, away into the darkness of the West.

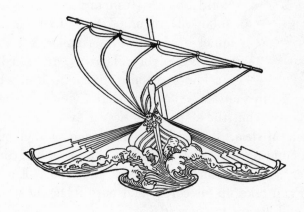

PART V.

HOW THE ARGONAUTS WERE DRIVEN INTO THE UN-- KNOWN SEA.

S O they fled away in haste to the west- ward: but Aietes manned his fleet and followed them.   And Lynceus the quick-eyed saw him coming, while he was still many a mile away, and cried, "I see a hundred ships, like a flock of white swans, far in the east."   And at that they rowed hard, like heroes; but the ships came nearer every hour.

Then Medeia, the dark witch-maiden, laid a cruel and a cunning plot; for she killed Absyrtus her young brother, and cast him into the sea, and said, " Ere my father can take up his corpse and bury it, he must wait long, and be left far behind."

And all the heroes shuddered, and looked one at the other for shame; yet they did not punish that dark witch-woman, because she had won for them the golden fleece.

And when Aietes came to the place, he saw the float- ing corpse; and he stopped a long while, and bewailed his son, and took him up, and went home.   But he sent on his sailors toward the westward, and bound them by a mighty curse: " Bring back to me that dark witch-woman, that she may die a dreadful death.   **But** if you return without her, you shall die by the same death yourselves."

So the Argonauts escaped for that time: but Father Zeus saw that foul crime; and out of the heavens he sent a storm, and swept the ship far from her course. Day after day the storm drove her, amid foam and blinding mist, till they knew no longer where they were, for the sun was blotted from the skies. And at last the ship struck on a shoal, amid low isles of mud and sand, and the waves rolled over her and through her, and the heroes lost all hope of life.

Then Jason cried to Hera: "Fair queen, who hast befriended us till now, why hast thou left us in our misery, to die here among unknown seas? It is hard to lose the honor which we have won with such toil and danger, and hard never to see Hellas again, and the pleasant bay of Pagasai."

Then out and spoke the magic bough which stood upon the Argo's beak: "Because Father Zeus is angry, all this has fallen on you; for a cruel crime has been done on board, and the sacred ship is foul with blood."

At that some of the heroes cried: "Medeia is the murderess. Let the witch-woman bear her sin, and die!" And they seized Medeia, to hurl her into the sea and atone for the young boy's death: but the magic bough spoke again: "Let her live till her crimes are full. Vengeance waits for her, slow and sure; but she must live, for you need her still. She must show you the way to her sister Circe, who lives among the islands of the West. To her you must sail, a weary way, and she shall cleanse you from your guilt."

Then all the heroes wept aloud when they heard the

sentence of the oak; for they knew that a dark journey lay before them, and years of bitter toil. And some upbraided the dark witch-woman, and some said, " Nay, we are her debtors still; without her we should never have won the fleece." But most of them bit their lips in silence, for they feared the witch's spells.

And now the sea grew calmer, and the sun shone out once more, and the heroes thrust the ship off the sandbank, and rowed forward on their weary course, under the guiding of the dark witch-maiden, into the wastes of the unknown sea.

Whither they went I cannot tell, nor how they came to Circe's isle. Some say that they went to the westward, and up the Ister[1] stream, and so came into the Adriatic, dragging their ship over the snowy Alps. And others say that they went southward, into the Red Indian Sea, and past the sunny lands where spices grow, round Æthiopia toward the West; and that at last they came to Libya, and dragged their ship across the burning sands, and over the hills into the Syrtes, where the flats and quicksands spread for many a mile, between rich Cyrene and the Lotus-eaters' shore. But all these are but dreams and fables, and dim hints of unknown lands.

But all say that they came to a place where they had to drag their ship across the land nine days with ropes and rollers, till they came into an unknown sea. And the best of all the old songs tells us, how they went away toward the North, till they came to the slope of Caucasus, where it sinks into the sea; and to the narrow Cimmerian Bosphorus,[2] where the Titan

---

[1] The Danube.   [2] Between the Crimæa and Circassia.

swam across upon the bull; and thence into the lazy waters of the still Mæotid lake.[1] And thence they went northward ever, up the Tanais, which we call Don, past the Geloni and Sauromatai, and many a wandering shepherd-tribe, and the one-eyed Arimaspi, of whom old Greek poets tell, who steal the gold from the Griffins, in the cold Rhiphaian[2] hills.

And they passed the Scythian archers, and the Tauri who eat men, and the wandering Hyperboreai, who feed their flocks beneath the pole-star, until they came into the northern ocean, the dull dead Cronian Sea.[3] And there Argo would move on no longer; and each man clasped his elbow, and leaned his head upon his hand, heart-broken with toil and hunger, and gave himself up to death. But brave Ancaios the helmsman cheered up their hearts once more, and bade them leap on land, and haul the ship with ropes and rollers for many a weary day, whether over land, or mud, or ice, I know not, for the song is mixed and broken like a dream. And it says next, how they came to the rich nation of the famous long-lived men; and to the coast of the Cimmerians, who never saw the sun, buried deep in the glens of the snow mountains; and to the fair land of Hermione, where dwelt the most righteous of all nations; and to the gates of the world below, and to the dwelling-place of dreams.

And at last Ancaios shouted — " Endure a little while, brave friends, the worst is surely past; for I can see the pure west wind ruffle the water, and hear the roar of ocean on the sands. So raise up the mast, and set the sail, and face what comes like men."

---

[1] The Sea of Azov.   [2] The Ural Mountains ?   [3] The Baltic ?

Then out spoke the magic bough — " Ah, would that I had perished long ago, and been whelmed by the dread blue rocks, beneath the fierce swell of the Euxine !   Better so, than to wander forever, disgraced by the guilt of my princes ; for the blood of Absyrtus still tracks me, and woe follows hard upon woe.   And now some dark horror will clutch me, if I come near the Isle of Ierne.[1]   Unless you will cling to the land, and sail southward and southward forever, I shall wander beyond the Atlantic, to the ocean which has no shore."

Then they blest the magic bough, and sailed southward along the land.   But ere they could pass Ierne, the land of mists and storms, the wild wind came down, dark and roaring, and caught the sail, and strained the ropes.   And away they drove twelve nights, on the wide wild western sea, through the foam. and over the rollers, while they saw neither sun nor stars.   And they cried again, " We shall perish, for we know not where we are.   We are lost in the dreary damp darkness, and cannot tell north from south."

But Lynceus the long-sighted called gayly from the bows — " Take heart again, brave sailors ; for I see a pine-clad isle, and the halls of the kind Earth-mother, with a crown of clouds around them."

But Orpheus said, " Turn from them, for no living man can land there : there is no harbor on the coast, but steep-walled cliffs all round."

So Ancaios turned the ship away ; and for three days more they sailed on, till they came to Aiaia, Circe's home, and the fairy island of the west.[2]

[1] Britain ?   [2] The Azores ?

And there Jason bid them land, and seek about for any sign of living man. And as they went inland, Circe met them, coming down toward the ship; and they trembled when they saw her; for her hair, and face, and robes, shone like flame.

And she came and looked at Medeia; and Medeia hid her face beneath her veil.

And Circe cried, "Ah, wretched girl, have you forgotten all your sins, that you come hither to my island, where the flowers bloom all the year round? Where is your aged father, and the brother whom you killed? Little do I expect you to return in safety with these strangers whom you love. I will send you food and wine: but your ship must not stay here, for it is foul with sin, and foul with sin its crew."

And the heroes prayed her, but in vain, and cried, "Cleanse us from our guilt!" But she sent them away and said, "Go on to Malea, and there you may be cleansed, and return home."

Then a fair wind rose, and they sailed eastward, by Tartessus on the Iberian shore, till they came to the Pillars of Hercules, and the Mediterranean Sea. And thence they sailed on through the deeps of Sardinia, and past the Ausonian islands, and the capes of the Tyrrhenian shore, till they came to a flowery island, upon a still bright summer's eve. And as they neared it, slowly and wearily, they heard sweet songs upon the shore. But when Medeia heard it, she started, and cried, "Beware, all heroes, for these are the rocks of the Sirens. You must pass close by them, for there is no other channel; but those who listen to that song are lost."

Then Orpheus spoke, the king of all minstrels —
"Let them match their song against mine. I have
charmed stones, and trees, and dragons, how much
more the hearts of men!" So he caught up his lyre,
and stood upon the poop, and began his magic song.

And now they could see the Sirens, on Anthemousa,
the flowery isle; three fair maidens sitting on the
beach, beneath a red rock in the setting sun, among
beds of crimson poppies and golden asphodel. Slowly
they sung and sleepily, with silver voices, mild and
clear, which stole over the golden waters, and into the
hearts of all the heroes, in spite of Orpheus's song.

And all things stayed around and listened; the gulls
sat in white lines along the rocks; on the beach great
seals lay basking, and kept time with lazy heads;
while silver shoals of fish came up to hearken, and
whispered as they broke the shining calm. The Wind
overhead hushed his whistling, as he shepherded his
clouds towards the west; and the clouds stood in mid
blue, and listened dreaming, like a flock of golden sheep.

And as the heroes listened, the oars fell from their
hands, and their heads drooped on their breasts, and
they closed their heavy eyes; and they dreamed of
bright still gardens, and of slumbers under murmuring
pines, till all their toil seemed foolishness, and they
thought of their renown no more.

Then one lifted his head suddenly, and cried, "What
use in wandering forever? Let us stay here and rest
awhile." And another, "Let us row to the shore, and
hear the words they sing." And another, "I care not
for the words, but for the music. They shall sing me
to sleep, that I may rest."

And Butes, the son of Pandion, the fairest of all mortal men, leapt out and swam toward the shore, crying, "I come, I come, fair maidens, to live and die here, listening to your song."

Then Medeia clapped her hands together, and cried, "Sing louder, Orpheus, sing a bolder strain; wake up these hapless sluggards, or none of them will see the land of Hellas more."

Then Orpheus lifted his harp, and crashed his cunning hand across the strings; and his music and his voice rose like a trumpet through the still evening air; into the air it rushed like thunder, till the rocks rang and the sea; and into their souls it rushed like wine, till all hearts beat fast within their breasts.

And he sung the song of Perseus, how the Gods led him over land and sea, and how he slew the loathly Gorgon, and won himself a peerless bride; and how he sits now with the Gods upon Olympus, a shining star in the sky, immortal with his immortal bride, and honored by all men below.

So Orpheus sang, and the Sirens, answering each other across the golden sea, till Orpheus's voice drowned the Sirens, and the heroes caught their oars again.

And they cried, "We will be men like Perseus, and we will dare and suffer to the last. Sing us his song again, brave Orpheus, that we may forget the Sirens and their spell."

And as Orpheus sang, they dashed their oars into the sea, and kept time to his music, as they fled fast away; and the Sirens' voices died behind them, in the hissing of the foam along their wake.

But Butes swam to the shore, and knelt down before

the Sirens, and cried, " Sing on ! sing on ! " But he could say no more ; for a charmed sleep came over him, and a pleasant humming in his ears ; and he sank all along upon the pebbles, and forgot all heaven and earth, and never looked at that sad beach around him, all strewn with the bones of men.

Then slowly rose up those three fair sisters, with a cruel smile upon their lips ; and slowly they crept down towards him, like leopards who creep upon their prey ; and their hands were like the talons of eagles, as they stept across the bones of their victims to enjoy their cruel feast.

But fairest Aphrodite saw him from the highest Idalian peak, and she pitied his youth and his beauty, and leapt up from her golden throne ; and like a falling star she cleft the sky, and left a trail of glittering light, till she stooped to the Isle of the Sirens, and snatched their prey from their claws. And she lifted Butes as he lay sleeping, and wrapt him in a golden mist ; and she bore him to the peak of Lilybæum ; and he slept there many a pleasant year.

But when the Sirens saw that they were conquered, they shrieked for envy and rage, and leapt from the beach into the sea, and were changed into rocks until this day.

Then they came to the straits by Lilybæum, and saw Sicily, the three-cornered island, under which Enceladus the giant lies groaning day and night, and when he turns the earth quakes, and his breath bursts out in roaring flames from the highest cone of Ætna, above the chestnut woods. And there Charybdis caught them in its fearful coils of wave, and rolled mast-high about

them, and spun them round and round; and they could
go neither back nor forward, while the whirlpool
sucked them in.

And while they struggled they saw near them, on the
other side the strait, a rock stand in the water, with a
peak wrapt round in clouds; a rock which no man
could climb, though he had twenty hands and feet, for
the stone was smooth and slippery, as if polished by
man's hand; and half way up a misty cave looked out
toward the west.

And when Orpheus saw it, he groaned, and struck
his hands together. And "Little will it help to us,"
he cried, "to escape the jaws of the whirlpool; for in
that cave lives Scylla, the sea-hag with a young whelp's
voice; my mother warned me of her ere we sailed away
from Hellas; she has six heads, and six long necks, and
hides in that dark cleft. And from her cave she fishes
for all things which pass by, for sharks, and seals, and
dolphins, and all the herds of Amphitrite. And never
ship's crew boasted that they came safe by her rock;
for she bends her long necks down to them, and every
mouth takes up a man. And who will help us now?
For Hera and Zeus hate us, and our ship is foul with
guilt; so we must die, whatever befalls."

Then out of the depths came Thetis, Peleus's silver-
footed bride, for love of her gallant husband, and all
her nymphs around her; and they played like snow-
white dolphins, diving on from wave to wave, before
the ship, and in her wake, and beside her, as dolphins
play. And they caught the ship, and guided her, and
passed her on from hand to hand, and tossed her
through the billows, as maidens toss the ball. And

when Scylla stooped to seize her, they struck back her
ravening heads, and foul Scylla whined, as a whelp
whines, at the touch of their gentle hands. But she
shrank into her cave affrighted; for all bad things
shrink from good; and Argo leapt safe past her, while
a fair breeze rose behind. Then Thetis and her nymphs
sank down to their coral caves beneath the sea, and
their gardens of green and purple, where live flowers
bloom all the year round; while the heroes went on
rejoicing, yet dreading what might come next.

After that they had rowed on steadily for many a
weary day, till they saw a long high island, and beyond
it a mountain land. And they searched till they found
a harbor, and there rowed boldly in. But after awhile
they stopped, and wondered; for there stood a great
city on the shore, and temples and walls and gardens,
and castles high in air upon the cliffs. And on either
side they saw a harbor, with a narrow mouth, but
wide within; and black ships without number, high
and dry upon the shore.

Then Ancaius, the wise helmsman, spoke, "What
new wonder is this? I know all isles, and harbors,
and the windings of all seas; and this should be Cor-
cyra, where a few wild goatherds dwell. But whence
come these new harbors, and vast works of polished
stone?"

But Jason said, "They can be no savage people. We
will go in and take our chance."

So they rowed into the harbor, among a thousand
black-beaked ships, each larger far than Argo, toward
a quay of polished stone. And they wondered at that
mighty city, with its roofs of burnished brass, and long

and lofty walls of marble, with strong palisades above. And the quays were full of people, merchants, and mariners, and slaves, going to and fro with merchandise among the crowd of ships. And the heroes' hearts were humbled, and they looked at each other and said, "We thought ourselves a gallant crew when we sailed from Iolcos by the sea: but how small we look before this city, like an ant before a hive of bees."

Then the sailors hailed them roughly from the quay, "What men are you? — we want no strangers here, nor pirates. We keep our business to ourselves."

But Jason answered gently, with many a flattering word, and praised their city and their harbor, and their fleet of gallant ships. "Surely you are the children of Poseidon, and the masters of the sea; and we are but poor wandering mariners, worn out with thirst and toil. Give us but food and water, and we will go on our voyage in peace."

Then the sailors laughed and answered, "Stranger, you are no fool; you talk like an honest man, and you shall find us honest too. We are the children of Poseidon, and the masters of the sea; but come ashore to us, and you shall have the best that we can give."

So they limped ashore, all stiff and weary, with long ragged beards and sunburnt cheeks, and garments torn and weather-stained, and weapons rusted with the spray, while the sailors laughed at them (for they were rough-tongued, though their hearts were frank and kind). And one said, "These fellows are but raw sailors; they look as if they had been sea-sick all the day." And another, "Their legs have grown crooked with much rowing, till they waddle in their walk like ducks."

At that Idas the rash would have struck them; but Jason held him back, till one of the merchant kings spoke to them, a tall and stately man.

"Do not be angry, strangers; the sailor boys must have their jest. But we will treat you justly and kindly, for strangers and poor men come from God; and you seem no common sailors by your strength, and height, and weapons. Come up with me to the palace of Alcinous, the rich sea-going king, and we will feast you well and heartily; and after that you shall tell us your name."

But Medeia hung back, and trembled, and whispered in Jason's ear, "We are betrayed, and are going to our ruin; for I see my countrymen among the crowd; dark-eyed Colchi in steel mail-shirts, such as they wear in my father's land."

"It is too late to turn," said Jason. And he spoke to the merchant king — "What country is this, good sir; and what is this new-built town?"

"This is the land of the Phæaces, beloved by all the Immortals; for they come hither and feast like friends with us, and sit by our side in the hall. Hither we came from Liburnia to escape the unrighteous Cyclopes; for they robbed us, peaceful merchants, of our hard-earned wares and wealth. So Nausithous, the son of Poseidon, brought us hither, and died in peace; and now his son Alcinous rules us, and Arete the wisest of queens."

So they went up across the square, and wondered still more as they went; for along the quays lay in order great cables, and yards, and masts, before the fair temple of Poseidon, the blue-haired king of the seas. And round the square worked the shipwrights, as many in number as ants, twining ropes, and hewing timber, and smoothing long yards and oars. And the Minuai went on in silence through clean white marble streets, till they came to the hall of Alcinous, and they wondered then still more. For the lofty palace shone aloft in the sun, with walls of plated brass, from the threshold to the innermost chamber, and the doors were of silver and gold. And on each side of the doorway sat living dogs of gold, who never grew old or died, so well Hephaistus had made them in his forges in smoking Lemnos, and gave them to Alcinous to guard his gates by night. And within, against the walls, stood thrones on either side, down the whole length of the hall, strewn with rich glossy shawls; and on them the merchant kings of those crafty sea-roving Phæaces sat eating and drinking in pride, and feasting there all the year round. And boys of molten gold stood each on a polished altar, and held torches in their hands, to give light all night to the guests. And round the house sat fifty maid-servants, some grinding the meal in the mill, some turning the spindle, some weaving at the loom, while their hands twinkled as they passed the shuttle, like quivering aspen leaves.

And outside before the palace a great garden was walled round, filled full of stately fruit-trees, with olives and sweet figs, and pomegranates, pears, and apples, which bore the whole year round. For the rich southwest wind fed them, till pear grew ripe on pear, fig on fig, and grape on grape, all the winter and the spring. And at the further end gay flower-beds bloomed through all seasons of the year; and two fair fountains rose, and

ran, one through the garden-grounds, and one beneath
the palace gate, to water all the town.   Such noble
gifts the heavens had given to Alcinous the wise.

So they went in, and saw him sitting, like Poseidon,
on his throne, with his golden sceptre by him, in garments stiff with gold, and in his hand a sculptured
goblet, as he pledged the merchant kings; and beside
him stood Arete, his wise and lovely queen, and leaned
against a pillar, as she spun her golden threads.

Then Alcinous rose, and welcomed them, and bade
them sit and eat; and the servants brought them tables,
and bread, and meat, and wine.

But Medeia went on trembling toward Arete the fair
queen, and fell at her knees, and clasped them, and cried
weeping as she knelt, —

"I am your guest, fair queen, and I entreat you by
Zeus from whom prayers come.   Do not send me back
to my father, to die some dreadful death; but let me
go my way, and bear my burden.   Have I not had
enough of punishment and shame?"

"Who are you, strange maiden? and what is the
meaning of your prayer?"

"I am Medeia, daughter of Aietes, and I saw my
countrymen here to-day; and I know that they are
come to find me, and take me home to die some dreadful death."

Then Arete frowned, and said — "Lead this girl in,
my maidens; and let the kings decide, not I."

And Alcinous leapt up from his throne, and cried,
"Speak, strangers, who are you?   And who is this
maiden?"

"We are the heroes of the Minuai," said Jason;

"and this maiden has spoken truth. We are the men who took the Golden Fleece, the men whose fame has run round every shore. We came hither out of the ocean, after sorrows such as man never saw before. We went out many, and come back few, for many a noble comrade have we lost. So let us go, as you should let your guests go, in peace; that the world may say, 'Alcinous is a just king.'"

But Alcinous frowned, and stood deep in thought; and at last he spoke —

"Had not the deed been done, which is done, I should have said this day to myself, 'It is an honor to Alcinous, and to his children after him, that the far-famed Argonauts are his guests.' But these Colchi are my guests, as you are; and for this month they have waited here with all their fleet; for they have hunted all the seas of Hellas, and could not find you, and dared neither go further, nor go home."

"Let them choose out their champions, and we will fight them, man for man."

"No guest of ours shall fight upon our island; and if you go outside, they will outnumber you. I will do justice between you; for I know and do what is right."

Then he turned to his kings, and said: "This may stand over till to-morrow. To-night we will feast our guests, and hear the story of all their wanderings, and how they came hither out of the ocean."

So Alcinous bade the servants take the heroes in, and bathe them, and give them clothes. And they were glad when they saw the warm water, for it was long since they had bathed. And they washed off the sea-salt from their limbs, and anointed themselves from head to foot with oil, and combed out their golden hair. Then they came back again into the hall, while the merchant-kings rose up to do them honor. And each man said to his neighbor: "No wonder that these men won fame. How they stand now like Giants, or Titans, or Immortals come down from Olympus, though many a winter has worn them, and many a fearful storm. What must they have been when they sailed from Iolcos, in the bloom of their youth, long ago?"

Then they went out to the garden; and the merchant-princes said: "Heroes, run races with us. Let us see whose feet are nimblest."

"We cannot race against you, for our limbs are stiff from sea; and we have lost our two swift comrades, the sons of the north wind. But do not think us cowards: if you wish to try our strength, we will shoot, and box, and wrestle, against any men on earth."

And Alcinous smiled, and answered: "I believe you, gallant guests; with your long limbs and broad shoulders, we could never match you here. For we care nothing here for boxing, or shooting with the bow; but for feasts, and songs, and harping and dancing, and running races, to stretch our limbs on shore."

So they danced there and ran races, the jolly merchant kings, till the night fell, and all went in.

And then they ate and drank, and comforted their weary souls, till Alcinous called a herald, and bade him go and fetch the harper.

The herald went out, and fetched the harper, and led him in by the hand; and Alcinous cut him a piece of meat from the fattest of the haunch, and sent it to him, and said: "Sing to us, noble harper, and rejoice the heroes' hearts."

So the harper played and sang, while the dancers danced strange figures; and after that the tumblers showed their tricks, till the heroes laughed again.

Then, "Tell me, heroes," asked Alcinous, "you who have sailed the ocean round, and seen the manners of all nations, have you seen such dancers as ours here? or heard such music and such singing? We hold ours to be the best on earth."

"Such dancing we have never seen," said Orpheus; "and your singer is a happy man; for Phœbus himself must have taught him, or else he is the son of a Muse; as I am also, and have sung once or twice, though not so well as he."

"Sing to us, then, noble stranger," said Alcinous; "and we will give you precious gifts."

So Orpheus took his magic harp, and sang to them a stirring song of their voyage from Iolcos, and their dangers, and how they won the Golden Fleece; and of Medeia's love, and how she helped them, and went with them over land and sea; and of all their fearful dangers, from monsters, and rocks, and storms, till the heart of Arete was softened, and all the women wept. And the merchant kings rose up, each man from off his golden throne, and clapped their hands, and shouted: "Hail to the noble Argonauts, who sailed the unknown sea!"

Then he went on, and told their journey over the sluggish northern main, and through the shoreless outer ocean, to the fairy island of the west; and of the Sirens, and Scylla, and Charybdis, and all the wonders they had seen, till midnight passed, and the day dawned; but the kings never thought of sleep. Each man sat still and listened, with his chin upon his hand.

And at last when Orpheus had ended, they all went thoughtful out, and the heroes lay down to sleep, beneath the sounding porch outside, where Arete had strewn them rugs and carpets, in the sweet still summer night.

But Arete pleaded hard with her husband for Medeia, for her heart was softened. And she said: " The Gods will punish her, not we. After all, she is our guest and my suppliant, and prayers are the daughters of Zeus. And who, too, dare part man and wife, after all they have endured together?"

And Alcinous smiled. "The minstrel's song has charmed you; but I must remember what is right; for songs cannot alter justice; and I must be faithful to my name. Alcinous I am called, the man of sturdy sense, and Alcinous I will be." But for all that, Arete besought him, until she won him round.

So next morning he sent a herald, and called the kings into the square, and said; "This is a puzzling matter; remember but one thing. These Minuai live close by us, and we may meet them often on the seas; but Aietes lives afar off, and we have only heard his name. Which, then, of the two is it safer to offend, the men near us, or the men far off?"

The princes laughed, and praised his wisdom; and Alcinous called the heroes to the square, and the Colchi also; and they came and stood opposite each other: but Medeia stayed in the palace. Then Alcinous spoke, — "Heroes of the Colchi, what is your errand about this lady?"

" To carry her home with us, that she may die a shameful death : but if we return without her, we must die the death she should have died."

"What say you to this, Jason the Æolid?" said Alcinous, turning to the Minuai.

" I say," said the cunning Jason, " that they are come here on a bootless errand. Do you think that you can make her follow you, heroes of the Colchi? her, who knows all spells and charms? She will cast away your ships on quicksands, or call down on you Brimo the wild huntress; or the chains will fall from off her wrists, and she will escape in her dragon-car: or if not thus, some other way; for she has a thousand plans and wiles. And why return home at all, brave heroes, and face the long seas again, and the Bosphorus, and the stormy Euxine, and double all your toil? There is many a fair land round these coasts, which waits for gallant men like you. Better to settle there, and build a city, and let Aietes and Colchis help themselves."

Then a murmur rose among the Colchi, and some cried, " He has spoken well; " and some, " We have had enough of roving, we will sail the seas no more ! " And the chief said at last, " Be it so, then; a plague she has been to us, and a plague to the house of her father, and a plague she will be to you. Take her, since you are no wiser; and we will sail away toward the north."

Then Alcinous gave them food, and water, and garments, and rich presents of all sorts; and he gave the same to the Minuai, and sent them all away in peace.

So Jason kept the dark witch-maiden to breed him woe and shame: and the Colchi went northward into the Adriatic, and settled, and built towns along the shore.

Then the heroes rowed away to the eastward, to reach Hellas their beloved land; but a storm came down upon them, and swept them far away toward the south.   And they rowed till they were spent with struggling, through the darkness and the blinding rain, but where they were they could not tell, and they gave up all hope of life.   And at last they touched the ground, and when daylight came they waded to the shore; and saw nothing round but sand, and desolate salt pools; for they had come to the quicksands of the Syrtis, and the dreary treeless flats, which lie between Numidia and Cyrene, on the burning shore of Africa. And there they wandered starving for many a weary day, ere they could launch their ship again, and gain the open sea.   And there Canthus was killed while he was trying to drive off sheep, by a stone which a herds-man threw.

And there too Mopsus died, the seer who knew the voices of all birds: but he could not foretell his own end, for he was bitten in the foot by a snake, one of those which sprang from the Gorgon's head when Perseus carried it across the sands.

At last they rowed away toward the northward, for many a weary day, till their water was spent, and their food eaten; and they were worn out with hunger and thirst.   But at last they saw a long steep island, and a blue peak high among the clouds; and they knew it for the peak of Ida, and the famous land of Crete. And they said, " We will land in Crete, and see Minos, the just king, and all his glory and his wealth; at least he will treat us hospitably, and let us fill our water-casks upon the shore."

But when they came nearer to the island they saw a wondrous sight upon the cliffs. For on a cape to the westward stood a giant, taller than any mountain pine; who glittered aloft against the sky like a tower of burnished brass. He turned and looked on all sides round him, till he saw the Argo and her crew; and when he saw them he came toward them, more swiftly than the swiftest horse, leaping across the glens at a bound, and striding at one step from down to down. And when he came abreast of them he brandished his arms up and down, as a ship hoists and lowers her yards, and shouted with his brazen throat like a trumpet from off the hills — "You are pirates, you are robbers! If you dare land here, you die."

Then the heroes cried, "We are no pirates. We are all good men and true; and all we ask is food and water:" but the giant cried the more —

"You are robbers, you are pirates all; I know you; and if you land, you shall die the death."

Then he waved his arms again as a signal, and they saw the people flying inland, driving their flocks before them, while a great flame arose among the hills. Then the giant ran up a valley and vanished; and the heroes lay on their oars in fear.

But Medeia stood watching all, from under her steep black brows, with a cunning smile upon her lips, and a cunning plot within her heart. At last she spoke: I know this giant. I heard of him in the East. Hephaistos the Fire King made him, in his forge in Ætna beneath the earth, and called him Talus, and gave him to Minos for a servant, to guard the coast of Crete. Thrice a day he walks round the island, and never stops to sleep; and if strangers land he leaps into his furnace, which flames there among the hills; and when he is red-hot he rushes on them, and burns them in his brazen hands."

Then all the heroes cried, "What shall we do, wise Medeia? We must have water, or we die of thirst. Flesh and blood we can face fairly; but who can face this red-hot brass?"

"I can face red-hot brass, if the tale I hear be true. For they say that he has but one vein in all his body, filled with liquid fire; and that this vein is closed with a nail; but I know not where that nail is placed. But if I can get it once into these hands, you shall water your ship here in peace."

Then she bade them put her on shore, and row off again, and wait what would befall.

And the heroes obeyed her unwillingly; for they were ashamed to leave her so alone; but Jason said, "She is dearer to me than to any of you, yet I will trust her freely on shore; she has more plots than we dream of, in the windings of that fair and cunning head."

So they left the witch-maiden on the shore; and she stood there in her beauty all alone, till the giant strode back red-hot from head to heel, while the grass hissed and smoked beneath his tread.

And when he saw the maiden alone, he stopped; and she looked boldly up into his face without moving, and began her magic song: —

"Life is short, though life is sweet; and even men

of brass and fire must die. The brass must rust, the
fire must cool, for time gnaws all things in their turn.
Life is short, though life is sweet; but sweeter to live
forever; sweeter to live ever youthful like the Gods,
who have ichor in their veins; ichor which gives life,
and youth, and joy, and a bounding heart."

Then Talus said, " Who are you, strange maiden?
and where is this ichor of youth?"

Then Medeia held up a flask of crystal, and said,
"Here is the ichor of youth. I am Medeia the en-
chantress; my sister Circe gave me this, and said,
'Go and reward Talus the faithful servant, for his
fame is gone out into all lands.' So come, and I
will pour this into your veins, that you may live forever young."

And he listened to her false words, that simple Talus,
and came near; and Medeia said, " Dip yourself in the
sea first, and cool yourself, lest you burn my tender
hands; then show me where the nail in your vein is,
that I may pour the ichor in."

Then that simple Talus dipped himself in the sea, till
it hissed, and roared, and smoked; and came and knelt
before Medeia, and showed her the secret nail.

And she drew the nail out gently; but she poured no
ichor in; and instead the liquid fire spouted forth, like
a stream of red-hot iron. And Talus tried to leap up,
crying, "You have betrayed me, false witch-maiden!"
But she lifted up her hands before him, and sang, till
he sank beneath her spell. And as he sank, his brazen
limbs clanked heavily, and the earth groaned beneath
his weight; and the liquid fire ran from his heel, like
a stream of lava to the sea; and Medeia laughed, and

called to the heroes, "Come ashore, and water your ship in peace."

So they came, and found the giant lying dead; and they fell down, and kissed Medeia's feet; and watered their ship, and took sheep and oxen, and so left that inhospitable shore.

At last, after many more adventures, they came to the Cape of Malea, at the southwest point of the Peloponnese. And there they offered sacrifices, and Orpheus purged them from their guilt. Then they rowed away again to the northward, past the Laconian shore, and came all worn and tired by Sunium, and up the long Eubœan Strait, until they saw once more Pelion, and Aphetai, and Iolcos by the sea.

And they ran the ship ashore; but they had no strength left to haul her up the beach; and they crawled out on the pebbles, and sat down, and wept till they could weep no more. For the houses and the trees were all altered; and all the faces which they saw were strange; and their joy was swallowed up in sorrow, while they thought of their youth, and all their labor, and the gallant comrades they had lost.

And the people crowded round, and asked them, "Who are you, that you sit weeping here?"

"We are the sons of your princes, who sailed out many a year ago. We went to fetch the Golden Fleece; and we have brought it, and grief therewith. Give us news of our fathers and our mothers, if any of them be left alive on earth."

Then there was shouting and laughing, and weeping; and all the kings came to the shore, and they led away the heroes to their homes, and bewailed the valiant dead.

Then Jason went up with Medeia to the palace of his uncle Pelias. And when he came in, Pelias sat by the hearth, crippled and blind with age; while opposite him sat Æson, Jason's father, crippled and blind likewise; and the two old men's heads shook together, as they tried to warm themselves before the fire.

And Jason fell down at his father's knees, and wept, and called him by his name. And the old man stretched his hands out, and felt him, and said, "Do not mock me, young hero. My son Jason is dead long ago at sea."

"I am your own son Jason, whom you trusted to the Centaur upon Pelion; and I have brought home the Golden Fleece, and a princess of the Sun's race for my bride. So now give me up the kingdom, Pelias my uncle, and fulfil your promise as I have fulfilled mine."

Then his father clung to him like a child, and wept, and would not let him go; and cried, "Now I shall not go down lonely to my grave. Promise me never to leave me till I die."

PART VI.

WHAT WAS THE END OF THE HEROES.

AND now I wish that I could end my story pleasantly; but it is no fault of mine that I cannot. The old songs end it sadly, and I believe that they are right and wise; for though the heroes were purified at Malea, yet sacrifices cannot make bad hearts good, and Jason had taken a wicked wife, and he had to bear his burden to the last.

And first she laid a cunning plot, to punish that poor old Pelias, instead of letting him die in peace.

For she told his daughters, "I can make old things young again; I will show you how easy it is to do."

So she took an old ram and killed him, and put him in a caldron with magic herbs; and whispered her spells over him, and he leapt out again a young lamb. So that "Medeia's caldron" is a proverb still, by which we mean times of war and change, when the world has become old and feeble, and grows young again through bitter pains.

Then she said to Pelias's daughters, "Do to your

father as I did to this ram, and he will grow young and strong again." But she only told them half the spell; so they failed, while Medeia mocked them; and poor old Pelias died, and his daughters came to misery. But the songs say she cured Æson, Jason's father, and he became young and strong again.

But Jason could not love her, after all her cruel deeds. So he was ungrateful to her, and wronged her: and she revenged herself on him. And a terrible revenge she took — too terrible to speak of here. But you will hear of it yourselves when you grow up, for it has been sung in noble poetry and music; and whether it be true or not, it stands forever as a warning to us, not to seek for help from evil persons, or to gain good ends by evil means. For if we use an adder even against our enemies, it will turn again and sting us.

But of all the other heroes there is many a brave tale left, which I have no space to tell you, so you must read them for yourselves; — of the hunting of the boar in Calydon, which Meleager killed; and of Heracles's twelve famous labors; and of the seven who fought at Thebes; and of the noble love of Castor and Polydeuces, the twin Dioscouroi; how when one died, the other would not live without him, so they shared their immortality between them; and Zeus changed them into the twin stars, which never rise both at once.

And what became of Cheiron, the good immortal beast? That too is a sad story; for the heroes never saw him more. He was wounded by a poisoned arrow, at Pholoe among the hills, when Heracles opened the

fatal wine-jar, which Cheiron had warned him not to
touch.   And the Centaurs smelt the wine, and flocked
to it, and fought for it with Heracles: but he killed
them all with his poisoned arrows, and Cheiron was
left alone.   Then Cheiron took up one of the arrows,
and dropped it by chance upon his foot; and the
poison ran like fire along his veins, and he lay down,
and longed to die; and cried, "Through wine I perish,
the bane of all my race.   Why should I live forever in
this agony?   Who will take my immortality that I
may die?"

Then Prometheus answered, the good Titan, whom
Heracles had set free from Caucasus, "I will take your
immortality and live forever, that I may help poor
mortal men."   So Cheiron gave him his immortality,
and died, and had rest from pain.   And Heracles and
Prometheus wept over him, and went to bury him on
Pelion: but Zeus took him up among the stars, to live
forever, grand and mild, low down in the far southern
sky.

And in time the heroes died, all but Nestor the
silver-tongued old man; and left behind them valiant
sons, but not so great as they had been.   Yet their
fame, too, lives till this day; for they fought at the
ten years' siege of Troy; and their story is in the book
which we call Homer, in two of the noblest songs on
earth; the Iliad, which tells us of the siege of Troy,
and Achilles's quarrel with the kings: and the Odyssey,
which tells the wanderings of Odysseus, through many
lands for many years; and how Alcinous sent him
home at last, safe to Ithaca his beloved island, and to
Penelope his faithful wife, and Telemachus his son,

and Euphorbus the noble swineherd, and the old dog who licked his hand and died. We will read that sweet story, children, by the fire some winter night. And now I will end my tale.

THE ODYSSEY; OR, THE ADVEN-
TURES OF ULYSSES

By ALFRED J. CHURCH.

CHAPTER I.

THE CYCLOPS.

WHEN the great city of Troy was taken, all the chiefs who had fought against it set sail for their homes. But there was wrath in heaven against them, for indeed they had borne themselves haughtily and cruelly in the day of their victory. Therefore they did not all find a safe and a happy return. For one was shipwrecked, and another was shamefully slain by his false wife in his palace, and others found all things at home troubled and changed, and were driven to seek new dwellings elsewhere. And some, whose wives and friends and people had been still true to them through those ten long years of absence, were driven far and wide about the world before they saw their native land again. And of all, the wise Ulysses was he who wandered farthest and suffered most.

He was well-nigh the last to sail, for he had tarried

174

many days to do pleasure to Agamemnon, lord of all
the Greeks. Twelve ships he had with him — twelve
he had brought to Troy — and in each there were some
fifty men, being scarce half of those that had sailed in
them in the old days, so many valiant heroes slept the
last sleep by Simoïs and Scamander, and in the plain
and on the sea-shore, slain in battle, or by the shafts of
Apollo.

First they sailed north-west to the Thracian coast,
where the Ciconians dwelt, who had helped the men of
Troy. Their city they took, and in it much plunder,
slaves and oxen, and jars of fragrant wine, and might
have escaped unhurt, but that they stayed to hold
revel on the shore. For the Ciconians gathered their
neighbors, being men of the same blood, and did battle
with the invaders, and drove them to their ships. And
when Ulysses numbered his men, he found that he had
lost six out of his ship.

Scarce had he set out again when the wind began to
blow fiercely; so, seeing a smooth sandy beach, they
drave the ships ashore and dragged them out of reach
of the waves, and waited till the storm should abate.
And the third morning being fair, they sailed again and
journeyed prosperously till they came to the very end
of the great Peloponnesian land, where Cape Malea
looks out upon the southern sea. But contrary cur-
rents baffled them, so that they could not round it,
and the north wind blew so strongly that they must
fain drive before it. And on the tenth day they came
to the land where the lotus grows — a wondrous fruit,
of which whosoever eats cares not to see country or
wife or children again. Now the Lotus-eaters, for so

they call the people of the land, were a kindly folk, and gave of the fruit to some of the sailors, not meaning them any harm, but thinking it to be the best that they had to give. These, when they had eaten, said that they would not sail any more over the sea; which, when the wise Ulysses heard, he bade their comrades bind them and carry them, sadly complaining, to the ships.

Then, the wind having abated, they took to their oars, and rowed for many days till they came to the country where the Cyclopes dwell. Now, a mile or so from the shore there was an island, very fair and fertile, but no man dwells there or tills the soil, and in the island a harbor where a ship may be safe from all winds, and at the head of the harbor a stream falling from the rock, and whispering alders all about it. Into this the ships passed safely, and were hauled up on the beach, and the crews slept by them, waiting for the morning. And the next day they hunted the wild goats, of which there was great store on the island, and feasted right merrily on what they caught, with draughts of red wine which they had carried off from the town of the Ciconians.

But on the morrow, Ulysses, for he was ever fond of adventure, and would know of every land to which he came what manner of men they were that dwelt there, took one of his twelve ships and bade row to the land. There was a great hill sloping to the shore, and there rose up here and there a smoke from the caves where the Cyclopes dwelt apart, holding no converse with each other, for they were a rude and savage folk, but ruled each his own household, not caring for others. Now

very close to the shore was one of these caves, very
huge and deep, with laurels round about the mouth,
and in front a fold with walls built of rough stone, and
shaded by tall oaks and pines. So Ulysses chose out
of the crew the twelve bravest, and bade the rest guard
the ship, and went to see what manner of dwelling this
was, and who abode there. He had his sword by his
side, and on his shoulder a mighty skin of wine, sweet-
smelling and strong, with which he might win the
heart of some fierce savage, should he chance to meet
with such, as indeed his prudent heart forecasted that
he might.

So they entered the cave, and judged that it was the
dwelling of some rich and skilful shepherd. For within
there were pens for the young of the sheep and of the
goats, divided all according to their age, and there were
baskets full of cheeses, and full milkpails ranged along
the wall. But the Cyclops himself was away in the
pastures. Then the companions of Ulysses besought
him, that he would depart, taking with him, if he would,
a store of cheeses and sundry of the lambs and of the
kids. But he would not, for he wished to see, after
his wont, what manner of host this strange shepherd
might be. And truly he saw it to his cost!

It was evening when the Cyclops came home, a
mighty giant, twenty feet in height, or more. On his
shoulder he bore a vast bundle of pine logs for his fire,
and threw them down outside the cave with a great
crash, and drove the flocks within, and closed the
entrance with a huge rock, which twenty wagons and
more could not bear. Then he milked the ewes and all
the she-goats, and half of the milk he curdled for

cheese, and half he set ready for himself, when he
should sup.   Next he kindled the fire with the pine
logs, and the flame lighted up all the cave, showing
him Ulysses and his comrades.

"Who are ye?" cried Polyphemus, for that was the
giant's name.   "Are ye traders, or, haply, pirates?"

For in those days it was not counted shame to be
called a pirate.

Ulysses shuddered at the dreadful voice and shape,
but bore him bravely, and answered, "We are no
pirates, mighty sir, but Greeks, sailing back from Troy,
and subjects of the great King Agamemnon, whose
fame is spread from one end of heaven to the other.
And we are come to beg hospitality of thee in the name
of Zeus, who rewards or punishes hosts and guests
according as they be faithful the one to the other, or
no."

"Nay," said the giant, "it is but idle talk to tell me
of Zeus and the other gods. We Cyclopes take no
account of gods, holding ourselves to be much better
and stronger than they.   But come, tell me where have
you left your ship?"

But Ulysses saw his thought when he asked about
the ship, how he was minded to break it, and take
from them all hope of flight.   Therefore he answered
him craftily —

"Ship have we none, for that which was ours King
Poseidon brake, driving it on a jutting rock on this
coast, and we whom thou seest are all that are escaped
from the waves."

Polyphemus answered nothing, but without more
ado caught up two of the men, as a man might catch

up the whelps of a dog, and dashed them on the
ground, and tore them limb from limb, and devoured
them, with huge draughts of milk between, leaving not
a morsel, not even the very bones. But the others,
when they saw the dreadful deed, could only weep and
pray to Zeus for help. And when the giant had ended
his foul meal, he lay down among his sheep and slept.

Then Ulysses questioned much in his heart whether
he should slay the monster as he slept, for he doubted
not that his good sword would pierce to the giant's
heart, mighty as he was. But, being very wise, he
remembered that, should he slay him, he and his comrades would yet perish miserably. For who should
move away the great rock that lay against the door
of the cave? So they waited till the morning. And
the monster woke, and milked his flocks, and afterwards,
seizing two men, devoured them for his meal. Then he
went to the pastures, but put the great rock on the
mouth of the cave, just as a man puts down the lid upon
his quiver.

All that day the wise Ulysses was thinking what he
might best do to save himself and his companions, and
the end of his thinking was this: there was a mighty
pole in the cave, green wood of an olive tree, big as a
ship's mast, which Polyphemus purposed to use, when
the smoke should have dried it, as a walking staff. Of
this he cut off a fathom's length, and his comrades
sharpened it and hardened it in the fire, and then hid
it away. At evening the giant came back, and drove
his sheep into the cave, nor left the rams outside, as he
had been wont to do before, but shut them in. And
having duly done his shepherd's work, he made his cruel

feast as before. Then Ulysses came forward with the
wine-skin in his hand and said —

"Drink, Cyclops, now that thou hast feasted. Drink,
and see what precious things we had in our ship. But
no one hereafter will come to thee with such like, if
thou dealest with strangers as cruelly as thou hast dealt
with us."

Then the Cyclops drank, and was mightily pleased,
and said, "Give me again to drink, and tell me thy
name, stranger, and I will give thee a gift such as a
host should give. In good truth this is a rare liquor.
We, too, have vines, but they bear not wine like this,
which indeed must be such as the gods drink in
heaven."

Then Ulysses gave him the cup again, and he drank.
Thrice he gave it to him, and thrice he drank, not
knowing what it was, and how it would work within
his brain.

Then Ulysses spake to him. "Thou didst ask my
name, Cyclops. Lo! my name is No Man. And now
that thou knowest my name, thou shouldst give me thy
gift."

And he said, "My gift shall be that I will eat thee
last of all thy company."

And as he spake he fell back in a drunken sleep.
Then Ulysses bade his comrades be of good courage,
for the time was come when they should be delivered.
And they thrust the stake of olive wood into the fire
till it was ready, green as it was, to burst into flame,
and they thrust it into the monster's eye; for he had
but one eye, and that in the midst of his forehead, with
the eyebrow below it. And Ulysses leant with all his

force upon the stake, and thrust it in with might and main. And the burning wood hissed in the eye, just as the red-hot iron hisses in the water when a man seeks to temper steel for a sword.

Then the giant leapt up, and tore away the stake, and cried aloud, so that all the Cyclopes who dwelt on the mountain side heard him and came about his cave, asking him, "What aileth thee, Polyphemus, that thou makest this uproar in the peaceful night, driving away sleep? Is any one robbing thee of thy sheep, or seeking to slay thee by craft or force?"

And the giant answered, "No Man slays me by craft."

"Nay, but," they said, "if no man does thee wrong, we cannot help thee. The sickness which great Zeus may send, who can avoid? Pray to our father, Poseidon, for help."

Then they departed; and Ulysses was glad at heart for the good success of his device, when he said that he was No Man.

But the Cyclops rolled away the great stone from the door of the cave, and sat in the midst stretching out his hands, to feel whether perchance the men within the cave would seek to go out among the sheep.

Long did Ulysses think how he and his comrades should best escape. At last he lighted upon a good device, and much he thanked Zeus for that this once the giant had driven the rams with the other sheep into the cave. For, these being great and strong, he fastened his comrades under the bellies of the beasts, tying them with osier twigs, of which the giant made his bed. One ram he took, and fastened a man beneath it, and

two others he set, one on either side. So he did with
the six, for but six were left out of the twelve who had
ventured with him from the ship. And there was one
mighty ram, far larger than all the others, and to this
Ulysses clung, grasping the fleece tight with both his
hands. So they waited for the morning. And when
the morning came, the rams rushed forth to the pasture; but the giant sat in the door and felt the back
of each as it went by, nor thought to try what might
be underneath. Last of all went the great ram. And
the Cyclops knew him as he passed, and said —

" How is this, thou, who art the leader of the flock?
Thou art not wont thus to lag behind. Thou hast
always been the first to run to the pastures and streams
in the morning, and the first to come back to the fold
when evening fell; and now thou art last of all. Perhaps thou art troubled about thy master's eye, which
some wretch — No Man, they call him — has destroyed,
having first mastered me with wine. He has not
escaped, I ween. I would that thou couldst speak,
and tell me where he is lurking. Of a truth I would
dash out his brains upon the ground, and avenge me of
this No Man."

So speaking, he let him pass out of the cave. But
when they were out of reach of the giant, Ulysses loosed
his hold of the ram, and then unbound his comrades.
And they hastened to their ship, not forgetting to drive
before them a good store of the Cyclops' fat sheep.
Right glad were those that had abode by the ship to
see them. Nor did they lament for those that had
died, though they were fain to do so, for Ulysses forbade,
fearing lest the noise of their weeping should betray

them to the giant, where they were. Then they all
climbed into the ship, and sitting well in order on the
benches, smote the sea with their oars, laying-to right
lustily, that they might the sooner get away from the
accursed land. And when they had rowed a hundred
yards or so, so that a man's voice could yet be heard by
one who stood upon the shore, Ulysses stood up in the
ship and shouted —

"He was no coward, O Cyclops, whose comrades thou
didst so foully slay in thy den. Justly art thou pun-
ished, monster, that devourest thy guests in thy dwelling. May the gods make thee suffer yet worse things
than these!"

Then the Cyclops, in his wrath, broke off the top of
a great hill, a mighty rock, and hurled it where he had
heard the voice. Right in front of the ship's bow it
fell, and a great wave rose as it sank, and washed the
ship back to the shore. But Ulysses seized a long pole
with both hands and pushed the ship from the land, and
bade his comrades ply their oars, nodding with his head,
for he was too wise to speak, lest the Cyclops should
know where they were. Then they rowed with all
their might and main.

And when they had gotten twice as far as before,
Ulysses made as if he would speak again; but his comrades sought to hinder him, saying, "Nay, my lord,
anger not the giant any more. Surely we thought
before we were lost, when he threw the great rock, and
washed our ship back to the shore. And if he hear thee
now, he may crush our ship and us, for the man throws
a mighty bolt, and throws it far."

But Ulysses would not be persuaded, but stood up and

said, " Hear, Cyclops ! If any man ask who blinded thee, say that it was the warrior Ulysses, son of Laertes, dwelling in Ithaca."

And the Cyclops answered with a groan, " Of a truth, the old oracles are fulfilled, for long ago there came to this land one Telemus, a prophet, and dwelt among us even to old age. This man foretold to me that one Ulysses would rob me of my sight. But I looked for a great man and a strong, who should subdue me by force, and now a weakling has done the deed, having cheated me with wine. But come thou hither, Ulysses, and I will be a host indeed to thee. Or, at least, may Poseidon give thee such a voyage to thy home as I would wish thee to have. For know that Poseidon is my sire. May be that he may heal me of my grievous wound."

And Ulysses said, " Would to God I could send thee down to the abode of the dead, where thou wouldst be past all healing, even from Poseidon's self."

Then Cyclops lifted up his hand to Poseidon and prayed —

" Hear me, Poseidon, if I am indeed thy son and thou my father. May this Ulysses never reach his home ! or, if the Fates have ordered that he should reach it, may he come alone, all his comrades lost, and come to find sore trouble in his house ! "

And as he ended he hurled another mighty rock, which almost lighted on the rudder's end, yet missed it as by a hair's breadth. So Ulysses and his comrades escaped, and came to the island of the wild goats, where they found their comrades, who indeed had waited long for them, in sore fear lest they had perished. Then Ulysses divided amongst his company all the sheep which they had taken from the Cyclops. And all, with one consent, gave him for his share the great ram which had carried him out of the cave, and he sacrificed it to Zeus. And all that day they feasted right merrily on the flesh of sheep and on sweet wine, and when the night was come, they lay down upon the shore and slept.

CHAPTER II.

THE ISLAND OF ÆOLUS — THE LÆSTRYGONS — CIRCE.

FTER sailing awhile, they came to the island of Æolus, who is the king of the winds, and who dwelt there with his children, six sons and six daughters. Right well did Æolus entertain them, feasting them royally for a whole month, while he heard from Ulysses the story of all that had been done at Troy. And when Ulysses prayed him that he would help him on his way homewards, Æolus hearkened to him, and gave him the skin of an ox, in which he had bound all contrary winds, so that they should not hinder him. But he let a gentle west wind blow, that it might carry him and his comrades to their home. For nine days it blew and now they were near to Ithaca, their country, so that they saw lights burning in it, it being night-time. But now, by an ill chance, Ulysses fell asleep, being wholly wearied out, for he had held the helm for nine days, nor trusted it to any of his comrades. And while he slept, his comrades, who had cast eyes of envy on the great ox-hide, said one to another —

"Strange it is how men love and honor this Ulysses whithersoever he goes. And now he comes back from Troy with much spoil, but we with empty hands. Let

us see what it is that Æolus hath given, for doubtless
in this ox-hide is much silver and gold."

So they loosed the great bag of ox-hide, and lo! all
the winds rushed out, and carried them far away from
their country. But Ulysses, waking with the tumult,
doubted much whether he should not throw himself
into the sea and so die. But he endured, thinking it
better to live. Only he veiled his face and so sat, while
the ships drave before the winds, till they came once
more to the island of Æolus. Then Ulysses went to
the palace of the king, and found him feasting with his
wife and children, and sat him down on the threshold.
Much did they wonder to see him, saying, " What evil
power has hindered thee, that thou didst not reach thy
country and home ? "

Then he answered, " Blame not me, but the evil
counsels of my comrades, and sleep, which mastered me
to my hurt. But do ye help me again."

But they said, " Begone ; we may not help him whom
the gods hate ; and hated of them thou surely art."

So Æolus sent him away. Then again they launched
their ships and set forth, toiling wearily at the oars, and
sad at heart.

Six days they rowed, nor rested at night, and on the
seventh they came to Lamos, which was a city of the
Læstrygons, in whose land the night is as the day, so
that a man might earn double wage, if only he wanted
not sleep — shepherd by day and herdsman by night.
There was a fair haven with cliffs about it, and a narrow mouth with great rocks on either side. And within
are no waves, but always calm.

Now Ulysses made fast his ship to the rocks, but the

others entered the haven. Then he sent two men and
a herald with them, and these came upon a smooth
road by which wagons brought down wood from the
mountain to the city. Here they met a maiden, the
stalwart daughter of Antiphates, king of the land, and
asked of her who was lord of that country. Whereupon
she showed them her father's lofty palace. And they,
entering this, saw the maiden's mother, big as a mountain, horrible to behold, who straightway called to
Antiphates, her husband. The messengers, indeed, fled
to the ships; but he made a great shout, and the Læstrygons came flocking about him, giants, not men. And
these broke off great stones from the cliffs, each stone
as much as a man could carry, and cast them at the
ships, so that they were broken. And the men they
speared, as if they were fishes, and devoured them. So
it happened to all the ships in the haven. Ulysses
only escaped, for he cut the hawser with his sword, and
bade his men ply their oars, which indeed they did right
willingly.

After a while they came to the island of Ææa, where
Circe dwelt, who was the daughter of the Sun. Two
days and nights they lay upon the shore in great
trouble and sorrow. On the third, Ulysses took his
spear and sword and climbed a hill that there was, for
he wished to see to what manner of land they had
come. And having climbed it, he saw the smoke rising
from the palace of Circe, where it stood in the midst
of a wood. Then he thought awhile: should he go
straightway to the palace that he saw, or first return
to his comrades on the shore? And this last seemed
better; and it chanced that as he went he saw a great

stag which was going down to the river to drink, for
indeed the sun was now hot, and casting his spear at it
he pierced it through.   Then he fastened together the
feet with green withes and a fathom's length of rope,
and slinging the beast round his neck, so carried it to
the ship, leaning on his spear; for indeed it was heavy
to bear, nor could any man have carried it on the
shoulder with one hand.   And when he was come to
the ship, he cast down his burden.   Now the men were
sitting with their faces muffled, so sad were they.   But
when he bade them be of good cheer, they looked up
and marvelled at the great stag.   And all that day
they feasted on deer's flesh and sweet wine, and at
night lay down to sleep on the shore.   But when morning was come, Ulysses called them all together and
spake —

"I know not, friends, where we are.   Only I know,
having seen smoke yesterday from the hill, that there
is a dwelling in this island."

It troubled the men much to hear this, for they
thought of the Cyclops and of the Læstrygons; and
they wailed aloud, but there was no counsel in them.
Wherefore Ulysses divided them into two companies,
setting Eurylochus over the one and himself over the
other, and shook lots in a helmet who should go and
search out the island, and the lot of Eurylochus leapt
out.   So he went, and comrades twenty and two with
him.   And in an open space in the wood they found
the palace of Circe.   All about were wolves and lions;
yet these harmed not the men, but stood up on their
hind legs, fawning upon them, as dogs fawn upon their
master when he comes from his meal.   And the men

were afraid. And they stood in the porch and heard the voice of Circe as she sang with a lovely voice and plied the loom. Then said Polites, who was dearest of all his comrades to Ulysses —

"Some one within plies a great loom, and sings with a loud voice. Some goddess is she, or woman. Let us make haste and call."

So they called to her, and she came out and beckoned to them that they should follow. So they went, in their folly. And she bade them sit, and mixed for them a mess, red wine, and in it barley-meal and cheese and honey, and mighty drugs withal, of which, if a man drank, he forgot all that he loved. And when they had drunk she smote them with her wand. And lo! they had of a sudden the heads and the voices and the bristles of swine, but the heart of a man was in them still. And Circe shut them in sties, and gave them mast and acorns and cornel to eat.

But Eurylochus fled back to the ship. And for a while he could not speak, so full was his heart of grief, but at the last he told the tale of what had befallen. Then Ulysses took his silver-studded sword and his bow, and bade Eurylochus guide him by the way that he had gone.

Nor would he hearken when Eurylochus would have hindered him, but said, " Stay here by the ship, eating and drinking, if it be thy will, but I must go, for necessity constrains me."

And when he had come to the house, there met him Hermes of the golden wand, in the shape of a fair youth, who said to him —

" Art thou come to rescue thy comrades that are now

swine in Circe's house? Nay, but thou shalt never go back thyself. Yet, stay; I will give thee such a drug as shall give thee power to resist all her charms. For when she shall have mixed thee a mess, and smitten thee with her wand, then do thou rush upon her with thy sword making as if thou wouldst slay her. And when she shall pray for peace, do thou make her swear by the great oath that binds the gods that she will not harm thee."

Then Hermes showed Ulysses a certain herb, whose root was black, but the flower white as milk. "Moly," the gods call it, and very hard it is for mortal man to find. Then Ulysses went into the house, and all befell as Hermes had told him. For Circe would have changed him as she had changed his comrades. Then he rushed at her with his sword, and made her swear the great oath which binds the gods that she would not harm him.

But afterwards, when they sat at meat together, the goddess perceived that he was silent and ate not. Wherefore she said, "Why dost thou sit, Ulysses, as though thou wert dumb? Fearest thou any craft of mine? Nay, but that may not be, for have I not sworn the great oath that binds the gods?"

And Ulysses said, "Nay, but who could think of meat and drink when such things had befallen his companions?"

Then Circe led the way, holding her wand in her hand, and opened the doors of the sties, and drove out the swine that had been men. Then she rubbed on each another mighty drug, and the bristles fell from their bodies and they became men, only younger and fairer than before. And when they saw Ulysses they clung to him and wept for joy, and Circe herself was moved with pity.

Then said she, " Go, Ulysses, to thy ship, and put away all the goods and tackling in the caves that are on the shore, but come again hither thyself, and bring thy comrades with thee."

Then Ulysses went. Right glad were they who had stayed to see him, glad as are the calves who have been penned in the fold-yard when their mothers come back in the evening. And when he told them what had been, and would have them follow him, they were all willing, save only Eurylochus, who said, —

" O ye fools, whither are we going? To the dwelling of Circe, who will change us all into swine, or wolves or lions, and keep us in prison, even as the Cyclops did! For was it not this same foolhardy Ulysses that lost our comrades there ?"

Then was Ulysses very wroth, and would have slain Eurylochus, though near of kin to him. But his comrades hindered him, saying, " Let him abide here and keep the ship, if he will. But we will go with thee to the dwelling of Circe."

Then Ulysses forbore. Nor did Eurylochus stay behind, but followed with the rest. So they went to the dwelling of Circe, who feasted them royally, so that they remained with her for a whole year, well content.

But when the year was out they said to Ulysses, " It were well to remember thy country, if it is indeed the will of the gods that thou shouldst return thither."

Then Ulysses besought Circe that she would send

him on his way homewards, as indeed she had promised to do. And she answered —

"I would not have you abide in my house unwillingly. Yet must thou first go another journey, even to the dwellings of the dead, there to speak with the seer Tiresias."

But Ulysses was sore troubled to hear such things, and wept aloud, saying, "Who shall guide us in this journey? — for never yet did ship make such a voyage as this."

Then said Circe, "Seek no guide; only raise the mast of thy ship and spread the white sails, and sit in peace. So shall the north wind bear thee to the place on the ocean shore where are the groves of Persephone, tall poplars and willows. There must thou beach thy ship. And after that thou must go alone."

Then she told him all that he must do if he would hold converse with the dead seer Tiresias, and hear what should befall him. So the next morning he roused his companions, telling them that they should now return. But it chanced that one of them, Elpenor by name, was sleeping on the roof, for the coolness, being heavy with wine. And when he heard the stir of his comrades, he rose up, nor thought of the ladder, but fell from the roof and brake his neck. And the rest being assembled, Ulysses told them how they must take another journey first, even to the dwellings of the dead. This they were much troubled to hear yet they made ready the ship and departed.

CHAPTER III.

THE REGIONS OF THE DEAD — SCYLLA — THE OXEN OF THE SUN — CALYPSO.

O they came to the place of which Circe had told them. And when all things had been rightly done, Ulysses saw spirits of the dead. First of all came Elpenor, and he marvelled much to see him, saying —

"How camest thou hither? — on foot, or in the ship?"

Then he answered, telling how he had died, and he said, "Now, as thou wilt go back, I know, to the island of Circe, suffer me not to remain unburied, but make above me a mound of earth, for men in aftertimes to see and put upon it my oar, with which I was wont to row while I yet lived."

These things Ulysses promised that he would do. Afterwards came the spirit of Tiresias, holding a sceptre of gold in his hand. And when Ulysses asked him of his return, he said —

"Thy return shall be difficult, because of the anger of Poseidon, whose son thou madest blind. Yet, when thou comest to the island of the Three Capes, where feed the oxen of the Sun, if thou leave these unhurt, thou and thy comrades shall return to Ithaca. But otherwise they shall perish, and thou shalt return, after

long time, in a ship not thine own, and shalt find in
thy palace, devouring thy goods, men of violence,
suitors of thy wife. These thou shalt slay, openly or
by craft. Nor yet shalt thou rest, but shalt go to a
land where men know not the sea, nor eat their meat
with salt; and thou shalt carry thy oar on thy shoulder.
And this shall be a sign to thee, when another wayfarer, meeting thee, shall ask whether it be a winnow-
ing fan that thou bearest on thy shoulder; then shalt
thou fix thy oar in the earth, and make a sacrifice to
Poseidon, and so return. So shalt thou die at last in
peace."

Then Tiresias departed. After this he saw his
mother, and asked how it fared with his home in
Ithaca, and she told him all. And many others he saw,
wives and daughters of the heroes of old time. Also
there came King Agamemnon, who told him how
Ægisthus, with Clytemnestra, his wicked wife, had
slain him in his own palace, being newly returned
from Troy. Fain would the king have heard how it
fared with Orestes, his son, but of this Ulysses could
tell him nothing. Then came the spirit of Achilles,
and him Ulysses comforted, telling him how bravely
and wisely his son Neoptolemus had borne himself in
Troy.

Also he saw the spirit of Ajax, son of Telamon; but
Ajax spake not to him, having great wrath in his heart,
because of the arms of Achilles. For the two, Ajax and
Ulysses, had contended for them, Achilles being dead,
before the assembly of the Greeks, and the Greeks had
given them to Ulysses, whereupon Ajax being very
wroth, had laid hands upon himself.

And having seen many other things, Ulysses went back to his ship, and returned with his companions to the island of Circe. And being arrived there, first they buried Elpenor, making a mound over him, and setting up on it his oar, and afterwards Circe made them a feast. But while the others slept she told to Ulysses all that should befall him, saying —

"First thou wilt come to the island of the Sirens, who sing so sweetly, that whosoever hears them straightway forgets wife and child and home. In a meadow they sit, singing sweetly, but about them are bones of men. Do thou, then, close with wax the ears of thy companions, and make them bind thee to the mast, so that thou mayest hear the song and yet take no hurt. And do thou bid them, when thou shalt pray to be loosed, not to hearken, but rather to bind thee the more. And this peril being past, there lie others in thy path, of which thou must take thy choice. For either thou must pass between the rocks which the gods call the Wanderers — and these close upon all that passes between them, even the very doves in their flight, nor has any ship escaped them, save only the ship Argo, which Hera loved — or thou must go through the strait, where there is a rock on either hand. In the one rock dwells Scylla, in a cave so high above the sea that an archer could not reach it with his arrow. A horrible monster is she. Twelve unshapely feet she hath, and six long necks, and on each a head, with three rows of teeth. In the cave she lies, but her heads are without, fishing for sea-dogs and dolphins, or even a great whale, if such should chance to go by. Think not to escape her, Ulysses, for, of a truth, with each

head will she take one of thy companions. But the
other rock is lower and more flat, with a wild fig-tree
on the top. There Charybdis thrice a day draws in the
dark water, and thrice a day sends it forth. Be not
thou near when she draws it in; not even Poseidon's
self could save thee. Choose rather to pass near to
Scylla, for it is better to lose six of thy companions than
that all should perish."

Then said Ulysses, "Can I not fight with this Scylla,
and so save my companions?"

But Circe answered, "Nay, for she is not of mortal
race. And if thou linger to arm thyself, thou wilt but
lose six others of thy companions. Pass them with all
the speed that may be, and call on Crataïs, who is the
mother of Scylla, that she may keep her from coming
the second time. Then wilt thou come to the island
of the Three Capes, where feed the oxen of the Sun.
Beware that thy companions harm them not."

The next day they departed. Then Ulysses told his
companions of the Sirens, and how they should deal
with him. And after a while, the following wind that
had blown ceased, and there was a great calm; so they
took down the sails and laid them in the ship, and put
forth the oars to row. Then Ulysses made great cakes
of wax, kneading them (for the sun was now hot), and
put into the ears of his companions. And they bound
him to the mast and so rowed on. Then the Sirens
sang —

> " Hither, Ulysses, great Achaian name,
> Turn thy swift keel, and listen to our lay;
> Since never pilgrim near these regions came,
> In black ship on the azure field astray,

But heard our sweet voice ere he sailed away,
And in his joy passed on with ampler mind.
We know what labors were in ancient day
Wrought in wide Troia, as the gods assigned ;
We know from land to land all toils of all mankind."[1]

Then Ulysses prayed that they would loose him,
nodding his head, for their ears were stopped ; but they
plied their oars, and Eurylochus and Perimedes put
new bonds upon him.

After this they saw a smoke and surf, and heard a
mighty roar, and their oars dropped out of their hands
for fear; but Ulysses bade them be of good heart, for
that by his counsel they had escaped other dangers in
past time.   And the rowers he bade row as hard as
they might.   But to the helmsman he said, " Steer the
ship outside the smoke and the surf, and steer close to
the cliffs, lest the ship shoot off unawares and lose us."

But of Scylla he said nothing, fearing lest they
should lose heart and cease rowing altogether.   Then
he armed himself, and stood in the prow waiting till
Scylla should appear.

But on the other side Charybdis was sucking in the
water with a horrible noise, and with eddies so deep
that a man might see the sand at the bottom.   But
while they looked trembling at this, Scylla caught six
of the men from the ship, and Ulysses heard them call
him by his name as the monster carried them away.
And never, he said in after days, did he see with his
eyes so piteous a sight.

But after this they came to the land where fed the
oxen of the Sun.   And Ulysses said, " Let us pass by

[1] Worsley.

this island, for there shall we find the greatest evil that we have yet suffered." But they would not hearken; only they said that the next day they would sail again.

Then spake Ulysses, " Ye constrain me, being many to one. Yet promise me this, that ye will not take any of the sheep or oxen, for if ye do great trouble will come to us."

So they promised. But for a whole month the south wind blew and ceased not. And their store of meat and drink being spent, they caught fishes and birds, as they could, being sore pinched with hunger. And at last it chanced that Ulysses, being weary, fell asleep. And while he slept, his companions, Eurylochus persuading them, took of the oxen of the Sun, and slew them, for they said that their need was great, and that when they came to their own land they would build a temple to the Sun to make amends. But the Sun was very wroth with them. And a great and dreadful thing happened, for the hides crept, and the meat on the spits bellowed.

Six days they feasted on the oxen, and on the seventh they set sail. But when they were now out of sight of land, Zeus brought up a great storm over the sea, and a mighty west wind blew, breaking both the forestay and the backstay of the mast, so that it fell. And after this a thunderbolt struck the ship, and all the men that were in it fell overboard and died. But Ulysses lashed the mast to the keel with the backstay, and on these he sat, borne by the winds across the sea.

All night was he borne along, and in the morning he came to Charybdis. And it chanced that Charybdis was then sucking in the water; but Ulysses, springing up, clung to a wild fig-tree that grew from the rock, but could find no rest for his feet, nor yet could climb into the tree. All day long he clung, waiting till the raft should come forth again; and at evening, at the time when a judge rises from his seat after judging many causes, the raft came forth. Then he loosed his hands and fell, so that he sat astride upon the raft.

After this he was borne for nine days upon the sea, till he came to the island Ogygia, where dwelt the goddess Calypso.

CHAPTER IV.

TELEMACHUS AND PENELOPE.

N this island of Ogygia Ulysses abode seven years, much against his will, thinking always of his home and his wife and his young son. And when the seven years were ended, Athene, who had ever loved him much, spake to Zeus, complaining much that one so wise had been so long balked of his return.

Then said Zeus that it should not be so any longer, for that Poseidon must give up his wrath against the man, if all the other gods were of one mind.

Then said Athene to Zeus, "Do thou send Hermes, thy messenger, to Calypso, that she let Ulysses depart, and I will go to Ithaca to Telemachus, to bid him go search for his father; for indeed it is but seemly that he should do so, now that he is come to man's estate."

So she went to Ithaca, and there she took upon her the form of Mentor, who was chief of the Paphians.

Now there were gathered in the house of Ulysses many princes from the islands, suitors of the Queen Penelope, for they said that Ulysses was dead, and that she should choose another husband. These were gathered together, and were sitting, playing draughts and feasting. And Telemachus sat among them, vexed at heart, for they wasted his substance, neither was he

master in his house. But when he saw the guest at
the door, he rose from his place and welcomed him, and
made him sit down, and commanded that they should
give him food and wine. And when he had ended his
meal, Telemachus asked him of his business.

Thereupon the false Mentor said, " My name is
Mentor, and I am King of the Paphians, and I am sailing to Cyprus for copper, taking iron in exchange.
Now I have been long time the friend of this house, of
thy father and thy father's father, and I came trusting
to see thy father, for they told me that he was here.
But now I see that some god has hindered his return,
for that he lives I know full well."

And after this the two had much talk together, and
Athene gave good counsel to Telemachus, and chiefly
that he should go to Pylos, to old Nestor, and to Sparta,
where Menelaus dwelt, if haply he might hear aught of
his father in this place or in that. And after this she
departed ; and as she went, Telemachus knew her who
she was.

The next day the people of Ithaca were called to an
assembly. And Telemachus stood up among them and
said —

" I have great trouble in my heart, men of Ithaca, for
first my father is not, whom ye all loved ; and next,
the princes of the islands come hither, making suit to
my mother, but she waits ever for her husband, when
he shall return. And they devour all our substance,
nor is Ulysses here to defend it, and I, in truth, am
not able. And this is a grievous wrong, and not to be
borne."

Then he dashed his sceptre on the ground, and sat

down weeping. And Antinous, who was one of the
suitors, rose up and said —

"Nay, Telemachus, blame not us, but blame thy
mother, who indeed is crafty above all women. For
now this is the fourth year that we have come suing
for her hand, and she has cheated us with hopes. Hear
now this that she did. She set up a great warp for
weaving, and said to us, ' Listen, ye that are my suitors. Hasten not my marriage till I finish this web to
be a burial cloth for Laertes, for indeed it would be foul
shame if he who has won great possessions should lack
this honor.' So she spake, and for three years she
cheated us, for what she wove in the day she undid at
night. But when the fourth year was come, one of her
maidens told us of the matter, and we came upon her
by night and found her undoing the web, even what she
had woven in the day. Then did she finish it, much
against her will. Send away, therefore, thy mother,
and bid her marry whom she will. But till this be
done we will not depart."

Then answered Telemachus, "How can I send her
away against her will, who bare me and brought me
up? Much forfeit must I pay to Icarus, her father;
ay, and the curses of my mother would abide on me.
Wherefore I cannot do this thing."

So he spake; and there came two eagles, which flew
abreast till they came over the assembly. Then did
they wheel in the air, and shook out from each many
feathers, and tare each other, and so departed.

Then cried Alitherses, the soothsayer, " Beware, ye
suitors, for great trouble is coming to you, and to others
also. And as for Ulysses, I said when he went to Troy

that he should return after twenty years; and so it shall be."

And when the suitors would not listen, Telemachus said, " Yet give me a ship and twenty rowers, that I may go to Pylos and to Sparta, if haply I may hear news of my father."

But this also they would not, and the assembly was dismissed.

But Telemachus went out to the sea-shore, and prayed to Athene that she would help him. And while he prayed, lo! she stood by him, having the shape of a certain Mentes, who indeed had spoken on his behalf in the assembly. And she said —

" Thou art not, I trow, without spirit and wit, and art like to be a true son of Ulysses and Penelope. Wherefore I have good hopes that this journey of which thou speakest will not be in vain. But as for the suitors, think not of them, for they lack wisdom, nor know the doom that is even now close upon them. Go, therefore, and talk with the suitors as before, and get ready meat for a journey, wine and meal. And I will gather men who will offer themselves freely for the journey, and find a ship also, the best in Ithaca."

Then Telemachus returned to the house. And Antinous caught him by the hand and said, " Eat and drink, Telemachus, and we will find a ship and rowers for thee, that thou mayest go where thou wilt, to inquire for thy father."

But Telemachus answered, " Think ye that I will eat and drink with you, who so shamefully waste my substance ? Be sure of this, that I will seek vengeance against you, and if you deny me a ship, I will even go with another man's."

So he spake, and dragged his hand from the hand of Antinous.

And another of the suitors said, " Now will Telemachus go and seek help against us from Pylos or from Sparta, or may be he will put poison in our cups, and so destroy us."

And another said, " Perchance he also will perish, as his father has perished. Then should we have much labor, even dividing all his substance, but the house should we give to his mother and to her husband."

So they spake, mocking him. But he went to the chamber of his father, in which were ranged many casks of old wine, and store of gold and bronze, and clothing and olive oil; and of these things the prudent Euryclea, who was the keeper of the house, had care. To her he spake, " Mother, make ready for me twelve jars of wine, not of the best, but of that which is next to it, and twenty measures of barley-meal. At even will I take them, when my mother sleeps, for I go to Pylos and Sparta, if perchance I may hear news of my father."

But the old woman said, weeping, " What meanest thou, being an only son, thus to travel abroad ? Wilt thou perish, as thy father has perished ? For this evil brood of suitors will devise means to slay thee and divide thy goods. Thou hadst better sit peaceably at home."

Then Telemachus said, " 'Tis at the bidding of the gods I go. Only swear that thou wilt say nought to my mother till eleven or twelve days be past, unless perchance she should ask concerning me."

And the old woman sware it should be so. And

Telemachus went again among the suitors. But Athene, meanwhile, taking his shape, had gathered together a crew, and also had borrowed a ship for the voyage. And lest the suitors should hinder the thing, she caused a deep sleep to fall upon them, that they slept where they sat. Then she came in the shape of Mentor to the palace, and called Telemachus forth, saying, " The rowers are ready ; let us go."

So they two went together and came to the ship. And they sat on the stern together, and the rowers sat upon the benches. Then Athene caused a west wind to blow, and they raised the mast and set the sail, and all night long the ship ran before the wind.

CHAPTER V.

NESTOR AND MENELAUS.

N the morning they came to Pylos. And lo! there was a great sacrifice to Poseidon on the shore, nine companies of men, and five hundred men in each company, and to each nine oxen. And Nestor was there with his sons; and when he saw the two travellers he bade them welcome, and caused them to sit down and to eat and drink, not forgetting to pour out of the wine to King Poseidon. And this they did, praying that he would help them in the matter whereon they had come from their home.

And when the feast was ended, Nestor asked them of their name and business. So Telemachus told him that he was come seeking news of his father Ulysses. And Nestor praised him much that he spake so wisely, but of his father he could tell him nothing, only that he had stayed a while at Troy to do pleasure to King Agamemnon. Diomed, he said, had returned safe, and he himself to Pylos, and the Myrmidons, with the son of Achilles, and Philoctetes also, and Idomeneus. And Menelaus also had come back to his home, after wanderings many and great. But of Ulysses no one knew anything at all. Then they talked of many things, and specially of King Agamemnon, how he had been slain and also avenged.

And when evening was come, Athene indeed departed (and they knew her as she went for a goddess), but Telemachus remained, for he would go (for so Nestor advised) to Sparta, to inquire of King Menelaus, being the latest returned of all the kings.

On the morrow Nestor held a sacrifice to Athene, and on the morrow after that Nestor bade his men yoke horses to a chariot, and Pisistratus, who was the youngest of his sons, took the reins, and Telemachus rode with him. And all that day they journeyed; and when the land grew dark they came to the city of Pheræ, where Diocles, son of Orsilochus, was king, and there they rested; and the next day, travelling again, came to Lacedæmon, to the palace of King Menelaus.

And it chanced that Menelaus had made a great feast that day, for his daughter Hermione, the child of the fair Helen, was married to Neoptolemus, the son of Achilles, to whom she had been promised at Troy; and he had also taken a wife for his son Megapenthes. And the two stayed their chariot at the door, and one spied them, and said to Menelaus —

"Lo! here are two strangers who are like the children of kings. Shall we keep them here, or send them to another?"

But Menelaus was wroth, and said, "Shall we, who have eaten so often of the bread of hospitality, send these strangers to another? Nay, but unyoke their horses and bid them sit down to meat."

So the two lighted from the chariot, and after the bath they sat down to meat. And when they had ended the meal, Telemachus, looking round at the hall, said to his companion —

"See the gold and the amber, and the silver and the ivory. This is as the hall of Olympian Zeus."

This he spake with his face close to his comrade's ear, but Menelaus heard him and said —

"With the halls of the gods nothing mortal may compare. And among men also there may be the match of these things. Yet I have wandered far, and got many possessions in many lands. But woe is me! while I gather these things my brother was foully slain in his house. Would that I had but the third part of this wealth of mine, so that they who perished at Troy were alive again! And most of all I mourn for the great Ulysses, for whether he be alive or dead no man knows."

But Telemachus wept to hear mention of his father, holding up his purple cloak before his eyes. This Menelaus saw, and knew him who he was, and pondered whether he should wait till he should himself speak of his father, or should rather ask him of his errand. But while he pondered there came in the fair Helen, and three maidens with her, of whom one set a couch for her to sit, and one spread a carpet for her feet, and one bare a basket of purple wool, but she herself had a distaff of gold in her hand. And when she saw the strangers she said —

"Who are these, Menelaus? Never have I seen such likeness in man or woman as this one bears to Ulysses. Surely 'tis his son Telemachus, whom he left an infant at home when ye went to Troy for my sake!"

Then said Menelaus, "It must indeed be so, lady. For these are the hands and feet of Ulysses, and the look of his eyes and his hair. And but now, when I made mention of his name, he wept."

Then said Pisistratus, " King Menelaus, thou speakest truth. This is indeed the son of Ulysses, who is come to thee, if haply thou canst help him by word or deed."

And Menelaus answered, " Then is he the son of a man whom I loved right well. I thought to give him a city in this land, bringing him from Ithaca with all his goods. Then might we often have companied together, nor should aught have divided us but death itself. But these things the gods have ordered otherwise."

At these words they all wept — the fair Helen and Telemachus and Menelaus ; nor could Pisistratus refrain himself, for he thought of his dear brother Antilochus, whom Memnon, son of the Morning, slew at Troy. But the fair Helen put a mighty medicine in the wine whereof they drank — nepenthé men call it. So mighty is it that whosoever drinks of it, that day he weeps not, though father and mother die, and though men slay brother or son before his eyes. Polydamna, wife of King Thoas, had given it to her in Egypt, where indeed many medicines grow that are mighty both for good and ill.

And after this she said, " It were long to tell all the wise and valiant deeds of Ulysses. One thing, however, ye shall hear, and it is this : while the Greeks were before Troy he came into the city, having disguised himself as a beggar-man, yea, and he had laid many blows upon himself, so that he seemed to have been shamefully entreated. I only knew him who he was, and questioned him, but he answered craftily. And afterwards, when I had bathed him and anointed him

with oil, I swore that I would not tell the thing till he
had gone back to the camp. So he slew many Trojans
with the sword, and learnt many things. And while
other women in Troy lamented, I was glad, for my
heart was turned again to my home."

Then Menelaus said, "Thou speakest truly, lady.
Many men have I seen, and travelled over many lands,
but never have I seen one who might be matched with
Ulysses. Well do I remember how, when I and other
chiefs of the Greeks sat in the horse of wood, thou
didst come, Deïphobus following thee. Some god who
loved the sons of Troy put the thing into thy heart.
Thrice didst thou walk round our hiding-place and call
by name to each one of the chiefs, likening thy voice in
marvellous fashion to the voice of his wife. Then would
Diomed and I have either risen from our place or
answered thee straightway. But Ulysses hindered us,
so saving all the Greeks."

But Telemachus said, "Yet all these things have not
kept him, but that he has perished."

And now it was the hour of sleep. And the next
day Menelaus asked Telemachus of his business.

Then Telemachus said, "I have come, if haply thou
canst tell me aught of my father. For certain suitors
of my mother devour my goods, nor do I see any help.
Tell me therefore true, sparing me not at all, but saying
if thou knowest anything of thyself, or hast heard it
from another."

And Menelaus answered, "It angers me to hear of
these cowards who would lie in a brave man's bed. So
a hind lays its young in a lion's den, but when he comes
he slays both her and them. So shall it be with these

in the day when Ulysses shall come back.   But as to
what thou askest me, I will answer clearly and without
turning aside.   I was in Egypt, the gods hindering my
voyage because I had not offered due sacrifice.   Now
there is an island, Pharos men call it, a day's journey
from the shore for a swift ship with a fair wind blowing.   And in this I tarried against my will, the wind
being contrary, ay, and should have died, but that
Idothea, daughter of old Proteus, had pity on me.
For she found me sitting alone while my companions
fished with hooks, for hunger pressed them sore.   And
she said, 'Art thou altogether a fool, stranger, and
without spirit, that thou sittest thus helpless, and
seekest no deliverance, while the hearts of thy companions faint within them?'   And I said, 'I tarry here
against my will, for some god hinders my voyage, and
thou, if thou be of the immortals, canst tell me whom I
have offended.'   Then she made answer, 'There is an
old man of the sea who knows all things: his name is
Proteus, and he is my father.   And if thou couldst lie
in ambush and take him, he would tell thee how thou
mayest return to thy home, ay, and tell thee all, be it
good or evil, that has befallen thee there.'   And when
I would fain know how I might lie in ambush and take
him, seeing that it was hard for a mortal to master a
god, she said, 'At noonday he comes to sleep in his
caves, and his herd of seals comes with him.   Thou
must take three of thy companions whom thou judgest
to be bravest, and I will hide you.   Now the old man
counts the seals, and when he has told the number he
lies down in the midst.   Then take heart and rush
upon him, thou and thy companions.   Much will he

try to escape, making himself into all kinds of moving things, and into water and into fire. But when he shall ask of thy errand, being such in shape as thou sawest him lie down, then may ye loose him, and he will tell thee what thou wouldst know.' The next day came Idothea, bringing with her the skins of four seals which she had newly slain. Holes she made in the sand of the sea, and bade us sit in them, putting upon us the skins. It would have been a dreadful ambush for us, so evil was the smell of the seals, but the goddess gave us ambrosia, that we might hold under our nostrils, and the sweet savor prevailed against the smell. And at noon the old man came and counted the seals, and lay down to sleep. Then we rushed upon him; and the old man made himself now a lion, and now a snake and a leopard and a boar, and after this water, and then a tree in leaf. But still we held him. And at the last he asked me what I would. So I told him. And he said that I must first return over the sea to Egypt, and make due offerings to the gods. And when he had said this, I asked him of the chiefs, my friends, whether they had come back safe from Troy. And he said, 'Two only of the chiefs have perished; but those that fell in battle thou knowest thyself. Ajax, son of Oïleus, was shipwrecked, and yet might have lived, but he spake blasphemously, so that Poseidon smote the rock whereon he sat, and he drank the salt water and perished. And thy brother Agamemnon was slain at a feast by the false Ægisthus.' Then I said, 'There is yet another of whom I would hear.' And he answered, 'I saw the son of Laertes weeping in the island of Calypso, who keeps him against his will, nor can he

depart, having neither ship nor rowers.' And after
this the old man departed, and I, when I had done that
which was commanded, and had made a great tomb for
Agamemnon, my brother, came back hither. And now
I would that thou shouldest stay here awhile, and I will
give thee horses and a chariot, and a cup from which
thou mayest pour out wine to the gods."

Then Telemachus answered, "I thank thee for the
horses, but we may not keep such beasts in Ithaca, for
it is rocky, and fit only for pasturing of goats."

And Menelaus said, smiling, "Thou speakest well
and wisely; but at least I will give thee other things,
many and seemly, instead of the horses."

Now it had been made known meanwhile to the
suitors in Ithaca that Telemachus was gone upon this
journey seeking his father, and the thing displeased
them much. And after that they had held counsel
about the matter, it seemed best that they should lay
in ambush against him, which should slay him as he
came back to his home. So Antinous took twenty
men and departed, purposing to lie in wait in the strait
between Ithaca and Samos.

Nor was this counsel unknown to Penelope, for the
herald Medan had heard it, and he told her how that
Telemachus had gone seeking news of his father, and
how the suitors purposed to slay him as he returned.
And she called her women, old and young, and rebuked
them, saying, "Wicked that ye were, that knew that
he was about to go, and did not rouse me from
my bed. Surely I had kept him, eager though he
was, from his journey, or he had left me dead behind
him!"

Then said Euryclea, "Slay me, if thou wilt, but I will hide nothing from thee. I knew his purpose, and I furnished him with such things as he needed. But he made me swear that I would not tell thee till the eleventh or the twelfth day was come. But go with thy maidens and make thy prayer to Athene that she will save him from death; and indeed I think that this house is not altogether hated by the gods."

Then Penelope, having duly prepared herself, went with her maidens to the upper chamber, and prayed aloud to Athene that she would save her son. And the suitors heard her praying, and said, "Surely the queen prays, thinking of her marriage, nor knows that death is near to her son."

Then she lay down to sleep, and had neither eaten nor drunk. And while she slept Athene sent her a dream in the likeness of her sister Iphthime, who was the wife of Eumelus, son of Alcestis. And the vision stood over her head and spake, "Sleepest thou, Penelope? The gods would not have thee grieve, for thy son shall surely return."

And Penelope said, "How camest thou here, my sister? For thy dwelling is far away. And how can I cease to weep when my husband is lost? And now my son is gone, and I am sore afraid for him, lest his enemies slay him."

But the vision answered, "Fear not at all; for there is a mighty helper with him, even Athene, who has bid me tell thee these things."

Then Penelope said, "If thou art a goddess, tell me this. Is my husband yet alive?"

But the vision answered, "That I cannot say, whether

he be alive or dead." And so saying, it vanished into air.

And Penelope woke from her sleep, and her heart was comforted.

CHAPTER VI.

ULYSSES ON HIS RAFT.

WHILE Telemachus was yet sojourning in Sparta, Zeus sent Hermes to Calypso, to bid her that she should let Ulysses go. So Hermes donned his golden sandals, and took his wand in his hand, and came to the island of Ogygia, and to the cave where Calypso dwelt. A fair place it was. In the cave was burning a fire of sweet-smelling wood, and Calypso sat at her loom and sang with a lovely voice. And round about the cave was a grove of alders and poplars and cypresses, wherein many birds, falcons and owls and sea-crows, were wont to roost; and all about the mouth of the cave was a vine with purple clusters of grapes; and there were four fountains which streamed four ways through meadows of parsley and violet. But Ulysses was not there, for he sat, as was his wont, on the sea-shore, weeping and groaning because he might not see wife and home and country.

And Calypso spied Hermes, and bade him come within, and gave him meat and drink, ambrosia and nectar, which are the food of the gods. And when he had ended his meal, she asked him of his errand. So he told her that he was come, at the bidding of Zeus, in the matter of Ulysses, for that it was the pleasure of the gods that he should return to his native country, and that she should not hinder him any more. It vexed Calypso much to hear this, for she would fain have kept Ulysses with her always, and she said —

" Ye gods are always jealous when a goddess loves a mortal man. And as for Ulysses, did not I save him when Zeus had smitten his ship with a thunderbolt, and all his comrades had perished ? And now let him go — if it pleases Zeus. Only I cannot send him, for I have neither ship nor rowers. Yet will I willingly teach him how he may safely return."

And Hermes said, " Do this thing speedily, lest Zeus be wroth with thee."

So he departed. And Calypso went seeking Ulysses, and found him on the shore of the sea, looking out over the waters, as was his wont, and weeping, for he was weary of his life, so much did he desire to see Ithaca again. She stood by him and said —

" Weary not for thy native country, nor waste thyself with tears. If thou wilt go, I will speed thee on thy way. Take therefore thine axe and cut thee beams, and join them together, and make a deck upon them, and I will give thee bread and water and wine, and clothe thee also, so that thou mayest return safe to thy native country, for the gods will have it so."

" Nay," said Ulysses, " what is this that thou sayest ? Shall I pass in a raft over the dreadful sea, over which even ships go not without harm ? I will not go against thy will; but thou must swear the great oath of the gods that thou plannest no evil against me."

Then Calypso smiled and said, "These are strange words. By the Styx I swear that I plan no harm against thee, but only such good as I would ask myself, did I need it; for indeed my heart is not of iron, but rather full of compassion."

Then they two went to the cave and sat down to meat, and she set before him food such as mortal men eat, but she herself ate ambrosia and drank nectar, as the gods are wont. And afterwards she said —

"Why art thou so eager for thy home? Surely if thou knewest all the trouble that awaits thee, thou wouldst not go, but wouldst rather dwell with me. And though thou desirest all the day long to see thy wife, surely I am not less fair than she."

"Be not angry," Ulysses made reply. "The wise Penelope cannot indeed be compared to thee, for she is a mortal woman and thou art a goddess. Yet is my home dear to me, and I would fain see it again."

The next day Calypso gave him an axe with a handle of olive wood, and an adze, and took him to the end of the island, where there were great trees, long ago sapless and dry, alder and poplar and pine. Of these he felled twenty, and lopped them, and worked them by the line. Then the goddess brought him a gimlet, and he made holes in the logs and joined them with pegs. And he made decks and side-planking also; also a mast and a yard, and a rudder wherewith to turn the raft. And he fenced it about with a bulwark of osier against the waves. The sails, indeed, Calypso wove, and Ulysses fitted them with braces and halyards and sheets. And afterwards, with ropes, he moored the raft to the shore.

On the fourth day all was finished, and on the fifth

day he departed. And Calypso gave him goodly garments, and a skin of wine, and a skin of water, and
rich provender in a wallet of leather. She sent also a
fair wind blowing behind, and Ulysses set his sails and
proceeded joyfully on his way; nor did he sleep, but
watched the sun and the stars, still steering, as indeed
Calypso had bidden, to the left. So he sailed for seven-
teen days, and on the eighteenth he saw the hills of
Phæacia and the land, which had the shape of a shield.

But Poseidon spied him as he sailed, and was wroth
to see him so near to the end of his troubles. Wherefore he sent all the winds of heaven down upon him.
Sore troubled was Ulysses, and said to himself, " It was
truth that Calypso spake when she said how that I
should suffer many troubles returning to my home.
Would that I had died that day when many a spear
was cast by the men of Troy over the dead Achilles.
Then would the Greeks have buried me ; but now shall
I perish miserably."

And as he spake a great wave struck the raft and
tossed him far away, so that he dropped the rudder
from his hand. Nor for a long time could he rise, so
deep was he sunk, and so heavy was the goodly clothing
which Calypso had given him. Yet at the last he rose,
and spat the salt water out of his mouth, and, so brave
was he, sprang at the raft and caught it and sat
thereon, and was borne hither and thither by the
waves. But Ino saw him and pitied him — a woman
she had been, and was now a goddess of the sea — and
came and sat upon the waves, saying —

" Luckless mortal, why doth Poseidon hate thee so ?
He shall not slay thee, though he fain would do it.

Put off these garments and swim to the land of Phæacia, putting this veil under thy breast. And when thou
art come to the land, loose it from thee, and cast it
into the sea; but when thou castest it, look away."

But Ulysses doubted what this might be, and thought
that he would yet stay on the raft while the timbers
held together, for that the land was far away. But as
he thought, yet another great wave struck it, and scattered the timbers. And he sat upon one of them, as a
man sits upon a horse; and then he stripped off the
garments which Calypso had given him, and so, leaping
into the sea, made to swim to the land.

And Poseidon saw him, and said, "Get to the shore
if thou canst, but even so thou art not come to the end
of thy troubles."

So for two days and two nights he swam, Athene
helping him, for otherwise he had perished. But on
the third day there was a calm, and he saw the land
from the top of a great wave, for the waves were yet
high, close at hand. Dear as a father to his son, rising
up from grievous sickness, so dear was the land to
Ulysses. But when he came near he heard the waves
breaking along the shore, for there was no harbor
there, but only cliffs and rugged rocks. And while he
doubted what he should do, a great wave bore him to
the shore. Then would he have perished, all his bones
being broken; but Athene put it in his heart to lay
hold of a great rock till the wave had spent itself.
And even then had he died, for the ebb caught him and
bore him far out to sea; but he bethought him that he
would swim along, if haply he might see some landing-
place. And at last he came to the mouth of a river,

where there were no rocks. Then at last he won his
way to the land. His knees were bent under him and
his hands dropped at his side, and the salt water ran
out of his mouth and nostrils. Breathless was he and
speechless; but when he came to himself, he loosed the
veil from under his breast and cast it into the sea.

Then he lay down on the rushes by the bank of the
river and kissed the earth, thinking within himself,
"What now shall I do? for if I sleep here by the river,
I fear that the dew and the frost may slay me; for indeed in the morning-time the wind from the river blows
cold. And if I go up to the wood, to lay me down to
sleep in the thicket, I fear that some evil beast may
devour me."

But it seemed better to go to the wood. So he went.
Now this was close to the river, and he found two
bushes, of wild olive one, and of fruitful olive the other.
So thickly grown together were they, that the winds
blew not through them, nor did the sun pierce them,
nor yet the rain. Thereunder crept Ulysses, and found
great store of leaves, shelter enough for two or three,
even in a great storm. Then, even as a man who
dwells apart from others cherishes his fire, hiding it
under the ashes, so Ulysses cherished his life under the
leaves. And Athene sent down upon his eyelids deep
sleep, that might ease him of his toil.

CHAPTER VII.

NAUSICAA AND ALCINOUS.

NOW the king of Phæacia was Alcinous, and he had five sons and one daughter, Nausicaa. To her, where she slept with her two maidens by her, Athene went, taking the shape of her friend, the daughter of Dymas, and said—

"Why hath thy mother so idle a daughter, Nausicaa? Lo! thy garments lie unwashed, and thy wedding must be near, seeing that many nobles in the land are suitors to thee. Ask then thy father that he give thee the wagon with the mules, for the laundries are far from the city, and I will go with thee."

And when the morning was come, Nausicaa awoke, marvelling at the dream, and went seeking her parents. Her mother she found busy with her maidens at the loom, and her father she met as he was going to the council with the chiefs of the land. Then she said, "Give me, father, the wagon with the mules, that I may take the garments to the river to wash them. Thou shouldest always have clean robes when thou goest to the council; and there are my five brothers also, who love to have newly washed garments at the dance."

But of her own marriage she said nothing. And her father, knowing her thoughts, said, "It is well. The men shall harness the wagon for thee."

So they put the clothing into the wagon. And her mother put also food and wine, and olive oil also, wherewith she and her maidens might anoint themselves after the bath. So they climbed into the wagon and went to the river. And then they washed the clothing, and spread it out to dry on the rocks by the sea. And after that they had bathed and anointed themselves, they sat down to eat and drink by the river side; and after the meal they played at ball, singing as they played, and Nausicaa, fair as Artemis when she hunts on Taygetus or Erymanthus wild goats and stags, led the song. But when they had nearly ended their play, the princess, throwing the ball to one of her maidens, cast it so wide that it fell into the river. Whereupon they all cried aloud, and Ulysses awoke. And he said to himself, "What is this land to which I have come? Are they that dwell therein fierce or kind to strangers? Just now I seemed to hear the voice of nymphs, or am I near the dwelling of men?"

Then he twisted leaves about his loins, and rose up and went towards the maidens, who indeed were frighted to see him (for he was wild of aspect), and fled hither and thither. But Nausicaa stood and fled not. Then Ulysses thought within himself, should he go near and clasp her knees, or, lest haply this should anger her, should he stand and speak? And this he did, saying —

"I am thy suppliant, O queen. Whether thou art a goddess, I know not. But if thou art a mortal, happy thy father and mother, and happy thy brothers, and happiest of all he who shall win thee in marriage. Never have I seen man or woman so fair. Thou art like a young palm-tree that but lately I saw in Delos, springing by the temple of the god. But as for me, I have been cast on this shore, having come from the island Ogygia. Pity me, then, and lead me to the city, and give me something, a wrapper of this linen, maybe, to put about me. So may the gods give thee all blessings!"

And Nausicaa made answer, "Thou seemest, stranger, to be neither evil nor foolish; and as for thy plight, the gods give good fortune or bad, as they will. Thou shalt not lack clothing or food, or anything that a suppliant should have. And I will take thee to the city. Know also that this land is Phæacia, and that I am daughter to Alcinous, who is king thereof."

Then she called to her maidens, "What mean ye, to flee when ye see a man? No enemy comes hither to harm us, for we are dear to the gods, and also we live in an island of the sea, so that men may not approach to work us wrong; but if one cometh here overborne by trouble, it is well to succor him. Give this man, therefore, food and drink, and wash him in the river, where there is shelter from the wind."

So they brought him down to the river, and gave him a tunic and a cloak to clothe himself withal, and also olive-oil in a flask of gold. Then, at his bidding, they departed a little space, and he washed the salt from his skin and out of his hair, and anointed himself, and put on the clothing. And Athene made him taller and fairer to see, and caused the hair to be thick

on his head, in color as a hyacinth.   Then he sat down
on the sea-shore, right beautiful to behold, and the
maiden said —

"Not without some bidding of the gods comes this
man to our land.   Before, indeed, I deemed him un-
comely, but now he seems like to the gods.   I should
be well content to have such a man for a husband, and
maybe he might will to abide in this land.   But give
him, ye maidens, food and drink."

So they gave him, and he ate ravenously, having
fasted long.   Then Nausicaa bade yoke the mules, and
said to Ulysses —

"Follow thou with the maidens, and I will lead the
way in the wagon.   For I would not that the people
should speak lightly of me.   And I doubt not that were
thou with me some one of the baser sort would say,
'Who is this stranger, tall and fair, that cometh with
Nausicaa?   Will he be her husband?   Perchance it is
some god who has come down at her prayer, or a man
from far away;   for of us men of Phæacia she thinks
scorn.'   It would be shame that such words should be
spoken.   And indeed it is ill-done of a maiden who,
father and mother unknowing, companies with men.
Do thou, then, follow behind, and when we are come to
the city, tarry in a poplar grove that thou shalt see
('tis the grove of Athene) till I shall have come to
my father's house.   Then follow; and for the house,
that any one, even a child, can show thee, for the other
Phæacians dwell not in such.   And when thou art
come within the doors, pass quickly through the hall
to where my mother sits, close to the hearth in her
seat, and my father's hard by, where he sits with the

wine cup in his hand, as a god. Pass him by and lay hold of her knees, and pray her that she give thee safe return to thy country."

It was evening when they came to the city. And Nausicaa drove the wagon to the palace. Then her brothers came out to her, and loosed the mules and carried in the clothing. Then she went to her chamber, where Eurymedusa, who was her nurse, lighted a fire and prepared a meal. Meanwhile Ulysses came from the grove, and lest any one should see him, Athene spread a mist about him, and when he had now reached the city, she took the shape of a young maiden carrying a pitcher, and met him.

Then Ulysses asked her, "My child, canst thou tell me where dwells Alcinous? for I am a stranger in this place."

And she answered, "I will show thee, for indeed he dwells nigh to my own father. But be thou silent, for we Phæacians love not strangers over much." Then she led him to the palace. A wondrous place it was, with walls of brass and doors of gold, hanging on posts of silver; and on either side of the door were dogs of gold and silver, the work of Hephæstus, and against the wall, all along from the threshold to the inner chamber, were set seats, on which sat the chiefs of the Phæacians, feasting; and youths wrought in gold stood holding torches in their hands, to give light in the darkness. Fifty women were in the house grinding corn and weaving robes, for the women of the land are no less skilled to weave than are the men to sail the sea. And round about the house were gardens beautiful exceedingly, with orchards of fig, and apple, and pear, and pomegranate, and olive. Drought hurts them not, nor frost, and harvest comes after harvest without ceasing. Also there was a vineyard; and some of the grapes were parching in the sun, and some were being gathered, and some again were but just turning red. And there were beds of all manner of flowers; and in the midst of all were two fountains which never failed.

These things Ulysses regarded for a space, and then passed into the hall. And there the chiefs of Phæacia were drinking their last cup to Hermes. Quickly he passed through them, and put his hands on the knees of Arete and said—and as he spake the mist cleared from about him, and all that were in the hall beheld him—

"I am a suppliant to thee, and to thy husband, and to thy guests. The gods bless thee and them, and grant you to live in peace, and that your children should come peacefully after you. Only, do you send me home to my native country."

And he sat down in the ashes of the hearth. Then for a space all were silent, but at the last spake Echeneus, who was the oldest man in the land—

"King Alcinous, this ill becomes you that this man should sit in the ashes of the hearth. Raise him and bid him sit upon a seat, and let us pour out to Father Zeus, who is the friend of suppliants, and let the keeper of the house give him meat and drink."

And Alcinous did so, bidding his eldest born, Laodamas, rise from his seat. And an attendant poured water on his hands, and the keeper of the house gave him meat and drink. Then, when all had poured out to Father Zeus, King Alcinous said that they would

take counsel on the morrow about sending this stranger
to his home. And they answered that it should be so,
and each went to his home. Only Ulysses was left in
the hall, and Alcinous and Arete with him. And
Arete saw his cloak and tunic, that she and her
maidens had made them, and said —

"Whence art thou, stranger? and who gave thee
these garments?"

So Ulysses told her how he had come from the
island of Calypso, and what he had suffered, and how
Nausicaa had found him on the shore, and had guided
him to the city.

But Alcinous blamed the maiden that she had not
herself brought him to the house. "For thou wast her
suppliant," he said.

"Nay," said Ulysses; "she would have brought me,
but I would not, fearing thy wrath." For he would
not have the maiden blamed.

Then said Alcinous, "I am not one to be angered for
such cause. Gladly would I have such a one as thou
art to be my son-in-law, and I would give him house
and wealth. But no one would I stay against his will.
And as for sending thee to thy home, that is easy; for
thou shalt sleep, and they shall take thee meanwhile."

And after this they slept. And the next day the
king called the chiefs to an assembly, and told them of
his purpose, that he would send this stranger to his
home, for that it was their wont to show such kindness
to such as needed it. And he bade fifty and two of
the younger men make ready a ship, and that the
elders should come to his house, and bring Demodocus,
the minstrel, with them, for that he was minded to

make a great feast for this stranger before he departed.
So the youths made ready the ship. And afterwards
there were gathered together a great multitude, so that
the palace was filled from the one end to the other.
And Alcinous slew for them twelve sheep and eight
swine and two oxen. And when they had feasted to
the full, the minstrel sang to them of how Achilles
and Ulysses had striven together with fierce words at a
feast, and how King Agamemnon was glad, seeing that
so the prophecy of Apollo was fulfilled, saying that
when valor and counsel should fall out, the end of
Troy should come. But when Ulysses heard the song,
he wept, holding his mantle before his face.

This Alcinous perceived, and said to the chiefs,
"Now that we have feasted and delighted ourselves
with song, let us go forth, that this stranger may see
that we are skilful in boxing and wrestling and
running."

So they went forth, a herald leading Demodocus by
the hand, for the minstrel was blind. Then stood up
many Phæacian youths, and the fairest and strongest of
them all was Laodamas, eldest son to the king, and
after him Euryalus. And next they ran a race, and
Clytoneus was the swiftest. And among the wrestlers
Euryalus was the best, and of the boxers, Laodamas.
And in throwing the quoit Elatrius excelled, and in
leaping at the bar, Amphialus.

Then Laodamas, Euryalus urging him, said to Ulysses,
"Father, wilt thou not try thy skill in some game, and
put away the trouble from thy heart?"

But Ulysses answered, "Why askest thou this? I
think of my troubles rather than of sport, and sit

among you, caring only that I may see again my home."

Then said Euryalus, " And in very truth, stranger, thou hast not the look of a wrestler or boxer. Rather would one judge thee to be some trader, who sails over the sea for gain."

" Nay," answered Ulysses, " this is ill said. So true is it that the gods give not all gifts to all men, beauty to one and sweet speech to another. Fair of form art thou, no god could better thee ; but thou speakest idle words. I am not unskilled in these things, but stood among the first in the old days ; but since have I suffered much in battle and shipwreck. Yet will I make trial of my strength, for thy words have angered me."

Whereupon he took a quoit, heavier far than such as the Phæacians were wont to throw, and sent it with a whirl. It hurtled through the air, so that the brave Phæacians crouched to the ground in fear, and fell far beyond all the rest.

Then said Ulysses, " Come now, I will contend in wrestling or boxing, or even in the race, with any man in Phæacia, save Laodamas only, for he is my friend. I can shoot with the bow, and only Philoctetes could surpass me ; and I can cast a spear as far as other men can shoot an arrow. But as for the race, it may be that some one might outrun me, for I have suffered much on the sea."

But they all were silent, till the king stood up and said, " Thou hast spoken well. But we men of Phæacia are not mighty to wrestle or to box ; only we are swift of foot, and skilful to sail upon the sea. And we love

feasts, and dances, and the harp, and gay clothing, and
the bath.   In these things no man may surpass us."

Then the king bade Demodocus the minstrel sing
again.   And when he had done so, the king's two sons,
Alius and Laodamas, danced together; and afterwards
they played with the ball, throwing it into the air,
cloud high, and catching it right skilfully.

And afterwards the king said, " Let us each give
this stranger a mantle and a tunic and a talent of gold,
and let Euryalus make his peace with words and with
a gift."

And they all (now there were twelve princes, and
Alcinous the thirteenth) said that it should be so; also
Euryalus gave Ulysses a sword with a hilt of silver and
a scabbard of ivory.   And after this Ulysses went to
the bath, and then they all sat down to the feast.   But
as he went to the hall, Nausicaa, fair as a goddess, met
him and said —

" Hail, stranger ; thou wilt remember me in thy
native country, for thou owest me thanks for thy life."

And he answered, " Every day in my native country
will I remember thee, for indeed, fair maiden, thou
didst save my life."

And when they were set down to the feast, Ulysses
sent a portion of the chine which the king had caused
to be set before him to the minstrel Demodocus, with a
message that he should sing to them of the horse of
wood which Epeius made, Athene helping him, and how
Ulysses brought it into Troy, full of men of war who
should destroy the city.

Then the minstrel sang how that some of the Greeks
sailed away, having set fire to their tents, and some hid

themselves in the horse with Ulysses, and how the men
of Troy sat around, taking counsel what they should
do with it, and some judged that they should rip it
open, and some that they should throw it from the
hill-top, and others again that they should leave it to
be a peace-offering to the gods; and how the Greeks
issued forth from their lurking-place and spoiled the
city, and how Ulysses and Menelaus went to the house
of Deïphobus.

So he sang, and Ulysses wept to hear the tale. And
when Alcinous perceived that he wept, he bade Demodocus cease from his song, for that some that were there
liked it not. And to Ulysses he said that he should
tell them who was his father and his mother, and from
what land he came, and what was his name. All these
things Ulysses told them, and all that he had done and
suffered, down to the time when the Princess Nausicaa
found him on the river shore. And when he had
ended, King Alcinous bade that the princes should give
Ulysses yet other gifts; and after that they went each
man to his house to sleep.

The next day King Alcinous put all the gifts into
the ship. And when the evening was come Ulysses
bade farewell to the king and to the queen, and
departed.

CHAPTER VIII.

ULYSSES AND THE SWINEHERD.

NOW Ulysses slept while the ship was sailing to Ithaca. And when it was come to the shore he yet slept. Wherefore the men lifted him out, and put him on the shore with all his goods that the princes of the Phæacians had given him, and so left him. After a while he awoke, and knew not the land, for there was a great mist about him, Athene having contrived that it should be so, for good ends, as will be seen. Very wroth was he with the men of Phæacia, thinking that they had cheated him; nor did it comfort him when he counted his goods to find that of these he had lost nothing.

But as he walked by the sea, lamenting his fate, Athene met him, having the shape of a young shepherd, fair to look upon, such as are the sons of kings; and Ulysses, when he saw him, was glad, and asked him how men called the country wherein he was.

And the false shepherd said, " Thou art foolish, or, may be, hast come from very far, not to know this country. Many men know it, both in the east and in the west. Rocky it is, not fit for horses, nor is it very broad; but it is fertile land, and full of wine; nor does it want for rain, and a good pasture it is for oxen and goats; and men call it Ithaca. Even in Troy, which is very far, they say, from this land of Greece, men have heard of Ithaca."

This Ulysses was right glad to hear. Yet he was not minded to say who he was, but rather to feign a tale.

So he said, " Yes, of a truth, I heard of this Ithaca in Crete, from which I am newly come with all this wealth, leaving also as much behind for my children. For I slew Orsilochus, son of Idomeneus the king, because he would have taken from me my spoil. Wherefore I slew him, lying in wait for him by the way. Then made I covenant with certain Phœnicians that they should take me to Pylos or to Elis; which thing indeed they were minded to do, only the wind drave them hither, and while I slept they put me upon the shore, and my possessions with me, and departed to Sidon."

This pleased Athene much, and she changed her shape, becoming like a woman, tall and fair, and said to Ulysses —

" Right cunning would he be who could cheat thee. Even now in thy native country ceasest thou not from cunning words and deceits! But let these things be; for thou, I trow, art the wisest of mortal men, and I excel among the gods in counsel. For I am Athene, daughter of Zeus, who am ever wont to stand by thee and help thee. And now we will hide these possessions of thine; and thou must be silent, nor tell to any one who thou art, and endure many things, so that thou mayest come to thine own again."

But still Ulysses doubted, and would have the goddess tell him whether of a truth he had come back to his native land. And she, commending his prudence, scattered the mist that was about him.

Then Ulysses knew the land, and kissed the ground, and prayed to the Nymphs that they would be favorable to him. And after this, Athene guiding him, he hid away his possessions in a cave, and put a great stone on the mouth. Then the two took counsel together.

And Athene said, "Think, man of many devices, how thou wilt lay hands on these men, suitors of thy wife, who for three years have sat in thy house devouring thy substance. And she hath answered them craftily, making many promises, but still waiting for thy coming."

Then Ulysses said, "Truly I had perished, even as Agamemnon perished, but for thee. But do thou help me, as of old in Troy, for with thee at my side I would fight with three hundred men."

Then said Athene, "Lo! I will cause that no man shall know thee, for I will wither the fair flesh on thy limbs, and take the bright hair from thy head, and make thine eyes dull. And the suitors shall take no account of thee, neither shall thy wife nor thy son know thee. But go to the swineherd Eumæus, where he dwells by the fountain of Arethusa, for he is faithful to thee and to thy house. And I will hasten to Sparta, to the house of Menelaus, to fetch Telemachus, for he went thither, seeking news of thee."

Then Athene changed him into the shape of a beggar-man. She caused his skin to wither, and his hair to fall off, and his eyes to grow dim, and put on

him filthy rags, with a great stag's hide about his
shoulders, and in his hand a staff, and a wallet on his
shoulder, fastened by a rope.

Then she departed, and Ulysses went to the house
of Eumæus, the swineherd. A great courtyard there
was, and twelve sties for the sows, and four watchdogs,
big as wild beasts, for such did the swineherd breed.
He himself was shaping sandals, and of his men three
were with the swine in the fields, and one was driving
a fat beast to the city, to be meat for the suitors. But
when Ulysses came near, the dogs ran upon him, and
he dropped his staff and sat down, and yet would have
suffered harm, even on his own threshold; but the
swineherd ran forth and drave away the dogs, and
brought the old man in, and gave him a seat of brush-
wood, with a great goat-skin over it.

And Ulysses said, "Zeus and the other gods requite
thee for this kindness."

Then the two talked of matters in Ithaca, and
Eumæus told how the suitors of the queen were devouring the substance of Ulysses. Then the false beggar
asked him of the king, saying that perchance, having
travelled far, he might know such an one.

But Eumæus said, "Nay, old man, thus do all way-
farers talk, yet we hear no truth from them. Not a
vagabond fellow comes to this island but our queen
must see him, and ask him many things, weeping the
while. And thou, I doubt not, for a cloak or a tunic,
would tell a wondrous tale. But Ulysses, I know, is
dead, and either the fowls of the air devour him or the
fishes of the sea."

And when the false beggar would have comforted

him, saying he knew of a truth that Ulysses would yet
return, he hearkened not. Moreover, he prophesied
evil for Telemachus also, who had gone to seek news
of his father, but would surely be slain by the suitors,
who were even now lying in wait for him as he should
return. And after this he asked the stranger who he
was and whence he had come. Then Ulysses answered
him craftily —

"I am a Cretan, the son of one Castor, by a slave
woman. Now my father, while he lived, did by me as
by his other sons. But when he died they divided his
goods, and gave me but a small portion, and took my
dwelling from me. Yet I won a rich wife for myself,
for I was brave and of good repute. No man would
sooner go to battle or to ambush than I, and I loved
ships and spears and arrows, which some men hate, I
trow. Nine times did I lead my followers in ships
against strangers, and the tenth time I went with King
Idomeneus to Troy. And when the city of Priam had
perished, I went back to my native country, and there
for the space of one month I tarried with my wife, and
afterwards I sailed with nine ships to Egypt. On the
fifth day — for the gods gave us a prosperous voyage
— we came to the river of Egypt. There did my comrades work much wrong to the people of the land,
spoiling their fields, and leading into captivity their
wives and children; nor would they hearken to me
when I would have stayed them. Then the Egyptians
gathered an army, and came upon them, and slew some
and took others. And I, throwing down helmet and
spear and shield, hasted to the king of the land where
he sat in his chariot, and prayed that he would have

mercy on me, which thing he did. And with him I dwelt for seven years, gathering much wealth. But in the eighth year there came a trader of Phœnicia, who beguiled me, that I went with him to his country. And there I tarried for a year; and afterwards he carried me in his ship to Libya, meaning to sell me as a slave, but Zeus brake the ship, so that I was only left alive. Nine days did I float, keeping hold of the mast, and on the tenth a wave cast me on the land of Thesprotia, where King Pheidon kindly entreated me, giving me food and raiment. There did I hear tell of Ulysses; yea, and saw the riches which he had gathered together, which King Pheidon was keeping till he himself should come back from Dodona, from the oracle of Zeus. Thence I sailed in a ship for Dulichium, purposing to go to King Acastus, but the sailors were minded to sell me for a slave. Therefore they left me bound in a ship, but themselves took their supper on the shore. But in the meanwhile I brake my bonds, the gods helping me, and leaping into the sea, swam to the land and hid myself in a wood that was near."

All this tale did Ulysses tell; but Eumæus doubted whether these things were so, thinking rather that the beggar-man said these things to please him. After this they talked much, and when the swineherd's men were returned they all feasted together. And the night being cold, and there being much rain, Ulysses was minded to see whether one would lend him a cloak; wherefore he told this tale —

"Once upon a time there was laid an ambush near to the city of Troy. And Menelaus and Ulysses and I were the leaders of it. In the reeds we sat, and the night

was cold, and the snow lay upon our shields.   Now all
the others had cloaks, but I had left mine behind at the
ships.   So when the night was three parts spent I spake
to Ulysses, ' Here am I without a cloak ; soon, methinks,
shall I perish with the cold.'   Soon did he bethink him
of a remedy, for he was ever ready with counsel.   Therefore to me he said, ' Hush, lest some one hear thee,'
and to the others, ' I have been warned in a dream.
We were very far from the ships, and in peril.   Wherefore let some one run to the ships to King Agamemnon, that he send more men to help.'   Then Thoas, son
of Andræmon, rose up and ran, casting off his cloak,
and this I took, and slept warmly therein.   Were I this
night such as then I was, I should not lack such kindness even now."

Then said Eumæus, " This is well spoken, old man.
Thou shalt have a cloak to cover thee.   But in the
morning thou must put on thy own rags again.   Yet
perchance, when the son of Ulysses shall come, he will
give thee new garments."

After this they slept, but Eumæus tarried without,
keeping watch over the swine.

CHAPTER IX.

THE RETURN OF TELEMACHUS.

NOW all this time Telemachus tarried in Sparta with King Menelaus. To him went Athene, and warned him that he should return to his home, for that the suitors were devouring his substance, and that Penelope, his mother, was much pressed by her father and her brothers to marry Eurymachus, who indeed of all the suitors promised the largest. Also she warned him that the suitors had laid an ambush to slay him in the strait between Samos and Ithaca, and that he should keep clear of the island; and as soon as ever he came near to Ithaca he should land and go to the swineherd Eumæus, and send him to his mother, with tidings of his being safely arrived.

Then Telemachus woke Pisistratus, and would have departed forthwith, only Pisistratus urged him that he should stay till the morning. So when the morning was come he would take leave of Menelaus and Helen.

And first Menelaus said that he would go with him through all the land of Greece, whithersoever he would; but seeing that his heart was steadfastly set to return to his home, he gave him gifts that he might take with him, and Helen also gave him a gift, the fairest robe that she had.

Then they departed; and that night they came to Pheræ, and lodged with Diocles, the son of Orsilochus, and the next night to Pylos, where old Nestor dwelt. And the next day, while they were doing sacrifice to Athene, behold! there came one Theoclymenus, a seer, who dwelt in Argos, and there had slain a man, wherefore he had fled; and now, seeing Telemachus, and hearing who he was, he prayed that he would receive him into his ship. Which thing Telemachus was willing to do. So the two departed together. And when they were come to Ithaca, Telemachus bade the men take the ship to the city, saying that he was minded to see his farms, but that in the evening he would come to the city, and would feast them with flesh and wine. And Theoclymenus he bade join himself to Eurymachus, who, he said, was the best of those that were suitors to his mother. And as he spake there appeared a hawk on his right hand, and it struck a dove, even between him and the ship.

Then the seer called him aside and said, "This is a sign from the gods. There is no house in Ithaca more to be feared than thine."

Then Telemachus was glad, and commended the seer to Piræus, who was the most faithful of his followers. After this the ship sailed to the city, but Telemachus went to the dwelling of the swineherd Eumæus. And Ulysses heard the steps of a man, and, as the dogs barked not, said to Eumæus, "Lo! there comes some comrade or friend, for the dogs bark not."

And as he spake, Telemachus stood in the doorway,
and the swineherd let fall from his hand the bowl in
which he was mixing wine, and ran to him and kissed
his head and his eyes and his hands. As a father
kisses his only son coming back to him from a far
country after ten years, so did the swineherd kiss
Telemachus. And when Telemachus came in, the false
beggar, though indeed he was his father, rose, and
would have given place to him; but Telemachus suffered him not. And when they had eaten and drunk,
Telemachus asked of the swineherd who this stranger
might be.

Then the swineherd told him as he had heard, and
afterwards said, "I hand him to thee; he is thy suppliant: do as thou wilt."

But Telemachus answered, "Nay, Eumæus. For am
I master in my house? Do not the suitors devour it?
And does not my mother doubt whether she will abide
with me, remembering the great Ulysses, who was her
husband, or will follow some one of those who are suitors to her? I will give this stranger, indeed, food and
clothing and a sword, and will send him whithersoever
he will, but I would not that he should go among the
suitors, so haughty are they and violent."

Then said Ulysses, "But why dost thou bear with
these men? Do the people hate thee, that thou
canst not avenge thyself on them? and hast thou not
kinsmen to help thee? As for me, I would rather
die than see such shameful things done in house of
mine."

And Telemachus answered, "My people hate me not;
but as for kinsmen, I have none, for Acrisius had but

one son, Laertes, and he again but one, Ulysses, and
Ulysses had none other but me. Therefore do these
men spoil my substance without let, and, it may be, will
take my life also. These things, however, the gods
will order. But do thou, Eumæus, go to Penelope,
and tell her that I am returned, but let no man know
thereof, for there are that counsel evil against me; but
I will stay here meanwhile."

So Eumæus departed. But when he had gone
Athene came, like a woman tall and fair; but Telemachus saw her not, for it is not given all to see the
immortal gods; but Ulysses saw her, and the dogs saw
her, and whimpered for fear. She signed to Ulysses,
and he went forth, and she said —

"Hide not the matter from thy son, but plan with
him how ye may slay the suitors, and lo! I am with
you."

Then she made his garments white and fair, and his
body lusty and strong, and his face swarthy, and his
cheeks full, and his beard black. And when he was
returned to the house, Telemachus marvelled to see
him, and said —

"Thou art not what thou wast. Surely thou art
some god from heaven."

But Ulysses made reply, "No god am I, only thy
father, whom thou hast so desired to see."

And when Telemachus yet doubted, Ulysses told him
how that Athene had so changed him. Then Telemachus threw his arms about him, weeping, and both wept
together for a while. And afterwards Telemachus
asked him of his coming back. And Ulysses, when
he had told him of this, asked him how many were the

suitors, and whether they two could fight with them
alone.

Then said Telemachus, " Thou art, I know, a great
warrior, my father, and a wise, but this thing we cannot do; for these men are not ten, no, nor twice ten,
but from Dulichium come fifty and two, and from Samos four and twenty, and from Zacynthus twenty, and
from Ithaca twelve; and they have Medon the herald,
and a minstrel also and attendants."

Then said Ulysses, " Go thou home in the morning
and mingle with the suitors, and I will come as an old
beggar; and if they entreat me shamefully, endure to
see it, yea, if they drag me to the door. Only, if thou
wilt, speak to them prudent words; but they will not
heed thee, for indeed their doom is near. Heed this
also: when I give thee the token, take all the arms
from the dwelling and hide them in thy chamber. And
when they shall ask thee why thou doest thus, say that
thou takest them out of the smoke, for that they are
not such as Ulysses left behind him when he went to
Troy, but that the smoke had soiled them. Say, also,
that haply they might stir up strife sitting at their
cups, and that it is not well that arms should be at
hand, for that the very steel draws on a man to fight.
But keep two swords and two spears and two shields —
these shall be for thee and me. Only let no one know
of my coming back — not Laertes, nor the swineherd,
no, nor Penelope herself."

But after a while the swineherd came back from the
city, having carried his tidings to the queen. And this
she also had heard from the sailors of the ships. Also
the ship of the suitors which they had sent to lie in

wait for the young man was returned. And the suitors
were in great wrath and fear, because their purpose
had failed, and also because Penelope the queen knew
what they had been minded to do, and hated them
because of it.

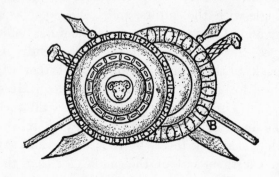

CHAPTER X.

ULYSSES IN HIS HOME.

THE next day Telemachus went to the city. But before he went he said to Eumæus that he should bring the beggar-man to the city, for that it was better to beg in the city than in the country. And the false beggar also said that he wished this. And Telemachus, when he was arrived, went to the palace and greeted the nurse Euryclea and his mother Penelope, who was right glad to see him, but to whom he told naught of what had happened. And after this he went to Piræus, and bade him keep the gifts which King Menelaus had given him till he should be in peace in his own house, and if things should fall out otherwise, that he should keep them for himself. And then he went to fetch the seer Theoclymenus, that he might bring him to the palace. And the seer, when he was come thither, prophesied good concerning Ulysses, how that he would certainly return and take vengeance for all the wrong that had been done to him.

Now in the meanwhile Eumæus and the false beggar were coming to the city. And when they were near to it, by the fountain which Ithacus and his brethren had made, where was also an altar of the Nymphs, Melanthius the goatherd met them, and spake evil to Eumæus, rebuking him that he brought this beggar to the city. And he came near and smote Ulysses with his foot on the thigh, but moved him naught from the path. And Ulysses thought a while, should he smite him with his club and slay him, or dash him on the ground. But it seemed to him better to endure.

But Eumæus lifted up his hands and said, "Oh, now may the Nymphs of the fountain fulfil this hope, that Ulysses may come back to his home, and tear from thee this finery of thine, wherein thou comest to the city, leaving thy flock for evil shepherds to devour!"

So they went on to the palace. And at the door of the court there lay the dog Argus, whom in the old days Ulysses had reared with his own hand. But ere the dog grew to his full, Ulysses had sailed to Troy. And, while he was strong, men used him in the chase, hunting wild goats and roe-deer and hares. But now he lay on a dunghill, and the lice swarmed upon him. Well he knew his master, and, for that he could not come near to him, wagged his tail and drooped his ears.

And Ulysses, when he saw him, wiped away a tear, and said, "Surely this is strange, Eumæus, that such a dog, being of so fine a breed, should lie here upon a dunghill."

And Eumæus made reply, "He belongeth to a master who died far away. For indeed when Ulysses had him of old, he was the strongest and swiftest of dogs; but now my dear lord has perished far away, and the careless women tend him not. For when the master is away the slaves are careless of their duty. Surely a man, when he is made a slave, loses half the virtue of a man."

And as he spake the dog Argus died. Twenty years had he waited, and he saw his master at the last.

After this the two entered the hall. And Telemachus, when he saw them, took from the basket bread and meat, as much as his hands could hold, and bade carry them to the beggar, and also to tell him that he might go round among the suitors, asking alms. So he went, stretching out his hand, as though he were wont to beg; and some gave, having compassion upon him and marvelling at him, and some asked who he was. But, of all, Antinous was the most shameless. For when Ulysses came to him and told him how he had had much riches and power in former days, and how he had gone to Egypt, and had been sold a slave into Cyprus, Antinous mocked him, saying —

"Get thee from my table, or thou shalt find a worse Egypt and a harder Cyprus than before."

Then Ulysses said, "Surely thy soul is evil though thy body is fair; for though thou sittest at another man's feast, yet wilt thou give me nothing."

But Antinous, in great wrath, took the stool on which he sat and cast it at him, smiting his right shoulder. But Ulysses stirred not, but stood as a rock. But in his heart he thought on revenge. So he went and sat down at the door. And being there, he said —

"Hear me, suitors of the queen! There is no wrath if a man be smitten fighting for that which is his own, but Antinous has smitten me because that I am poor. May the curse of the hungry light on him therefor, ere he come to his marriage day."

Also the other suitors blamed him that he had dealt so cruelly with this stranger. Also the queen was wroth when she heard it, as she sat in the upper chamber with her maidens about her.

But as the day passed on there came a beggar from the city, huge of bulk, mighty to eat and drink, but his strength was not according to his size. Arnæus was his name, but the young men called him Irus, because he was their messenger, after Iris, the messenger of Zeus. He spake to Ulysses —

"Give place, old man, lest I drag thee forth; the young men even now would have it so, but I think it shame to strike such an one as thee."

Then said Ulysses, "There is room for thee and for me; get what thou canst, for I do not grudge thee aught, but beware lest thou anger me, lest I harm thee, old though I am."

But Irus would not hear words of peace, but still challenged him to fight.

And when Antinous saw this he was glad, and said, "This is the goodliest sport that I have seen in this house. These two beggars would fight; let us haste and match them."

And the saying pleased them; and Antinous spake again: "Hear me, ye suitors of the queen! We have put aside these paunches of the goats for our supper. Let us agree then that whosoever of these two shall prevail, shall have choice of these, that which pleaseth him best, and shall hereafter eat with us, and that no one else shall sit in his place."

Then said Ulysses, "It is hard for an old man to fight with a young. Yet will I do it. Only do ye swear to me that no one shall strike me a foul blow while I fight with this man."

Then Telemachus said that this should be so, and
they all consented to his words. And after this Ulysses
girded himself for the fight. And all that were there
saw his thighs, how great and strong they were, and his
shoulders, how broad, and his arms, how mighty. And
they said one to another, "There will be little of Irus
left, so stalwart seems this beggar-man." But as for
Irus himself, he would have slunk out of sight, but they
that were set to gird him compelled him to come forth.

Then said the Prince Antinous, "How is this, thou
braggart, that thou fearest this old man, all woe-begone
as he is? Hearken thou to this. If this man prevails
against thee, thou shalt be cast into a ship and taken
to the land of King Echetus, who will cut off thy ears
and thy nose for his dogs to eat."

So the two came together. And Ulysses thought
whether he should strike the fellow and slay him out
of hand, or fell him to the ground. And this last
seemed the better of the two. So when Irus had dealt
his blow, he smote him on the jaw, and brake in the
bone, so that he fell howling on the ground, and the
blood poured amain from his mouth.

Then all the suitors laughed aloud. But Ulysses
dragged him out of the hall, and propped him by the
wall of the courtyard, putting a staff in his hand, and
saying, "Sit there, and keep dogs and swine from the
door, but dare not hereafter to lord it over men, lest
some worse thing befall thee."

Then Antinous gave him a great paunch, and Amphinomus gave two loaves, and pledged him in a cup,
saying, "Good luck to thee, father, hereafter, though
now thou seemest to have evil fortune."

And Ulysses made reply, "O Amphinomus, thou hast much wisdom, methinks, and thy father, I know, is wise. Take heed, therefore. There is naught feebler upon earth than man. For in the days of his prosperity he thinketh nothing of trouble, but when the gods send evil to him there is no help in him. I also trusted once in myself and my kinsmen, and now — behold me what I am! Let no man, therefore, do violence and wrong, for Zeus shall requite such deeds at the last. And now these suitors of the queen are working evil to him who is absent. Yet will he return some day and slay his enemies. Fly thou, therefore, while yet there is time, nor meet him when he comes."

So he spake, with kindly thought.

But his doom was on Amphinomus that he should die.

And that evening, the suitors having departed to their own dwellings, Ulysses and Telemachus took the arms from the hall, as they had also planned to do. And while they did so Telemachus said, "See, my father, this marvellous brightness that is on the pillars and the ceiling. Surely some god is with us."

And Ulysses made reply, "I know it: be silent. And now go to thy chamber and sleep, and leave me here, for I have somewhat to say to thy mother and her maidens."

And when the queen and her maidens came into the hall (for it was their work to cleanse it and make it ready for the morrow) Penelope asked him of his family and his country. And at first he made as though he would not answer, fearing, he said, lest he should trouble her with the story of that which he had suf-

fered. But afterwards, for she urged him, telling him
what she herself had suffered, her husband being lost
and her suitors troubling her without ceasing, he feigned
a tale that should satisfy her. For he told her how
that he was a man of Crete, a brother of King Idomeneus, and how he had given hospitality to Ulysses, what
time he was sailing to Troy with the sons of Atreus.

And when the queen, seeking to know whether he
spake the truth, asked him of Ulysses what manner of
man he was, and with what clothing he was clothed,
he answered her rightly, saying, "I remember me that
he had a mantle, twofold, woollen, of sea-purple, clasped
with a brooch of gold, whereon was a dog that held a
fawn by the throat ; marvellously wrought they were,
so hard held the one, so strove the other to be free.
Also he had a tunic, white and smooth, which the
women much admired to see. But whether some one
had given him these things I know not, for indeed
many gave him gifts, and I also, even a sword and a
tunic. Also he had a herald with him, one Eurybates,
older than him, dark-skinned, round in the shoulders,
with curly hair."

And Penelope, knowing these things to be true, wept
aloud, crying that she should see her husband no more.
But the false beggar comforted her, saying that Ulysses
was in the land of the Thesprotians, having much
wealth with him, only that he had lost his ships and
his comrades, yet nevertheless would speedily return.

Then Penelope bade her servants make ready a bed
for the stranger of soft mats and blankets, and also
that one of them should bathe him. But the mats and
blankets he would not have, saying that he would sleep

as before; and for the bathing, he would only that some old woman, wise and prudent, should do this. Wherefore the queen bade Euryclea, the keeper of the house, do this thing for him, for that he had been the comrade of her lord, and indeed was marvellously like to him in feet and hands.

And this the old woman was right willing to do, for love for her master, "for never," she said, "of all strangers that had come to the land, had come one so like to him." But when she had prepared the bath for his feet, Ulysses sat by the fire, but as far in the shadow as he might, lest the old woman should see a great scar that was upon his leg, and know him thereby.

Now the scar had chanced in this wise. He had come to see his grandfather Autolycus, who was the most cunning of men, claiming certain gifts which he had promised to him in the old days when, being then newly born, he was set on his grandfather's knees in the halls of Laertes, and his grandfather had given him this name. And on the day of his coming there was a great feast, and on the day after a hunting on Mount Parnassus. In this hunting, therefore, Ulysses came in the heart of the wood upon a place where lay a great wild boar, and the beast, being stirred by the noise, rose up, and Ulysses charged him with his spear, but before he could slay the beast it ripped a great wound just above the knee. And afterwards Ulysses slew it, and the young men bound up the wound, singing a charm to stanch the blood.

By this scar, then, the old nurse knew that it was Ulysses himself, and said, "O Ulysses, O my child, to think that I knew thee not!"

And she looked towards the queen, as meaning to tell the thing to her. But Ulysses laid his hand on her throat, "Mother, wouldst thou kill me? I am returned after twenty years; and none must know till I shall be ready to take vengeance."

And the old woman held her peace. And after this Penelope talked with him again, telling him her dreams, how she had seen a flock of geese in her palace, and how that an eagle had slain them, and when she mourned for the geese, lo! a voice that said, "These are thy suitors, and the eagle thy husband."

And Ulysses said that the dream was well. And then she said that on the morrow she must make her choice, for that she had promised to bring forth the great bow that was Ulysses', and whosoever should draw it most easily, and shoot an arrow best at a mark, he should be her husband.

And Ulysses made answer to her, "It is well, lady. Put not off this trial of the bow, for before one of them shall draw the string the great Ulysses shall come and duly shoot at the mark that shall be set."

After this Penelope slept, but Ulysses watched.

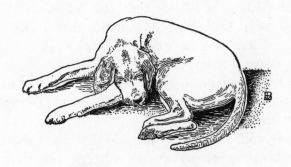

CHAPTER XI.

THE TRIAL OF THE BOW.

HE next day many things cheered Ulysses for that which he had to do; for first Athene had told him that she would stand at his side, and next he heard the thunder of Zeus in a clear sky, and last it chanced that a woman who sat at the mill grinding corn, being sore weary of her task, and hating the suitors, said, "Grant, Father Zeus, that this be the last meal which these men shall eat in the house of Ulysses!"

And after a while the suitors came and sat down, as was their wont, to the feast. And the servants bare to Ulysses, as Telemachus had bidden, a full share with the others. And when Ctesippus, a prince of Samos, saw this (he was a man heedless of right and of the gods), he said, "Is it well that this fellow should fare even as we? Look now at the gift that I shall give him." Whereupon he took a bullock's foot out of a basket wherein it lay, and cast it at Ulysses.

But he moved his head to the left and shunned it, and it flew on, marking the wall. And Telemachus cried in great wrath —

"It is well for thee, Ctesippus, that thou didst not strike this stranger. For surely, hadst thou done this thing, my spear had pierced thee through, and thy father had made good cheer, not for thy marriage, but for thy burial."

Then said Agelaus, " This is well said. Telemachus should not be wronged, no, nor this stranger. But, on the other hand, he must bid his mother choose out of the suitors whom she will, and marry him, nor waste our time any more."

And Telemachus said, " It is well. She shall marry whom she will. But from my house I will never send her against her will."

And the suitors laughed ; but their laughter was not of mirth, and the flesh which they ate dripped with blood, and their eyes were full of tears. And the eyes of the seer Theoclymenus were opened, and he cried —

" What ails you, miserable ones ? For your heads and your faces and your knees are covered with darkness, and the voice of groaning comes from you, and your cheeks are wet with tears. Also the walls and the pillars are sprinkled with blood, and the porch and the hall are full of shadows that move towards hell, and the sun has perished from the heaven, and an evil mist is over all."

But they laughed to hear him ; and Eurymachus said, " This stranger is mad ; let us send him out of doors into the market-place, for it seems that here it is dark."

Also they scoffed at Telemachus, but he heeded them not, but sat waiting till his father should give the sign.

After this Penelope went to fetch the great bow of Ulysses, which Iphitus had given to him. From the peg on which it hung she took it with its sheath, and sitting down, she laid it on her knees and wept over it, and after this rose up and went to where the suitors sat feasting in the hall. The bow she brought, and also the quiver full of arrows, and standing by the pillar of the dome, spake thus —

" Ye suitors who devour this house, making pretence that ye wish to wed me, lo! here is a proof of your skill. Here is the bow of the great Ulysses. Whoso shall bend it easiest in his hands, and shoot an arrow most easily through the helve-holes of the twelve axes that Telemachus shall set up, him will I follow, leaving this house, which I shall remember only in my dreams."

Then she bade Eumæus bear the bow and the arrows to the suitors. And the good swineherd wept to see his master's bow, and Philætius, the herdsman of the kine, wept also, for he was a good man, and loved the house of Ulysses.

Then Telemachus planted in due order the axes wherein were the helve-holes, and was minded himself to draw the bow; and indeed would have done the thing, but Ulysses signed to him that he should not. Wherefore he said, " Methinks I am too weak and young; ye that are elder should try the first."

Then first Leiodes, the priest, who alone among the suitors hated their evil ways, made trial of the bow. But he moved it not, but wearied his hands with it, for they were tender, and unwont to toil. And he said, " I cannot bend this bow; let some other try; but it shall be grief and pain to many this day, I trow."

And Antonius was wroth to hear such words, and bade Melanthius bring forth from the stores a roll of fat, that they might anoint the string and soften it withal. So they softened the string with fat, but not for that the more could they bend it, for they tried all of them in vain, till only Antinous and Eurymachus were left, who indeed were the bravest and the strongest of them all.

Now the swineherd and the herdsman of the kine had gone forth out of the yard, and Ulysses came behind them and said, "What would ye do if Ulysses were to come back to his home? Would ye fight for him, or for the suitors?"

And both said they would fight for him.

And Ulysses said, "It is even I who am come back in the twentieth year, and ye, I know, are glad at heart that I am come; nor know I of any one besides. And if ye will help me as brave men to-day, wives shall ye have, and possessions and houses near to mine own. And ye shall be brothers and comrades to Telemachus. And for a sign, behold this scar, which the wild boar made when I hunted with Autolycus."

Then they wept for joy and kissed Ulysses, and he also kissed them. And he said to Eumæus that he should bring the bow to him when the suitors had tried their fortune therewith; also that he should bid the women keep within doors, nor stir out if they should hear the noise of battle. And Philætius he bade lock the doors of the hall, and fasten them with a rope.

After this he came back to the hall, and Eurymachus had the bow in his hands, and sought to warm it at the fire. Then he essayed to draw it out, but could not. And he groaned aloud, saying, "Woe is me! not for loss of this marriage only, for there are other women to be wooed in Greece, but that we are so much weaker than the great Ulysses. This is indeed shame to tell."

Then said Antinous, " Not so; to-day is a holy day of the God of Archers; therefore we could not draw the bow. But to-morrow will we try once more, after due sacrifice to Apollo."

And this saying pleased them all; but Ulysses said, " Let me try this bow, for I would fain know whether I have such strength as I had in former days."

At this all the suitors were wroth, and chiefly Antinous, but Penelope said that it should be so, and promised the man great gifts if he could draw this bow.

But Telemachus spake thus, " Mother, the bow is mine to give or to refuse. And no man shall say me nay, if I will that this stranger make trial of it. But do thou go to thy chamber with thy maidens, and let men take thought for these things."

And this he said, for that he would have her depart from the hall forthwith, knowing what should happen therein. But she marvelled to hear him speak with such authority, and answered not, but departed. And when Eumæus would have carried the bow to Ulysses, the suitors spake roughly to him, but Telemachus constrained him to go. Therefore he took the bow and gave it to his master. Then went he to Euryclea, and bade her shut the door of the women's chambers and keep them within, whatsoever they might hear. Also Philætius shut the doors of the hall, and fastened them with a rope.

Then Ulysses handled the great bow, trying it, whether it had taken any hurt, but the suitors thought scorn of him. Then, when he had found it to be without flaw, just as a minstrel fastens a string upon his harp and strains it to the pitch, so he strung the bow without toil; and holding the string in his right hand, he tried its tone, and the tone was sweet as the voice of a swallow. Then he took an arrow from the quiver, and laid the notch upon the string and drew it, sitting as he was, and the arrow passed through every ring, and stood in the wall beyond. Then he said to Telemachus —

"There is yet a feast to be held before the sun go down."

And he nodded the sign to Telemachus. And forthwith the young man stood by him, armed with spear and helmet and shield.

CHAPTER XII.

THE SLAYING OF THE SUITORS.

THEN spake he among the suitors, "This labor has been accomplished. Let me try at yet another mark."

And he aimed his arrow at Antinous. But the man was just raising a cup to his lips, thinking not of death, for who had thought that any man, though mightiest of mortals, would venture on such a deed, being one among many? Right through the neck passed the arrowhead, and the blood gushed from his nostrils, and he dropped the cup and spurned the table from him.

And all the suitors, when they saw him fall, leapt from their seats; but when they looked, there was neither spear nor shield upon the wall. And they knew not whether it was by chance or of set purpose that the stranger had smitten him. But Ulysses then declared who he was, saying —

"Dogs, ye thought that I should never come back. Therefore have ye devoured my house, and made suit to my wife while I yet lived, and feared not the gods nor regarded men. Therefore a sudden destruction is come upon you all."

Then, when all the others trembled for fear, Eurymachus said, "If thou be indeed Ulysses of Ithaca, thou hast said well. Foul wrong has been done to thee in the house and in the field. But lo! he who was the mover of it all lies here, even Antinous. Nor was it so much this marriage that he sought, as to be king of this land, having destroyed thy house. But we will pay thee back for all that we have devoured, even twenty times as much.

But Ulysses said, "Speak not of paying back. My hands shall not cease from slaying till I have taken vengeance on you all."

Then said Eurymachus to his comrades, "This man will not stay his hands. He will smite us all with his arrows where he stands. But let us win the door, and raise a cry in the city; soon then will this archer have shot his last."

And he rushed on, with his two-edged knife in his hand. But as he rushed, Ulysses smote him on the breast with an arrow, and he fell forwards. And when Amphinomus came on, Telemachus slew him with his spear, but drew not the spear from the body, lest some one should smite him unawares.

Then he ran to his father and said, "Shall I fetch arms for us and our helpers?"

"Yea," said he, "and tarry not, lest my arrows be spent."

So he fetched from the armory four shields and four helmets and eight spears. And he and the servants, Eumæus and Philætius, armed themselves. Also Ulysses, when his arrows were spent, donned helmet and shield, and took a mighty spear in each hand. But Melanthius, the goatherd, crept up to the armory and brought down therefrom twelve helmets and shields, and spears as many. And when Ulysses saw that the suitors were arming themselves, he feared greatly, and said to his son —

"There is treachery here. It is one of the women, or, it may be, Melanthius, the goatherd."

And Telemachus said, "This fault is mine, my father, for I left the door of the chamber unfastened."

And soon Eumæus spied Melanthius stealing up to the chamber again, and followed him, and Philætius with him. There they caught him, even as he took a helmet in one hand and a shield in the other, and bound his feet and hands, and fastened him aloft by a rope to the beams of the ceiling.

Then these two went back to the hall, and there also came Athene, having the shape of Mentor. Still, for she would yet further try the courage of Ulysses and his son, she helped them not as yet, but changing her shape, sat on the roof-beam like unto a swallow.

And then cried Agelaus, "Friends, Mentor is gone, and helps them not. Let us not cast our spears at random, but let six come on together, if perchance we may prevail against them."

Then they cast their spears, but Athene turned them aside, one to the pillar and another to the door and another to the wall. But Ulysses and Telemachus and the two herdsmen slew each his man; and yet again they did so, and again. Only Amphimedon wounded Telemachus, and Ctesippus grazed the shoulder of Eumæus. But Telemachus struck down Amphimedon, and the herdsman of the kine slew Ctesippus, saying, "Take this, for the ox foot which thou gavest to our guest." And all the while Athene waved her flaming ægis-shield from above, and the suitors fell as birds are scattered and torn by eagles.

Then Leiodes, the priest, made supplication to Ulysses, saying, " I never wrought evil in this house, and would have kept others from it, but they would not. Naught have I done save serve at the altar; wherefore slay me not."

And Ulysses made reply, " That thou hast served at the altar of these men is enough, and also that thou wouldest wed my wife."

So he slew him ; but Phemius, the minstrel, he spared, for he had sung among the suitors in the hall, of compulsion, and not of good will ; and also Medon, the herald, bidding them go into the yard without. There they sat, holding by the altar and looking fearfully every way, for yet they feared that they should die.

So the slaughtering of the suitors was ended ; and now Ulysses bade cleanse the hall and wash the benches and the tables with water, and purify them with sulphur. And when this was done, that Euryclea, the nurse, should go to Penelope and tell her that her husband was indeed returned. So Euryclea went to her chamber and found the queen newly woke from slumber, and told her that her husband was returned, and how that he had slain the suitors, and how that she had known him by the scar where the wild boar had wounded him.

And yet the queen doubted, and said, " Let me go down and see my son, and these men that are slain, and the man who slew them."

So she went, and sat in the twilight by the other wall, and Ulysses sat by a pillar, with eyes cast down, waiting till his wife should speak to him. But she was sore perplexed; for now she seemed to know him, and now she knew him not, being in such evil case, for he had not suffered that the women should put new robes upon him.

And Telemachus said, " Mother, evil mother, sittest thou apart from my father, and speakest not to him? Surely thy heart is harder than a stone."

But Ulysses said, " Let be, Telemachus. Thy mother will know that which is true in good time. But now let us hide this slaughter for a while, lest the friends of these men seek vengeance against us. Wherefore let there be music and dancing in the hall, so that men shall say, ' This is the wedding of the queen, and there is joy in the palace,' and know not of the truth."

So the minstrel played and the women danced. And meanwhile Ulysses went to the bath, and clothed himself in bright apparel, and came back to the hall, and Athene made him fair and young to see. Then he sat him down as before, over against his wife, and said—

" Surely, O lady, the gods have made thee harder of heart than all women besides. Would other wife have kept away from her husband, coming back now after twenty years?"

And when she doubted yet, he spake again, " Hear thou this, Penelope, and know that it is I myself, and not another. Dost thou remember how I built up the bed in our chamber? In the court there grew an olive tree, stout as a pillar, and round it I built a chamber of stone, and spanned the chamber with a roof; and I

hung also a door, and then I cut off the leaves of the
olive, and planed the trunk, to be smooth and round;
and the bed I inlaid with ivory and silver and gold,
and stretched upon it an ox-hide that was ornamented
with silver."

Then Penelope knew him that he was her husband
indeed, and ran to him, and threw her arms about him
and kissed him, saying, "Pardon me, my lord, if I was
slow to know thee; for ever I feared, so many wiles
have men, that some one should deceive me, saying
that he was my husband. But now I know this, that
thou art he and not another."

And they wept over each other and kissed each
other. So did Ulysses come back to his home after
twenty years.

KING ARTHUR AND THE KNIGHTS
OF THE ROUND TABLE

CHAPTER I.

SIR GARETH'S TRIAL.

IT was in the old days of England, when instead of one King, there were many, who divided the country between them and constantly made war upon each other, to increase their possessions.

The noblest of all these Kings was Arthur. He was the son of Uther Pendragon, and he succeeded to the throne at a very early age, though not without great trouble, as the knights and barons said they would not be ruled over by a " beardless boy," and if he wanted his crown, he might fight for it. However, by the aid of an old man named Merlin, who was supposed to have magic powers, the rising insurrection was stopped, and young King Arthur was crowned with great pomp in London.

The King proved himself able not only to take the crown, but to keep it, and the other Kings found they had to be very respectful to him, and very careful not to encroach on his boundaries.

For the encouragement of feats of arms, and all sorts

of bravery, he founded the brotherhood of the Knights
of the Round Table, and any man who wished to join
it had first to prove his worth in tournament or fight.
They had also to take this oath : —

> "To reverence the King as if he were
>   Their conscience, and their conscience as their King;
>   To break the heathen, and uphold the Christ;
>   To ride abroad redressing human wrongs;
>   To speak no slander, no, nor listen to it;
>   To honor his own word, as if his God's;
>   To love one maiden only, cleave to her,
>   And worship her by years of noble deeds,
>   Until they won her."

The fame of the Table Round was spread far and
wide, and the secret ambition of many a young man
was that some day he might be found worthy to
join it.

There was a youth named Gareth, who lived at
home with his mother, who was Queen of Orkney.
He was much the youngest of all the boys, and his
mother clung to him and wanted to keep him with
her as long as she could, especially as her husband, old
King Lot, was childish and paralyzed, and could not
help her in any way.

But the boy's one idea was to go to the Court, win
great fame for himself, and be one of the splendid
Table Round. He was always begging his mother to
let him go, and she always had some good reason why
he should stay at home. Sometimes she said he was
too young, at others that it was cruel to leave her
alone. Still, day after day he persisted, and she began
to see that he was growing moody and discontented.

So, poor woman, she hit on a plan which she hoped would settle it once for all. She would tell him he might go, but on one condition — that condition should be an impossible one; and so the next time Gareth began to beg and implore her not to keep him wasting his youth at home, she said :

> " 'Ay, go then, an ye must: only one proof,
> Before thou ask the King to make thee knight,
> Of thine obedience and thy love to me,
>   Thy mother — I demand.'
> And Gareth cried,
> ' A hard one, or a hundred, so I go.
> Nay ! — quick — the proof to prove me to the quick ! ' "

And what do you think the test was? That he was to go in disguise to the Court and ask leave to serve in the kitchen, in return for his food ; not to tell his name, however much he might be pressed, and to stay in that position for twelve months and a day. Truly a hard condition for any young man of spirit.

Gareth thought for awhile, and then accepted the condition. " For," said he, " the thrall in person may be free in soul. And I shall see the jousts." The Queen was very sorry she had yielded so far as to make a condition ; she had hoped that Gareth would refuse indignantly ; but the mischief was done.

Early one morning Gareth left the castle, with two men who had waited on him since his birth, and set out on his journey. They were all three disguised as peasants, with rough, poor clothes, and met with no notice or adventures on their way. They knew the King was holding his Court at Camelot this year. He always kept the festival of Whitsuntide with great splendor, but not always in the same place. Camelot was the town we now call Winchester, and it was the capital of Arthur's kingdom.

As they neared the city, the serving-men were struck with amazement at the beauty and grandeur of the towers and roofs as they glistened in the sunshine. It seemed to them an enchanted city, and as they called to mind the strange stories of Merlin and his doings, they grew afraid and begged Gareth to turn back. But he only laughed at them, and so they came on to the great gate, which was a perfect marvel of carving. High up in the centre there was the statue of the Lady of the Lake, imposing and beautiful, and in one hand there was a sword, and in the other a censer, while on her breast was the sacred fish, the symbol of Christianity.   To right and left of this central figure were carved scenes showing Arthur's victories in battle. They passed under this wonderful gateway, and asked the way to the great hall.

Now it was Arthur's custom not to sit down to dinner till he had seen some adventure.

As Sir Gawaine, one of the knights, was gazing idly out of the window, he saw the three men approaching, and he went to the King and said: "Sire, go now to your dinner, for here comes the adventure."

It was rather clever of Gawaine, for it could have been nothing very uncommon, as strangers were constantly coming to the Court on some pretext or other.

Then the great Table Round was filled with a splendid company of brave and handsome knights, and the King sat in the midst.

The three men came into the hall. Gareth was in

the middle, and though he was so tall and well grown, he leaned on the shoulders of the others, as if he were weak and ill. The company made way for them, though they stared a great deal, and they went straight up to the King.

Then Gareth stepped in front of the others, made a low reverence, and said: " God bless you, and all your fair fellowship, and especially the fellowship of the Round Table. And I have come hither, sire, to ask of you three things. I will ask the first now, and leave the other two until this day twelve months, when you are again holding the feast at Pentecost."

" Well," said the King, " and what is your petition ? "

" This," said Gareth, plucking up heart, as he noticed the King's kind and frank expression. " This — that you will give me meat and drink in your kitchen for a year and a day."

" That is a very small matter," said the King; " if you had asked for horse and harness I would have given it, but as for food, that I have never refused to friend or foe — I give it you gladly. But now tell me your name and degree."

Gareth longed to tell the truth, but his promise to his mother held him fast, and so he answered respectfully :

" That I may not tell, Sire, and I entreat you of your kindness not to desire it of me."

" You shall have your way," said the King; and then he called Sir Kaye, the Seneschal, and charged him to provide all that was necessary for the stranger, and added that he should be treated as one of noble birth, " for I am quite sure," said he, " though he refuses to tell his name, he is noble."

"Indeed," said Sir Kaye, who was a very sour, sarcastic person, "that will not be needed, for if he had been noble he would have asked for horse and armor, and not for food alone. I will take care he has all he can eat, but he shall live in the kitchen, and help the serving-men, and that will be good enough for him. I warrant he has been brought up in some monastery, and they can feed him no longer, so he comes to us. As for a name, I shall call him Beaumains — that is to say, 'Fair Hands.'"

This was said in derision, for Launcelot had pointed out that, poorly as the youth was dressed, and as humble as was his petition, yet he was undoubtedly of noble birth, for his broad, open brow, fair hair, and well-formed hands were proof of it. Launcelot went so far as to say that although the Seneschal might know a horse or a hound when he saw one, he evidently did not know a man; and that he would do well to treat the stranger properly, or some day he might be ashamed of his conduct.

But Sir Kaye put aside Launcelot's kindly-meant advice, and had his own way. The two serving-men departed, and Gareth, or Beaumains, as we must now call him, was put among the kitchen-folk.

It was a very rough place for a lad of his breeding, and much rude joking went on at his expense; but he bore it all pleasantly, and did not even resent being set to wash the dishes. His whole heart and mind being set to go through the adventure, he remained firm and good-tempered through all.

There was one ray of brightness in Beaumain's hard life, and that was the kindness shown him by Gawaine,

who had been the first to see him, and Sir Launcelot of
the Lake.   All the knights admired Sir Launcelot, who
was in great favor with both the King and his lovely
Queen, Guinevere.   He was the most famous in all the
feats of strength and the most noted in the tournaments,
and with all this he was not proud, but gentle, cour-
teous and lovable.

He and Sir Gawaine took a great fancy to the handsome lad who bore himself so modestly and did his
daily work without complaint, and they did not like to
see him among the grooms and helpers, so they asked
him to come to their rooms privately, and promised to
see that he had better meals and better clothes.   But
though he felt their delicate kindness to the bottom of
his heart, he refused all offers of help, thanked them
warmly, and declared he needed nothing better than he
had.

The only one who was really unkind to him was Sir
Kaye, the Seneschal, who was constantly taunting him
with being so poor spirited as to serve in a kitchen in
return for food.   As Sir Kaye had the superintendence
of the household matters, he could make things very
unpleasant for Beaumains, and he seemed to take a pleasure in doing it.   He gave him extra and heavier tasks
than he gave the other youths : if more water was to
be fetched, or more logs of wood, it was always Beaumains who was told to do it.   " For," said Sir Kaye,
" if he is a fine gentleman, a little taking down will do
him good."   The only pleasure Beaumains had was to
try his luck in the different games, and he soon proved
both his strength and skill were beyond the common.
Whenever there was any tilting he was on fire to go,

and if Sir Kaye really could not find him another task he would reluctantly give him leave.

So the months passed on, till the sweet spring-time came again, and the Feast of Pentecost drew near. This year it was to be held at Caerleon-upon-Usk, in Wales, and all the Court proceeded there with much pomp: brave and handsome knights, and beautiful ladies, of whom Queen Guinevere was the sweetest and loveliest, with her golden hair, blue eyes, and complexion of lilies and roses. She wore a dress of pale green silk, like the first tender leaves of spring, and her slender waist was clasped by a golden girdle.

On Whitsunday all the Court went to service in the church in great state, the King and Queen sitting in the seats of honor, with the knights and dames around them. Then the feast was spread in the great hall with much magnificence, but first a little time was set apart for any who wished to appeal to the King for justice. Presently the ushers brought in a young and pretty girl, who seemed in the greatest distress, and begged for help. The King desired her to be calm and to tell her story. So she said she came on behalf of a lady who was besieged in her own castle by a knight of great prowess, and, having no one to defend her, she had sent to King Arthur for help.

"What is the lady's name?" said the King, "and who is the knight that besieges her?"

"That I may not tell you, sire," said she, and shut up her pretty lips with great decision.

"There are many knights here," returned the King, "who would gladly do battle for this lady; but if you will neither tell me her name, nor his who attacks her, they shall none of them go with my consent."

Just at this moment up came Beaumains, looking very tall and handsome, and with a sort of triumph in his bearing which transformed him, and he said to the King, making his reverence:

"Sir King, God thank you, I have now been twelve months and a day in your kitchen, and now I will ask my two gifts."

"With all my heart," said the King.

"First," said Beaumains, with a glance at the damsel, who was looking very displeased that her business should be set aside, "give me this adventure. Let *me* be the one to succor the distressed lady. Secondly, I pray you, let Sir Launcelot make me knight, and then I will ride on my way to the castle."

"Both these I grant," said the King.

Then the lady was very angry, and, with crimson cheeks and flashing eyes, she cried out: "What! shall I have none but he that is your kitchen page? — Then I will have none!" And in great wrath she turned and left the royal presence with scant ceremony, flung herself into the saddle, and rode away, followed by her servant.

Looking to the King for permission, Beaumains left the hall, and making his way into the courtyard, what did he find there? — a fine horse with rich trappings, and a suit of armor for himself, brought by one of the old serving-men who had attended him when he left home.

The man whispered that his royal mother had sent him with them, and with a message that he was released from his promise, as the time of trial was over.

Beaumains' heart beat high with delight. At last the weary time of waiting was over, and he might be

his own man again. His first thought was to go back
to the King and tell him all the story; then a curious
impulse came over him, and he decided to keep the
secret from all but Sir Launcelot, and force the haughty
beauty to respect him even as a kitchen page. So,
bidding the servant wait with the horse, he sought Sir
Launcelot, and made his petition that he would dub
him knight.

"Willingly," said Sir Launcelot; "but you must
tell me your name before I do this."

"My name is Gareth, and I am the youngest son of
the King and Queen of Orkney, and my mother would
let me come to the Court on one condition only, that I
should serve in the kitchen for a year and a day, and
tell my name to none, not even to the King."

"I am right glad," said Sir Launcelot; "I knew you
were noble all the while."

So then in haste Beaumains was made knight, and
he mounted his horse and rode after the haughty lady.

CHAPTER II.

GARETH AND LYNETTE.

THERE was much discussion among the knights, and some laughter, as they watched him go, and Sir Kaye, who had always been unfriendly, said:

" Now I will hie me after my boy of the kitchen, and see if he will know me for his master!"

Just as Beaumains overtook the lady, Sir Kaye came spurring up behind in great haste, crying, " Hold, Beaumains! know ye not me? We miss you by the kitchen fire."

" Yes," said Beaumains, " I know ye for an ungentle knight, and therefore look to yourself!"

With that they began to fight, and after a while Sir Kaye was wounded, and fell to the ground sorely humiliated.

Beaumains then came up to the lady, who had been watching the encounter, curious, in spite of her scorn, to see which would win. She gave him but a poor reception, however, calling him " kitchen knave," and declaring his beautiful new clothes had the odor of the dishes about them. She told him it was only by chance he had overcome Sir Kaye, who, as every one knew, was his master, and again declared she would not have him for her champion.

"Damsel," said Gareth, as we must now call him, "say to me what ye like. I have undertaken to King Arthur to achieve your adventure, and I shall finish it or die in attempting it."

"Fie on thee, kitchen knave!" cried Lynette, for that was the lady's name, "thou shalt meet one whom, for all the broth thou hast supped, thou darest not look in the face!"

"I shall try," said Gareth quietly.

Just then a man came rushing up to them. "Help! help!" cried he; "my master has been set on by six ruffians, overcome and bound, and I fear for his life."

"Show me the way," said Gareth. The man led him to where his master lay bound, and three of the robbers made off when they saw him coming. Gareth laid about him so fiercely that he soon had the three others disabled, but was only slightly wounded himself, owing to his great skill in arms; then he went back to the prostrate man, unbound him, and helped him to regain his horse. The knight was most grateful, and thanked Gareth heartily, and begged him to go with him to his castle and rest and refresh himself. He even wished to reward him, but this Gareth refused. "Sir," said he, "I will no reward have. I was this day made knight of the noble Sir Launcelot, and this is reward enough. I must follow the lady."

When he turned to Lynette, who had thought it prudent to retire a little while the fight was going on, she abused him worse than ever. But he took no notice of her raging, other than to assure her that his purpose was fixed to go on with her and rescue the unknown distressed lady.

Then the knight, seeing there was a wandering lady also, begged them both very earnestly to come to his castle and rest.   So they rode on together, and for once Lynette forbore to wrangle.

They went into the castle, where the knight ordered supper to be spread, and invited the two young people to sit down.   But when Gareth was given a place next to Lynette, she rose at once in anger, and declared that she would not sit down with a kitchen knave, as it was an insult to her dignity.

Gareth's face flushed, but, true to his resolve, he offered no objection.   The host settled the question by putting Gareth at a side table, and seated himself by him, leaving Lynette by herself, which was by no means what she wished.

Next morning, after breakfast, they thanked the good knight for his hospitality, and set off once more. They rode on and on till they came to a gloomy forest, through which Lynette led the way, and then they reached the banks of a river.   There was only one place where they could cross it in safety.   By the ford were two knights, who stood on the alert to prevent them crossing.   Again the lady tried her sharp tongue on her patient knight.

"Best go back," said she, "for you won't dare risk your bones!"

"Not I," said he; "not if there were six of them," and with that he rushed up to the ford.

Then there was another fight, long and hard, but in the end Gareth overcame his two assailants, and he and Lynette passed over the river in safety.   Small credit did he get at his lady's hands, however.   "Alas!" said

she, " that ever a kitchen page should have the fortune
to overcome two such doughty knights."

Gareth took no notice, and only suggested that they
should push on ; and seeing she could make no impression on him, she consented. After riding nearly all
day, they came to a strange place. There was a black
hawthorn, and on it hung a black banner; on the other
side there hung a black shield, and by it a long black
spear, and there was a great black horse fastened to it,
and hard by there was a black stone. On the stone
sat a knight all in black armor, and his name was the
Knight of the Black Lands.

When Lynette saw this, she advised Gareth to fly
down the valley, for his horse was not saddled.

" Nay, would you have me a coward ? " said Gareth,
smiling.

Then the Black Knight made ready to fight, and
after a short but sharp passage was overcome and
killed.

After this they rode on again, and presently they
met a knight dressed all in green, with a green shield
and a green spear. He, like the first, was anxious to
fight, and Gareth was nothing loth; so they set to with
great fierceness. Hard and quick came the blows, and
for a time the result seemed uncertain, when a fortunate stroke brought the Green Knight to the ground,
and Gareth stood over him, ready to kill him.

But Lynette, who had begun to respect her champion
in spite of herself, called out loudly to him that he was
to spare him.

" Nay," said Gareth, " not unless you ask me for
your sake to show mercy."

"Fair damsel," cried out the Green Knight, as she hesitated, "I beseech you, ask for my life, and I have thirty men at my command, and they shall all be at his orders, if he will but spare me."

So, much against her will, the proud Lynette was obliged to ask Gareth for her sake to spare the prostrate man, and Gareth agreed. The Green Knight, all his fire and fury gone, and aching horribly in all his bones, did homage to Gareth, and thanked Lynette for her intercession on his behalf. He also promised that he and his thirty knights should be ready at any time to do battle for King Arthur, if called upon. He begged them to spend the night at his castle, which they did, and supped together, the only trouble being that again Lynette refused to sit down next to Sir Gareth. But the Green Knight— and he was a good judge of men— settled the matter in the same way as the other host had done, and again Lynette sat by herself.

Next morning, after breakfast, the Green Knight wished them god-speed, and away they rode once more. After an hour's riding, they came to a beautiful castle, shining in the morning sunlight, and over the tower there hung fifty shields of different colors, for there was to be a great tournament next day. Now, the lord of the castle was looking out of a window, and saw the lady approaching, and Gareth, armed at all points.

"I will go down and engage with him," said he, "for I see he is a knight-errant." So he armed himself in blue from top to toe, and he had a blue shield and a blue spear. Then he sallied out to meet Gareth, and again there was a fight, and, as before, Gareth was the

victor, and held his adversary under his sword. The
Blue Knight cried out for mercy, and once more Lynette had to humble herself and beg for mercy, as she
did not wish the man to be killed at her feet. He had
fifty knights at his command, and he also promised to
lead them in King Arthur's service if needed. They
stayed the night, and in the morning they set off,
Lynette no longer riding in front in her haughty way,
but by Sir Gareth's side, for she was beginning to
acknowledge in her heart that, whatever his name
might be, he was a very fine fellow.

But now there was coming the greatest trial of all,
for at last, after all these delays, they drew near the
Castle Dangerous, where Dame Lyonors, who was really
Lynette's sister, was besieged. The three knights
whom Gareth had overcome were brothers of the Red
Knight of the Red Lands, and they had been given the
task of making an end on the way of any knight who
should come to the rescue. However, this valiant
youth was a match for them all, and even Lynette's
caution that they were nearing the castle did not cause
him the slightest fear. If he had a tremor, it was one
of pleasure, for the fire in Lynette's eyes was softened,
and there was quite a kindly tone in her voice as she
begged him to be careful, " For," said she, " I dread me
full sore lest that you should suffer some hurt or dam-
age, and that I would not have, for you are a brave
knight and a gentle, and I am truly sorry I used you
so roughly."

" Dear lady," said Gareth, " do not speak of it; for
you have done me no harm, and now I shall fight better
than ever I did, under the sunshine of your smile." So

on they rode in high spirits, and in the afternoon they came to a gloomy castle, and there was martial music sounding from within. Close by the entrance there was a sycamore tree, and on it hung a horn of ivory, the largest they had ever seen. Said Lynette, " The Knight of the Red Lands has hung it up there, and if any errant knight should come by and wish to fight, he must blow that horn, and then the Red Knight will come out and do battle with him."

" But I pray you, sir " — Lynette was growing civil — " do not blow it now, but wait till it is night, for from now till sunset he has the strength of seven, but after that time he has only what belongs to him of right."

" Oh, my lady," cried Gareth, " do not talk to me of fear; no matter what strength he may have, I will rescue your sister or die."

And with that he spurred his horse up to the sycamore tree, and blew such a blast on the horn that the castle rang with the sound. Then the Red Knight armed himself in haste, and all was blood red — his armor, spear, and shield. And he rode out of the castle gate to meet Gareth.

" Sir," said Lynette, " look that you be merry and bold, for here comes your deadly enemy, and at yonder window is my sister, Dame Lyonors, whom he holds in bondage."

" She is the fairest lady — save one — that I have ever seen," said Gareth, " and I am proud to do battle for her." And he looked up to the window with a bright smile, and Dame Lyonors smiled in return, and waved her hand.

Then the Red Knight called out in a great voice, "Leave, Sir Knight, thy looking, and beware of me, for she is my lady, and for her I have fought many battles."

"That may be," said Gareth, "but I warrant she cares little for your company, or she would not have sent to ask for help against you. I will rescue her from your hands, or die in the attempt."

"You had better take warning," said the Red Knight; "look in those trees yonder." And there hung upon the trees forty dead knights, and their shields and swords about their necks, and gilt spurs on their heels. "These doughty champions," said the Red Knight, with a grim smile, "all came hither on the same errand as yourself. Perhaps you would like to join them? I dare say I can find another tree!"

"Make ready," cried Gareth fiercely, "for I will parley no longer." He desired Lynette to stand away at a safe distance, and then the two rushed together with a tremendous onslaught.

Oh! but it was a long and a hard battle, by far the worst Gareth had fought, for the wicked knight had the strength of seven men. Suddenly Gareth fell to the ground and seemed unable to recover himself, and the Red Knight fell over him to hold him down.

Then Lynette burst out weeping, and cried, "Oh, Sir Beaumains! what is become of thy strength, in which we trusted?"

With that, liquid fire seemed to run through Gareth's veins. He flung off his enemy, sprang to his feet, and rushed upon him with renewed vigor. So fast and

furious were his strokes that the sword flew out of the
other's hand, and the next moment he was helpless on
the ground.

"Oh, noble knight, I yield me unto thy mercy,"
gasped the Red Knight.

Then Gareth said, "I ought not to save thy life, for
the sake of all those knights thou didst slay so shamefully."

"Stay thy hand," said the vanquished man, "and I
will tell thee why I treated them so. I once loved a
fair damsel, and her brother was slain, and she said it
was Sir Launcelot or Gawaine who did the deed, and
she made me promise that I should daily seek out those
of the Court, and put them to a shameful death as a
reprisal."

Then many barons and knights came to Gareth, begging him to spare the life of the Red Knight.

"I am willing to spare his life," said Gareth, " especially as all the wrong he has done was at a lady's
request ; and he shall go humbly to Dame Lyonors and
ask her pardon, and remove himself from this castle in
all haste. He shall also go to the Court, taking his
followers with him, and ask of the King pardon for the
foul wrong he has done to knighthood."

Lyonors was so grateful to her champion that he
might have married her, but all his heart was with
wilful Lynette, and soon the wedding was arranged.
King Arthur received the whole party, and when he
heard the story he praised Gareth till he made him
blush.

Then came the Queen of Orkney, and she scolded
them all round for not having known Gareth in spite

of his disguise; but when she heard how he had proved himself, and the charming bride he had won, she was comforted, and so all ended happily with wedding bells.

CHAPTER III.

LAUNCELOT AND ELAINE.

SIR LAUNCELOT was knight of most renown in all King Arthur's Table Round,
and his shield, with the lions on it, was so
well known that he sometimes had the fancy
to use a strange one, for some of the knights
thought he had magic power.

There was to be a great tournament held at Astolat,
now called Guildford.   At first Launcelot said he would
not ride in it, but both King Arthur and Queen Guinevere were anxious he should go, for they loved him
dearly; so they persuaded him to go.

He went to stay with an old knight, Sir Bernard of
Astolat, and he asked him if he could lend him a shield,
for his own was too well known.

"Gladly," said Sir Bernard; "I will lend you the
shield of my elder son, Sir Torre, and his brother,
Lavaine, shall go with you as your squire, and wait
on you."

Sir Bernard had two sons, and an only daughter,
named Elaine.   She was a lonely girl, her mother being dead, and her father and brothers often away from
home.   Much solitude had made her fanciful, and this
was increased by constant brooding over the stories she
heard of the knights and their wonderful doings.   So

when this strange knight came to lodge with her father, with his courtly presence and noble looks, her heart went out to him, and she "loved him with that love which was her doom."

No one in the house knew Sir Launcelot, for they had not been much at the Court, so his request about the shield excited no surprise. Elaine offered to take care of Launcelot's own shield, and he thanked her so pleasantly, that, blushing, she asked him if he would wear a favor of hers upon his helm, as the custom was. He told her he had never worn any lady's favor in that way, but remembering that his doing so for once would lessen the chance of his being known, he agreed, and she brought him a red sleeve, embroidered with pearls. With many kind words, he set off to the tournament.

Never had he fought as he fought that day. One knight after another went down before him, and every one was saying, "Who is the knight with the strange shield, and the red sleeve on his helm?" No one knew, however, and the day wore on. Towards the end Launcelot received such a frightful wound that he was forced to leave the field, instead of going to receive the reward of valor from the hands of the Queen; and Lavaine, Elaine's brother, went with him. He was so faint and weary that he could scarcely stagger into a little wayside hermitage, where the good man put him to bed and attended to his wounds.

But poor Sir Launcelot was very ill, and in a burning fever, and after a time, on Lavaine taking the news to Sir Bernard's household, Elaine, full of tender compassion, came to nurse him. Watching over his sick bed, her fatal love grew stronger, till it filled all her heart,

and when, in his ravings, she learnt that her hero was
the great Sir Launcelot, you may be sure it was not
lessened.

With Elaine and Sir Lavaine to nurse him, the sick
man began to mend after a time, and then with his
keen eyes he saw poor Elaine's hopeless love for him.
Very tenderly he told her he had no love to give, nor
should he ever marry.   For, alas! the whole of Sir
Launcelot's heart was fixed on Queen Guinevere, whom
he had been sent to fetch for her marriage with King
Arthur, and he thought her the only woman in the
world.

Elaine's tender, girlish heart broke when she found
she had loved in vain, and when at parting Launcelot
thanked and blessed her for bringing him back to life,
and hoped he should see her again, she smiled sadly,
for she knew well there would never be another meeting in this world.

Launcelot went away very sorrowfully, for he felt it
a bad return for all their care to break the heart of this
lovely girl, and yet he had done it quite in ignorance.

When he was gone, Elaine faded visibly from hour
to hour, and the old servants began to shake their
heads, and say she would not live long.   Last of all,
poor Sir Bernard and her brothers saw only too plainly
that the pretty fair-haired girl who had been their pet
and plaything was dying.

But all their love could not give her the one thing
she wanted — Launcelot's love.   Sometimes they heard
her crying, "Him or death," over and over, and their
hearts bled within them, for they could do nothing.
At last she called them all to her.   They thought her

better, for her sweet face, though pale, was calm.   She
smiled at them, and asked Sir Torre to write a letter,
which he did.   And this was what she said : —

"Most noble knight, Sir Launcelot, here lie I, slain for your
love, who would none of me.

"And unto all ladies I make my moan, and most of all to
Queen Guinevere, that they will pray for my soul.

"And you too, Sir Launcelot, pray for the repose of my soul."

Then she charged them, as they loved her, to dress
her all in white when she was dead, and lay her on a
bed, with this letter fast bound in her right hand.
And the bed was to be put in a barge, and that was to
be all draped with black cloth, and the man to steer it
was to be an old deaf and dumb servant who had
grown up in the house.

Weeping and praying, they received her last wishes;
and, with a smile, she died.   Then she was robed in a
fair white silken gown and laid on the bed, and that
was put in a barge, and so, with the silent serving-man
at the helm, lovely, hapless Elaine started on her last
journey.   The barge floated on and on till it reached
the landing-steps, and then, while the courtiers gathered around in astonishment, the bed was carried into
the hall, and Queen Guinevere bent her sweet face over
the dead girl.

The little cold hand still clasped the letter, which, on
being taken from her, proved to be for Sir Launcelot.
He was stricken with grief, for he never thought the
poor girl would die for love of him; and he could
hardly convince the King and Queen that he had really
been entirely blameless; but there was truth in his

eyes and his voice as he answered the questions put to
him, and all that could be done was to give Elaine the
fairest burying that could be devised for her.

And she was buried next morning with great pomp,
and Sir Launcelot walked next after her father and
brothers, and all the other knights followed him, and a
solemn service was sung. So died Elaine, in the flower
of her youth and beauty, and the memory of this was
always a sore grief to Sir Launcelot as long as he lived.

CHAPTER IV.

PRINCE GERAINT AND FAIR ENID.

ONE fine spring morning, when the Court was at Caerleon-upon-Usk, there was a great stag-hunt. The Queen, with only one attendant, set out so much later than the others, that she did not know in which direction they had gone. After fording the river Usk, she and her lady took their stand on a little hill, and listened for the baying of the hounds. As they waited, they heard the sound of galloping hoofs, and presently up came the noble Prince Geraint.

He looked, indeed, a gallant figure, as he rode up to salute the Queen. He was dressed in a beautiful suit of green and gold, with a purple scarf round his waist. He made a low reverence to the Queen, and she, smiling on him, replied: "You are late, Prince; later than we are."

"Yes, noble Queen," he said, "so late that I have but come to see the hunt, not to join it."

"Then wait with us," said the Queen graciously.

Nothing loth, Prince Geraint stayed, and they talked and laughed merrily together. Presently there came by on horseback three persons, a lady, a knight, and a dwarf. The knight had his vizor up, and the Queen, thinking she knew his face, sent her lady-in-waiting to ask the dwarf what was his master's name. The dwarf, an old and ill-tempered looking creature, answered, rudely, that she should not know.

" Then I will ask it of himself," said the damsel, and she spurred her horse to follow the knight, who was just on the point of disappearing in the wood.

" Thou shalt not ask it," cried out the dwarf, " for it matters not to thee," and he struck at the lady with his whip.

She wheeled about to avoid the blow, and hastened back to the Queen, to whom she told the story.

Geraint, all on fire at the insult, galloped up to the dwarf, but before the first words were out of his mouth, a stinging cut from the wretch's whip caught him on the cheek.

Geraint scorned to war with the servant, whose insolence was no doubt inspired by the master, and, returning to the Queen, he said :

" I will avenge this, my Queen, for in insulting your maiden he has struck at you. By your leave I will track the knight to his castle ; and though I have no arms upon me, I doubt not I can borrow all I need on the way. Then will I fight him, and will humble his pride, and teach him to respect your retinue. If I be not killed, I will return on the third day from now."

" Farewell, Prince," said Guinevere ; " I wish you safely back from this adventure ; and for your readiness to champion my cause, I promise that when you wed, no matter how humble a bride you choose — yes, even if she be a beggar from the hedge — I will clothe her for her bridal as though she were mine own daughter — 'tis a bargain."

With a bow and a smile, Geraint set off after the three, the lady, the knight, and the dwarf. Through one grassy glade after another, up and down, he galloped, keeping always a careful eye on those in front, who seemed unconscious that they were followed. After hours of riding, just as the sun was setting, he saw their figures for a moment outlined against the sky as they paused on the top of a hill, then, descending swiftly, they were lost to sight.

He put spurs to his tired and stumbling horse, and in a moment they were clattering through the stony street of a little town where he had never been before.

" So," he thought, " I have tracked him down at last — and now for supper," for he had tasted nothing since his morning meal.

He proceeded carefully down the rough roadway, dreading a stumble, for his horse was ready to drop. On the one side of the street was a large and gloomy fortress ; on the other, a half-ruined castle. The three in front passed into the courtyard of the fortress, and the great gate clanged to behind them with a sullen sound.

Three pressing wants presented themselves to Geraint — supper and bed for himself and his good horse, and a suit of armor. Where should he seek for them ?

There were two or three inns of far from tempting appearance, but on entering each in turn, he was told that the house was full.

The whole place was in a bustle — the blacksmiths' forges were all at work, sparks were flying, hammers clinking, and grooms were hissing and whistling as they rubbed down their masters' horses and scoured their armor.

"What is the meaning of all this?" he asked one of these youths, who, without pausing in his work, replied shortly, "The Sparrow-hawk."

Then he asked an old man, who staggered under the weight of a heavy sack of corn. The fellow grunted hoarsely, "Ugh! the Sparrow-hawk," and that was all.

Then Geraint, impatient and half angry, came to an armorer's, who sat, with bowed shoulders, riveting a helmet which he held on his knee. To the same question, the man said curtly, without looking at him, "Friend, he who works for the Sparrow-hawk has no time to answer idle questions;" whereat Prince Geraint flashed out, "Enough of your riddles and your sparrow-hawks! Speak! if ye be not like the rest, hawk-mad! Where can my horse and I find shelter for the night? — and arms, arms, arms, to fight my enemy? Speak!"

His fiery tone brought the armorer to his feet in a moment, and, seeing his visitor's splendid dress, he came forward, still grasping the helmet.

"Pardon me, oh stranger knight!" he said civilly. "There's a tournament here to-morrow, and hardly time for half the work which yet must needs be done. Arms, you need? — in truth, I hardly know; and shelter for the night? You may perchance find all you seek at Earl Yniol's, across the bridge; you can but try." Then in haste he turned to his work once more.

Geraint rode across the bridge, and saw on the other side the half-ruined castle he had noticed on first descending the hill. No servant kept the gate, which opened to his touch; and, leading his horse, he walked up a grass-grown path to an ancient-looking inner portal, where, surveying the sunset, he found a noble-looking old man, dressed in a faded suit that had once been splendid. It was Earl Yniol.

" Whither fare you ? " said he kindly.

" Sir," said Geraint, bowing low, " I and my tired horse seek shelter for the night, and my story you shall hear."

" Enter," said the Earl cordially ; " for though we are much fallen from our former estate, we have still a place for the stranger who needs it."

" Many thanks, fair sir," answered Geraint, touched by his courtesy; " so that I do not sup on sparrow-hawks, of which I have heard enough, the plainest fare will serve me. I have eaten no food for twelve hours or more."

The Earl smiled sadly. " We have no cause to love the Sparrow-hawk," he said ; " but come in, come in, without delay."

Then Geraint went into the castle court, and it was a scene of ruin on which he looked. Here a great part of a wall had fallen down, and ivy and flowers grew in the gaps of the stone ; there a tower stood with half its top crumbled away; the broken steps and grass-grown flagging — all lent an air of desolation. While he waited for his kindly host to announce his arrival, he heard, through an open window, the clear voice of a girl singing like a lark, so sweet and high were the notes.

It was the voice of Enid, Yniol's only daughter; and Geraint said to himself as he heard it : " Here, by God's grace, is the voice for me."

" Come," said the Earl, " Let us go in," and entering

the hall, which was dark and gloomy, he found an old
lady dressed in faded brocade, and, standing near her,
a lovely girl in the first bloom of youth.

" Enid," said the old Earl, " go fetch the stranger's
horse, and take him to his stall and feed him.   Then
go to the town and buy us meat and wine for supper."

Geraint sprang up, to forestall the maiden's services,
but the Earl waved him back.

" Friend," said he, " we are ruined, it is true, but
none the less we do not permit a guest to wait upon himself ; " and so the Prince said no more, though he hated
the idea of this girl acting as groom and messenger.

The three talked together till Enid returned from her
errand, with a lad behind her, carrying wine and meat,
bread and cakes.   Then the Earl and Countess sat
down with Geraint, and Enid waited on them, standing
behind their chairs; and she did all so sweetly and
willingly that Geraint began to love her : nevertheless,
he did not forget his errand, and as soon as his hunger
was satisfied, he told his name, and asked who might
the Sparrow-hawk be, of whom the townsfolk spoke
with bated breath.

" If he be the knight I saw ride into the gate of yon
castle," said he, " I have sworn to fight him, and
humble him, for his dwarf insulted the Queen's lady,
and when I would have remonstrated, struck at me
with his whip, and marked me, as you see.   I followed,
all unarmed as I was, and if you can lend me some
gear, I pray you let me have it, and we will see if
sparrow-hawks cannot be tamed."

" Are you Prince Geraint ? " cried the Earl; " then,
indeed, you are doubly welcome.   Your deeds are well

known in this house, and Enid has often heard me praise your doings, and ever asked to hear more. This Sparrow-hawk, who holds the town in awe, is my nephew, alas! and a worthless fellow.

"He cast his evil eye on Enid here, and because I refused her to him (who would not?), he sacked my house the night before her birthday, spread a foul slander that I had gold his father left him and kept it for myself, and holds me half a prisoner in mine own town, while he and his men riot about the streets, keeping the whole place in a ferment. I do not know if 'tis wisdom or cowardice, but I seem to have lost even the power of being angry with him."

"Lend me arms, sir," said Geraint, "and we will see who is the better man."

"My arms are old and rusty," said the Earl, "but such as they are, they are yours. The law of my nephew's tournament is somewhat curious. No man may tilt unless the lady he loves best is there. Two forks are fixed into the meadow-ground, over them is placed a silver wand, and over all a golden sparrow-hawk. The knight who would fain fight must claim that his lady is the fairest and worthiest there, and my nephew, being tall and big of bone, has ever won the victory for the lady with him, and overthrowing one good knight after another, has gained the name of Sparrow-hawk. But you, having no lady may not fight."

With sparkling eyes Geraint leaned towards his host. "Let me fight for your sweet daughter," said he earnestly, "for truly, though I have seen the fairest ladies of this land, she is the first that has touched my

heart. Should Heaven aid me in this fight, no other
maiden shall be my wife, if, indeed, you will give me
so great a prize."

The Earl gazed into the young man's face with surprise and pleasure, and gave consent, sudden as it
seemed; then calling the Countess, who was seated
some distance apart, he bade her seek Enid, and see if
her heart was turned towards the Prince.

Blushing and trembling, Enid heard all her mother
had to tell, and her only thought was wonder that so
great and mighty a prince, in green and gold, should
seek a simple maid like herself.

She lay awake all the night, too happy to sleep, and
in the morning she and her mother went their way to
the tournament.

All was set out as the Earl had described, and many
ladies watched from their raised seats. The Sparrow-
hawk was there, with a bold-looking beauty by his side,
and just as the Earl and Geraint, dressed in the rusty
armor, reached the field, he was preparing to hand
the silver wand and the golden bird to her saying:
" These two years have I won the prize, and for thee;
there is none that can stand against me — lo, it is
thine once more."

" Forbear!" cried Geraint, advancing in haste, " there
is a worthier;" and the bully, turning round, saw the
four — his uncle, aunt, the fair Enid, and Geraint.

With a scornful laugh he cried out, " Shalt fight for
it, then," and rushed at Geraint, without ceremony,
hoping to overthrow him at once by this sudden attack.

But he little knew his opponent, who had a rare
skill, and also great coolness. To and fro they clashed

together, the great blows ringing out, and for a time they seemed equally matched. Suddenly Geraint heard the Earl's voice crying out:

" Remember that great insult done to the Queen!" and with that word, a giant's strength seemed to possess him, and the next stroke clave the other's helmet, and laid him flat on the ground at his feet.

" Bending over him, with his foot upon his breast, Geraint said: " Thy name?"

" I am ashamed to tell it thee," groaned the wounded man. "Never have I been overthrown before. It is Edyrn, son of Nudd."

" Then," said Geraint sternly, " you will do these two things, or else I slay you on the spot. First you, with your lady and the dwarf, will ride to Arthur's Court, and there crave pardon for the insult done the Queen. Next, you will restore all that you robbed your kindred of, rebuilding what you destroyed, and you will take an oath never to repeat your crimes."

" My pride is broken," muttered Edyrn, " and Enid sees my fall. I will do thy will."

So Geraint let him rise, and, taking the glittering prize, he brought it to Enid, who, with shy, sweet eyes, thanked him prettily, remembering what his victory meant to her.

So the day ended, and the four, well pleased, sought the castle, and had a merry supper; while Edyrn, Sparrow-hawk no longer, made him ready to do Geraint's will. The Queen received him kindly, and forgave his wicked doings, and the fact of being mastered at last caused him to become a better man. He died in battle, fighting for his King.

Now there were brighter times for the Earl and all his house, for the news of Edyrn's downfall was spread abroad, and the townspeople, who had cringed to the Sparrow-hawk from fear, vied with each other in showing duty and kindness.   To the surprise of the Earl and Countess, Geraint held to his promise of returning to the Queen on the third day, in spite of the new joy that had come to him.   But he pleaded that Enid might ride with him and her father to the Court for the wedding.

It seemed a splendid thing to be married under Queen Guinevere's auspices, and Enid, seeing her parents approved, was glad to have it so.   But there was a little flaw in her joy.   All her pretty clothes were stolen when Edyrn sacked the house, and the only thing she had to wear was the faded silk she wore when Geraint first saw her.   She grew hot and cold by turns, as she pictured the haughty ladies of the Court, looking with scorn on the shabby girl in this poor dress.

While she fretted, her mother came to her smiling, holding a lovely gown of gold-embroidered silk.   It was the gown her parents had given her for her birthday present, and had, of course, disappeared with the other valuables.   After the tourney was over, many of their household goods had been brought back, this among them, fresh as ever.

But just as her mother had robed her in the lovely gown, her lover asked for her, and the Countess went to request him to wait for a few moments, and very naturally told the story.

To her utter surprise Geraint bade her carry this

message: " Tell her I beseech her, as she loves me, to ride with me in the faded silk she wore when first I saw her; I love it for her sake."

Poor Enid cried again, when she found the lovely dress must be doffed and the shabby one put on, but no thought of refusal crossed her mind; and soon she came to the hall, where Geraint awaited her, dressed in the same poor old silk.

Most lovingly Geraint kissed and thanked her, and told her: " The Queen made a request that when I should wed, she might adorn the bride, and I had the fancy that no other hand but hers should dress you. Therefore, I begged you to wear the faded silk. And, also, I longed to see if you loved me better than fine clothes. My sweet Enid, the Queen's words were, ' I will clothe her like the sun! ' "

So Enid was comforted; and a very happy party set forth to the Court. Queen Guinevere received Enid in the sweetest way, and at once set all her maids to work to prepare clothes for the wedding.

And all the Knights of the Round Table went to the wedding, and envied Geraint, and made pretty speeches to Enid, who looked her loveliest in a most exquisite gown of white silk and golden embroidery, which far outshone the dress she gave up at her lover's request. And they lived happily ever after.

CHAPTER V.

THE LAST BATTLE; OR, THE DEATH OF KING ARTHUR.

NOW, after many years, and more adventures than I have space to tell you, the peace of King Arthur's kingdom began to be troubled. This was mainly owing to an evil-disposed knight, called Sir Mordred, who was the King's nephew, his sister's son. He had always hated the King, and watched for an opportunity to harm him, though outwardly he professed the greatest affection. For years he had cherished the hope that if he could destroy the loyalty of the knights to King Arthur and each other, he might be able to gain a following and perhaps seize the throne. So he crept about the Court like a slow poison, dropping a word here and a suspicion there, till, as Tennyson says, "He left not Launcelot brave nor Galahad pure."

But for a long time he met with very little success, so strong was the devotion of the Knights of the Round Table to the King and each other. At last, however, he began to see a chance, and laid his plans with cunning. A number of the worthiest knights had gone away from the Court, each by a different way, on a quest called "The Quest of the Holy Grail," and with the best and truest of the brotherhood absent his task was easier.

By treachery he brought about a quarrel between Sir Launcelot and the King, and the former was dismissed the Court, though he had always been the greatest favorite and the one of all others nearest the King's heart.

Then Sir Launcelot left the Court in anger and bitterness, and those who thought him in the right followed him. This made the first breach. Next, news came that the kingdom was attacked on the northern shore, and King Arthur prepared to defend it. But Mordred's evil words had at last done their work, and he, breaking out in open revolt against his uncle, fled the Court, and a number of those whose hearts he had turned from the King went with him.

King Arthur learned, too late, what a traitor he had nurtured within the Court, and found himself not only harassed by invaders, but his kingdom torn by civil war. The poor King, grown old, bitterly lamented the absence of the true knights, Sir Percivale, Sir Galahad, Sir Gawaine, and others, but most of all he grieved over the loss of Sir Launcelot. Sad-hearted as he was, he led his army against the invaders, and day by day the battle raged.

Hearing of the troubles at home, Sir Percivale and Sir Gawaine left the quest and hurried back, but Sir Percivale died on the way. By this time Mordred's army was more to be dreaded than the northern invaders, and every day discontented knights joined themselves to his forces.

The King and his army were encamped near Salis-

bury, and there was to be a great battle. On the night
of Trinity Sunday the King had a very strange dream.
He thought he saw Sir Gawaine (who had been killed
in one of the first engagements after his return) alive
and well, and a great number of beautiful ladies with
him, all smiling and happy. In great amazement he
cried out: " Why, Gawaine, I thought thou wert dead!
How is it I see thee alive and well? and who are these
ladies with thee?"

" Sir," said Sir Gawaine, " these are the ladies for
whom I did battle when I was an errant knight, and
God has granted their prayer, and permitted them to
bring me to you that I may warn you of to-morrow.
For if you fight to-morrow with Sir Mordred you will
be slain, and the greater part of your people with you.
So God, of His most special grace, has sent me to you
to warn you that you put off the battle for a month,
and that shall be to your great gain. For in a month's
time Launcelot, whom you have banished, will come
with a great following, which he has gathered, and
fight for you, and by his hand Sir Mordred, the traitor,
shall die."

Then Sir Gawaine and the ladies vanished.

The King awoke, and called his knights and esquires
who slept near, and desired them to summon the elder
knights and the priests to him; he told them of the
vision, and it was agreed that King Arthur and Sir
Mordred were to have a parley together, and each was
only to bring fourteen men.

But King Arthur had not much faith in this truce,
and he warned his knights that if during the parley
they saw a single sword drawn they were to come on

and slay Sir Mordred at once. And Sir Mordred gave the same order to his followers.

Now, at first all went well, and after some wine had been brought the two leaders began to talk. Suddenly one of the knights with Sir Mordred felt an adder sting his foot, and he drew his sword to kill it. But at the sight of the drawn sword King Arthur's men made a rush, thinking it was the signal, and in a moment the two hosts were engaged in a desperate fight.

King Arthur mounted his horse when he found he could not prevent the fight, and the vision of the night was forgotten. This was the most terrible of all the many battles that had been fought; the two armies contended with a desperate fierceness which threatened the total destruction of both. The thickest of the fight was always about the King and Sir Mordred and both had received many serious wounds.

Heaps of slain lay about the field, and it was a dreadful sight on which the soft summer twilight closed. The King, exhausted with fatigue and his many wounds, had seated himself on the ground with his back against a tree. He gazed about to see what remained of his host, and lo! of all that gallant company there were but two left to him, Sir Lucan and his brother, Sir Bedivere.

"O great Heaven," said the King, "what has become of all my noble knights? Alas, that I should see this day! But now I would that I knew where that traitor Mordred is, that hath caused all this mischief."

Then looking about the field with his keen blue eyes, he saw where Sir Mordred leaned upon his sword by a heap of slain.

"Now," said the King to Sir Lucan, "give me my spear, for yonder is that traitor."

"Nay, my good lord," said Sir Lucan, "let him be for this day, and remember the vision ye had last night, and what the spirit of Sir Gawaine told you about the issue of this fight. Yet God in His great goodness has preserved your life so far. The victory is ours, for we have three left of our host, and Sir Mordred is alone alive of all his following. Therefore, if ye leave off now, this wicked day of destiny is done."

"Betide me death, betide me life," cried the King, "now I see him he shall not escape my hands!" and with that he gripped his spear in both hands, and rushed towards Sir Mordred, shouting, "Traitor! now is thy death-day come!"

And Sir Mordred came at the King with equal fierceness, but Arthur ran him through the body with his spear.

Sir Mordred felt this was his death-blow, but with one last despairing effort he struck the King's head with his sword, and it went through the helmet into the brain.

Down fell the wicked Sir Mordred, dead at last, and down went the King in a swoon, that looked like death.

Sir Lucan and Sir Bedivere took the stricken King up between them, weeping as they did so, and very feebly and painfully, for they, too, were badly wounded, they carried him off the field. They found a little half-ruined chapel, where they laid him and attended to his wounds. After a time he came to himself, but was so weak and faint they felt sure his end was near.

From the field they heard the sounds made by the half-drunken robbers, who were pillaging the bodies of the slain; and, with a thrill of horror, the faithful two begged the King to let them carry him to the nearest town, where perhaps a surgeon might be found, and they again took him up in their arms.

But with the effort poor Sir Lucan, who had been bleeding for a long time, suddenly fell to the ground, and when Sir Bedivere felt his heart he found he was dead.

Then King Arthur lamented bitterly the death of all his knights save one.

"My time is at hand," said he, "when I must go; therefore, Sir Bedivere, I ask of you one last service."

"Speak on, Sire," said Sir Bedivere, weeping.

"Take Excalibur, the magic sword, which was given me by the Lady of the Lake, and carry it to yonder mere, and throw it in, and bring me word what happens."

"My good lord, it shall be done," said Sir Bedivere, and he took the sword, which had been King Arthur's companion day and night, and departed on his errand. But as he went the matchless beauty of the sword tempted him. For it was like no other sword in the world: the pommel and hilt were a mass of precious stones, rubies, diamonds, sapphires, and emeralds.

The moon had risen by this time, and in its white beams the sword shone with a magical glory, and it seemed to say to him: "Hide me, and keep me, that you may have me for your own." So, forgetful of his promise, he hid the sword under a tree, and going back to the dying King, he said he had done his bidding.

"What did you see and hear?" said the King, lifting his heavy eyes to Sir Bedivere's face.

"I saw the reeds by the lake-side quiver, and I heard the rippling waters flow."

The blue eyes grew stern. "You are lying," said the King. "Now go, and do my command, spare not, but throw it in, and bring me word."

Sir Bedivere returned again, and took the sword in his hand. And yet it seemed a sin to throw away the noble blade, which had done such deeds, so once more he hid it, and came again to the King, saying he had done his will.

"What saw you?" said the King, "and what heard you?"

"Sir," said Sir Bedivere, trying vainly to look him in the face, "I saw nothing but the quivering reeds, and heard nothing but the rippling water."

Then the old strength and fire blazed up in King Arthur's eyes, and with a terrible voice he cried out: "Ah, miserable, unkind, untrue! you are lying to me still — to me, your King, wounded and helpless! Now, for the last time I bid you throw away the sword, and if you fail me again I shall arise and slay you with these hands, weak as I am!"

Then Sir Bedivere was bitterly ashamed, and went away with the determination to do the King's will.

He reached the mere for the third time, and, grasping the sword with both hands, he shut his eyes that he might not again be tempted, and with a mighty whirl he flung it far into the bosom of the lake. As it flew from his hand he opened his eyes and beheld a marvellous sight — a hand and arm clothed in white

glistening cloth caught Excalibur as it fell, brandished
it three times, as if in farewell, and drew it in beneath
the water.

Sir Bedivere stood gazing in wonder and awe for a
moment, then muttering, "The King knew of this,"
turned and hurried back.

Once more Arthur raised his eyes to Sir Bedivere's
face. "Now see I by thine eyes that this is done,"
said he faintly. Sir Bedivere told him what he had
seen. "Alas!" said the King, "I have tarried over
long. Take me on your shoulders and bear me to
yonder mere, for there be those who wait for me."

It was a terrible task for poor Sir Bedivere to carry
the King, who was now quite incapable of helping himself; but, with the strength born of desperation, he
managed to stagger along until he reached the borders
of the lake. Then they saw a funeral barge, draped in
black from stem to stern, and in it were many fair
ladies, all dressed in black hoods and veils, and they all
burst into weeping when they saw the King.

"Now put me into the barge," said the King, and so
he did, carefully; and there received him three Queens
with great mourning. And these three Queens sat
down, and in one of their laps King Arthur laid his
head. And then that Queen said, "Ah, dear brother,
why hast thou tarried so long from me?" And she
smoothed the damp hair from his brow, kissed him,
and wept bitterly.

And the other Queens drew near and joined their
tears to hers. One was King Arthur's sister, Morgan
Le Fay, the other was the Queen of North Wales, and
the third was the Queen of the Waste Lands. And

there was Nimue, who wedded Sir Pelleas, the Good
Knight, and the rest were their attendants. And so
then they rowed from the land, and Sir Bedivere cried
out as he saw them go: " Ah, my lord Arthur, what
will become of me now ye go from me, leaving me here
alone among mine enemies."

"Comfort thyself," said King Arthur, "and do as
well as thou mayest, for these will bear me into the
vale of Avilion, where the wind never blows loudly, and
where perpetual summer reigns."

Then the black-draped barge, with its sorrowful company, disappeared from Sir Bedivere's sight, and the
sound of wailings died on the wind; and as soon as he
had lost sight of the barge he wept and lamented, and,
taking to the forest, he travelled all night.

As day broke, he saw, between two hills, a little
chapel and an hermitage. Then Sir Bedivere was glad,
and, entering the chapel, he saw a hermit praying
devoutly beside a new-dug grave.

"Reverend sir," said Sir Bedivere, "what man is
there buried that ye pray so fast for?"

"My fair son," said the hermit, "I can only guess
who lies here; but last night at midnight there came
a great number of ladies, clothed in black, who brought
a dead body, and prayed me to bury it."

"Alas!" cried Sir Bedivere, "that was King Arthur," and he fell down in a swoon.

The hermit tended him carefully, and when he came
to himself, Sir Bedivere begged that he might live with
him all his days with fasting and prayers. "For," said
he, "from hence will I never go by my will, but will
spend what time remaineth to me in prayer for my lord
King Arthur."

So the knight put off his armor, and dressed himself in the poor clothes such as the hermit wore, and lived there till his death.

And when Queen Guinevere understood that the King and all that noble host were slain, she stole away by night from the Court, and five faithful ladies went with her. With the dawn they reached the Convent at Amesbury, and, summoning the portress, she begged audience of the Abbess. When admitted to the presence of the reverend mother, she said: " I have lost all that I hold dearest in this world, and crave to be allowed to live among you unknown by name."

Touched by her beauty and the earnestness of her entreaties, the Abbess granted her wish; and so Queen Guinevere, the pride of Arthur's Court, ended her life in prayer and fasting.

CHILDE HORN

THERE dwelt once in Southland a King named Altof, who was rich, powerful, and gentle. His Queen was named Gotthild, and they had a young son called Horn. The rain never rained, the sun never shone upon a fairer boy; his skin was like roses and lilies, and as clear as glass; and he was as brave as he was handsome. At fifteen years old his like was not to be seen in all the kingdoms around. He had a band of playfellows, twelve boys of noble birth, but not one of them could throw the ball so high as Horn. Out of the twelve, two were his special companions, and one of them, Athulf, was the best of the company, while the other, Figold, was altogether the worst.

It came to pass one summer morning that good King Altof was riding on the sea-shore with only two attendants, and he looked out to sea and saw fifteen ships lying in the offing. It was the heathen Vikings who had come from Northland, bent on plundering Christian lands. When these saw the three Norsemen, they swarmed on to shore like a pack of wolves, all armed and full of battle fury. They slew the King and his knights, and made themselves masters of the whole land.

Queen Gotthild wept much for her lord, and more for her son, Childe Horn, who could not now ascend his father's throne. She clad herself in mourning garments, the meanest she could find, and went to dwell in a cave, where she prayed night and day for her son, that he might be preserved from the malice of his enemies, at whose mercy he and his comrades lay. At first they thought to have slain him, but one of their leaders was touched by his glorious beauty, and so he said to the boy, "Horn, you are a fair stripling and a bold, and when you come to years, you and your band here, you are like to prove too many for us, so I am going to put you all in a boat and let it drift out to sea — where may the Gods preserve you, or else send you to the bottom; but, for all our sakes, you cannot remain here."

Then they led the boys down to the shore, placed them in a little skiff, and pushed it off from the land. All but Horn wrung their hands in fear. The waves rose high, and, as the boat was tossed up and down, the lads gave themselves up for lost, not knowing whither they were driven; but when the morning of the second day broke, Horn sprang up from where he sat in the forepart of the skiff, crying, "I hear the birds sing, and I see the grass growing green — we are at the land!" Then they sprang right gladly on shore, and Horn called after the boat as it floated away, "A good voyage to thee, little boat! May wind and wave speed thee back to Southland. Greet all who knew me, and chiefly the good Queen Gotthild, my mother. And tell the heathen King that some day he shall meet his death at my hand."

Then the boys went on till they came to a city, where reigned King Aylmer of Westland — whom God reward for his kindness to them. He asked them in mild words whence they came, " for in good sooth," said he, " never have I seen so well-favored a company " ; and Horn answered proudly, " We are of good Christian blood, and we come from Southland, which has just been raided by pagans, who slew many of our people, and sent us adrift in a boat, to be the sport of the winds and waves. For a day and a night we have been at sea without a rudder ; and now we have been cast upon your coast, you may enslave or slay us, but, if it please thee, show us mercy."

Then the good King asked, " What is your name, my child ? " and the boy answered, " Horn, at your pleasure, my Lord King ; and if you need a servant, I will serve you well and truly."

" Childe Horn," said the King, " you bear a mighty name for one so young and tender.

" Over hills and valleys oft the horn has rung,
In the royal palace long the horn has hung.
So shall thy name, O Hornchild, through every land resound,
And the fame of thy wondrous beauty in all the West be found."

So Horn found great favor with the King, and he put him in charge of Athelbrus, the house-steward, that he might teach him all knightly duties, and he spared no pains with him, nor yet with his companions; but well trained as they all were, Horn was far ahead of them both in stature and noble bearing. Even a stranger looking at him could guess his lofty birth, and the splendor of his marvellous beauty, lit up all the palace ; while he won all hearts, from the meanest grooms to the greatest of the court ladies.

Now the fairest thing in that lordly court was the King's only daughter, Riminild. Her mother was dead, and she was well-beloved of her father, as only children are. Not a word had she ever ventured to speak to Horn when she saw him among the other knights at the great feasts, but day and night she bore his image in her heart. One night she dreamed that he entered her apartments (and she wondered much at his boldness), and in the morning she sent for Athelbrus, the house-steward, and bade him conduct Horn into her presence. But he went to Athulf, who was the pure minded and true one of Horn's two chosen companions, while Figold, the other, was a wolf in sheep's clothing, and said to him, " You shall go with me in Horn's stead to the Princess."

So he went, and she, not recognizing him in the ill-lighted room, stretched out her hand to him, crying, " Oh, Horn, I have loved you long. Now plight me your troth."

But Athulf whispered to her, " Hold ! I am not Horn. I am but his friend, Athulf, as unlike him as may well be. Horn's little finger is fairer than my whole body ; and were he dead, or a thousand miles off, I would not play him false."

Then Riminild rose up in anger and glared upon the old steward, crying, " Athelbrus, you wicked man, out of my sight, or I shall hate you for evermore ! All shame and ill befall you if you bring me not Childe Horn himself ! "

" Lady and Princess," answered Athelbrus warily,

"listen, and I will tell you why I brought Athulf. The King entrusted Horn to my care, and I dread his anger. Now be not angry with me, and I will fetch him forthwith."

Then he went away, but, instead of Horn, this time he called Figold, the deceiver, and said to him, "Come with me, instead of Horn, to the royal Princess. Do not betray yourself, lest we both suffer for it."

Willingly went the faithless one with him, but to Figold the maid held not out her hand — well she knew that he was false, and she drove him from her presence in rage and fury. Athelbrus feared her anger, and said to himself, "To make my peace with her I must now send her the true Horn." He found him in the hall presenting the wine cup to the King, and whispered to him, "Horn, you are wanted in the Princess's apartments;" and when Horn heard this his hand holding the full goblet so trembled that the wine ran over the edge. He went straight into the presence of the royal maiden, and as he knelt before her his beauty seemed to light up the room.

"Fair befall thee and thy maidens, O Lady!" said he. "The house-steward has sent me hither to ask thy will."

Then Riminild stood up, her cheeks red as the dawn, and told him of her love; and Horn took counsel with himself how he should answer her.

"May God in heaven bless him whom thou weddest, whoever he may be," he said. "I am but a foundling, and the King's servant to boot — it would be against all rule and custom were he to wed me with thee."

When Riminild heard this her heart died within her,

and she fell fainting on the floor ; but Horn lifted her up, and advised her to request her father that he might now receive knighthood. " And then," said he, " I will win you by my brave deeds."

When she heard that, she recovered herself and said, " Take my ring here to Master Athelbrus, and bid him from me ask the King to make you a knight."

So Horn went and told all to Athelbrus, who sought the King forthwith, and said, " To-morrow is a festival; I counsel thee to admit Horn to knighthood." And the King was pleased, and said, " Good! Horn is well worthy of it. I will create him a knight to-morrow, and he himself shall confer it on his twelve companions."

The next day the newly knighted one went to Rimi-nild's bower, and told her that now he was her own true knight, and must go forth to do brave deeds in her name, and she said she would trust him evermore, and she gave him a gold ring with her name graven on it, which would preserve him from all evil. " Let this remind thee of me early and late," she said, " and thou canst never fall by treachery." And then they kissed each other, and she closed the door behind him, with tears.

The other knights were feasting and shouting in the King's hall, but Horn went to the stable, armed from head to foot. He stroked his coal-black steed, then sprang upon his back and rode off, his armor ringing as he went. Down to the seashore he galloped, singing joyously and praying God soon to send him the chance to do some deed of knightly daring, and there he met a band of pagan marauders, who had just landed from their pirate-ship. Horn asked them civilly what they wanted there, and one of the pagans answered insolently, "To conquer the land and slay all that dwell in it, as we did to King Altof, whose son now serves a foreign lord."

Horn, on hearing this, drew his sword and struck off the fellow's head; then he thought of his dead father and of his mother in her lonely cave; he looked on his ring and thought of Riminild, and dashed among the pirates, laying about him right and left, till, I warrant you, there were few of them left to tell the tale. "This," he cried, "is but the foretaste of what will be when I return to my own land and avenge my father's death!"

Then he rode back to the palace and told the King how he had slain the invaders, and "Here," he said, "is the head of their leader, to requite thee, O King, for granting me knighthood."

The next day the King went a-hunting in the forest, and the false Figold rode at his side, but Horn stayed at home. And Figold spoke to the King out of his wicked heart and said, "I warn thee, King Aylmer, Horn is plotting to dishonor thee — to rob thee of thy daughter and of thy kingdom to boot. He is even now plotting with her in her bower."

Then the King galloped home in a rage, and burst into Riminild's bower, and there, sure enough, he found Horn, as Figold had said. "Out of my land, base foundling!" he cried. "What have you to do with the young Queen here?"

And Horn departed without a word. He went to the stable, saddled his horse, then he girded on his

sword and returned to the palace; he crossed the hall
and entered Riminild's apartments for the last time.
"Lady," he said, "I must go forth to strange lands
for seven years; at the end of that time I will either
return or send a messenger; but if I do neither, you
may give yourself to another, nor wait longer for me.
Now kiss me a long farewell."

Riminild promised to be true to him, and she took a
gold ring from her finger, saying, "Wear this above
the other which I gave you, or if you grow weary of
them, fling them both away, and watch to see if its
two stones change color; for if I die, the one will turn
pale, and if I am false, the other will turn red."

"Riminild," said Childe Horn, "I am yours for evermore! There is a pool of clear water under a tree in
the garden — go there daily and look for my shadow in
the water. If you see it not, know that I am un-
altered; and if you see it, know that I no longer love
thee."

Then they embraced and kissed each other, and Horn
parted from her, and rode down to the coast, and took
passage on a ship bound for Ireland. When he landed
there, two of its King's sons met him, and took him to
their father, good King Thurstan, before whom Horn
bowed low, and the King bade him welcome, and
praised his beauty, and asked his name.

"My name is Good Courage," said Horn boldly, and
the King was well pleased.

Now, at Christmas, King Thurstan made a great
feast, and in the midst of it one rushed in crying,
"Guests, O King! We are besieged by five heathen
chiefs, and one of them proclaims himself ready to fight

any three of our knights single handed to-morrow at sunrise."

" That would be but a sorry Christmas service," said King Thurstan; "who can advise me how best to answer them?" Then Horn spoke up from his seat at the table, "If these pagans are ready to fight, one against three, what may not a Christian dare? I will adventure myself against them all, and one after another they shall go down before my good sword."

Heavy of heart was King Thurstan that night, and little did he sleep. But " Sir Good Courage " rose early and buckled on his armor. Then he went to the King and said, " Now, Sir King, come with me to the field, and I will show you in what coin to pay the demands of these heathen." So they rode on together in the twilight, till they came to a green meadow, where a giant was waiting for them. Horn greeted him with a blow that brought him to the ground at once, and ran another giant through the heart with his sword; and when their followers saw that their leaders were slain, they turned and fled back to the shore, but Horn tried to cut them off from their ships, and in the scrimmage the King's two sons fell. At this Horn was sore grieved, and he fell upon the pagans in fury, and slew them right and left, to avenge the King and himself.

Bitterly wept King Thurstan when his sons were brought home to him on their biers; there was great mourning for the young princes, who were buried with high honors in the vault under the church. Afterwards the King called his knights together and said to Horn, " Good Courage, but for you we were all dead men. I

will make you my heir; you shall wed my daughter
Swanhild, who is bright and beautiful as the sunshine,
and shall reign here after me."

So Horn lived there for six years, always under the
name of Good Courage, but he sent no messenger to
Riminild, not wishing any man to know his secret, and
consequently Riminild was in great sorrow on his
account, not knowing whether he was true to her or
not. Moreover, the King of a neighboring country
sought her hand in marriage, and her father now fixed
a day for the wedding.

One morning, as Horn was riding to the forest, he
saw a stranger standing by the wayside, who, on being
questioned, said, "I come from Westland, and I seek
the Knight Sir Horn. Riminild the maiden is in
sore heaviness of spirit, bewailing herself day and
night, for on Sunday next she is to be married to a
King."

Then was Horn's grief as great as that of Riminild.
His eyes overflowed with tears. He looked at his ring
with its colored stones; the one had not turned red,
but it seemed to him that the other was turning pale.
"Well knew my heart that you would keep your troth
with me, Riminild," said he to himself, "and that
never would that stone grow red; but this paling one
bodes ill. And you doubtless have often looked in the
garden pool for my shadow, and have seen naught there
but your own lovely image. *That* shadow shall never
come, O sweet love, Riminild, to prove to you that
your love is false, but he himself shall come and drive
all shadows away.

"And you, my trusty messenger," he said aloud,

" go back to maid Riminild and tell her that she shall indeed wed a King next Sunday, for before the church bells ring for service I will be with her."

The Princess Riminild stood on the beach and looked out to sea, hoping to see Horn coming in his helmet and shield to deliver her; but none came, save her own messenger, who was washed up on the shore — drowned! And she wrung her hands in her anguish.

Horn had gone immediately to King Thurstan, and, after saluting him, told him his real name and his present trouble. "And now, O King," said he, "I pray you to reward me for all my services by helping me to get possession of Riminild. Your daughter, Swanhild, will I give to a man the best and faithfullest ever called to the ranks of knighthood."

Then said the King, "Horn, follow your own counsel;" then he sent for his knights, and many of them followed Horn, so that he had a thousand or more at his command. The wind favored their course, and in a few hours the ships cast anchor on the shore of Westland. Horn left his forces in a wood while he went on to learn what was doing. Well did he know the way, and lightly did he leap over the stones. As he went he met a pilgrim, and asked him the latest news, who answered, "I come from a wedding feast — but the bride's true love is far away, and she only weeps. I could not stay to see her grief."

"May God help me!" said Horn; "but this is sorrowful news. Let us change garments, good pilgrim. I must go to this feast, and once there I vow I will give them something by which to remember Horn!"

He blackened his eyebrows, and took the pilgrim's hat and staff, and when he reached the gate of the palace, the porter was for turning him back, but Horn took him up and flung him over the bridge, and then went on to the hall where the feast was being held. He sat down among the lowest, on the beggars' bench, and glowered round from under his blackened eyebrows. At a distance he saw Riminild sitting like one in a dream; then she rose up to pour out mead and wine for the knights and squires, and Horn cried out, "Fair Queen, if ye would have God's blessing, let the beggar's turn come next."

She set down the flagon of wine, and poured him out brown beer in a jug, saying, "There, drink that off at a draught, thou boldest of beggar men!" But he gave it to the beggars, his companions, saying, "I am not come to drink jugs of beer, but goblets of wine. Fair Queen," he cried, "thou deemest me a beggar, but I am rather a fisherman, come to haul in my net, which I left seven years ago hanging from a fair hand here in Westland." Then was Riminild much troubled within herself, and she looked hard at Horn. She reached him the goblet and said, "Drink wine then, fisherman, and tell me who thou art."

He drank from the goblet, and then dropped into it the gold ring, and said, "Look, O Queen, at what thou findest in the goblet, and ask no more who I am." The Queen withdrew into her bower with her four maidens, and when she saw the gold ring that she had given to Horn, she was sore distressed, and cried out, "Childe Horn must be dead, for this is his ring."

She then sent one of her waiting-maids to command

the stranger to her presence, and Horn, all unrecognized, appeared before her. "Tell me, honest pilgrim, where thou gottest this ring?" she asked him.

"I took it," said he, "from the finger of a man whom I found lying sick unto death in a wood. Loudly he was bewailing himself and the lady of his heart, one Riminild, who should at this time have wedded him." As he spoke he drew his cap down over his eyes, which were full of tears.

Then Riminild cried, "Break, heart, in my bosom! Horn is no more — he who hath already caused thee so many tender pangs." She threw herself on her couch and called for a knife, to kill the bridegroom and herself.

Her maidens shrieked with fear, but Horn flung his arms around her and pressed her to his heart. Then he cast away hat and staff, and wiped the brown stain from his face, and stood up before his love in his own fair countenance, asking, "Dear love, Riminild, know you me not now? Away with your grief and kiss me — I am Horn! — Horn, your true lover and born slave."

She gazed into his eyes. At first she could not believe that it was he, but at last she could doubt no longer; she fell upon his neck, and in the sweet greetings that followed were two sick hearts made whole.

"Horn, you miscreant! how could you play me such a trick?"

"Have patience, sweet love, maid Riminild, and I will tell you all. Now let me go and finish my work, and when it is done I will come and rest at your side."

So he left her, and went back to the forest, and Riminild sent for Athulf, who met her with a doleful countenance. "Athulf!" she cried, "rejoice with me! Horn has come — I tell you Horn is here!"

"Alas!" said Athulf, "that cannot be. Who hath brought thee such an idle tale? Day and night have I stood here watching for him, but he came not, and much I fear me the noble Horn is dead."

"I tell you he is living," she said — "aye, and more alive than ever. Go to the forest and find him — he is there with all his faithful followers."

Athulf made haste to the forest, still unbelieving, but soon his heart bounded for joy, for there rode Horn in his shining armor at the head of his troops. Athulf rode to his side, and they returned together to the city, where Riminild was watching them from her turret. And Horn pointed to her and cried to his company, "Knights, yonder is my bride — help me to win her!"

Then was there a fierce storming of the gate — the shock of it shook Riminild's tower — and Horn and his heroes burst, all unheralded, into the King's hall. Fierce and furious was the bridal dance that followed; the tumult of it rose up to Riminild, and she prayed, "God preserve my lover in this wild confusion!"

Right merrily danced her dancer, and all unscathed he flashed through the hall, thanks to his true love and God's care. King Aylmer and the bridegroom confronted him, and the younger, the bridegroom King, asked him what he sought there. "I seek my bride," said he, "and if you do not give her up to me I will have your life."

"Better thou shouldst have the bride than that,"

said the other; " though I would sooner be torn in
pieces than give thee either." And he defended himself bravely, but it availed him naught. Horn struck
off his head from his shoulders, so that it bounded
across the hall. Then cried Horn to the other guests,
" The dance is over!" after which he proclaimed a
truce, and, throwing himself down on a couch, spake
thus to King Aylmer : " I was born in Southland, of a
royal race. The pagan Vikings slew King Altof, my
father, and put me out to sea with my twelve companions. You did train me for the order of knighthood,
and I have dishonored it by no unworthy deeds, though
you did drive me from your kingdom, thinking I meant
to disgrace you through your daughter. But that
which you credited me with I never contemplated.
Accept me then, O King, for your son-in-law. Yet will
I not claim my bride till I have won back my kingdom
of Southland. That will I accomplish quickly, with
the help of my brave knights and such others as I pray
you to lend me, leaving in pledge therefor the fairest
jewel in my crown, until King Horn shall be able
to place Queen Riminild beside him on his father's
throne."

As he spoke Riminild entered, and Horn took her
hand and led her to her father, and the young couple
stood before the old King — a right royal pair. Then
King Aylmer spoke jestingly, " Truly I once did chide
a young knight in my wrath, but never King Horn,
whom I now behold for the first time. Never would I
have spoken roughly to King Horn, much less forbidden
him to woo a Princess."

Then all the knights and lords came offering their

good wishes to the happy pair; and the old house-steward, Athelbrus, would have bent the knee to his former pupil, but Horn took the old man in his arms and embraced him, thanking him for all the pains he had taken with his breeding.

Horn's twelve companions came also, and did him homage as their sovereign, and he rejoiced to see them all, but especially Athulf the brave and true. "Athulf," he told him, " thou hast helped me to win my bride here, now come with me to Southland and help me to make a home for her. And you, too, shall win a lady — I have already chosen her; her name is Swanhild, and she will look fair even beside Riminild." Then did Athulf rejoice, but Figold, the traitor, was ready to sink into the ground with shame and envy.

Then Horn returned to his ship, taking Athulf with him, but Figold he left behind. Truly it is ill knowing what to do with a traitor, whether you take him to the field or leave him at home.

On went the ship before a favoring wind; the voyage lasted but four days. Horn landed at midnight, and he and Athulf went inland together. On the way they came upon a noble-looking knight asleep under his shield, upon which a cross was painted, and Horn cried to him, " Awake, and tell us what they are doing here. Thou seemest to be a Christian, I trow, else would I have hewn thee in pieces with my sword ! "

The good knight sprang up aghast, and said, "Against my will I am serving the heathen who rule here. I am keeping a place ready for Horn, the best loved of all heroes. Long I have wondered why he does not bestir himself to return and fight for his own. God

give him power so to do till he slay every one of these
miscreants. They put him out to sea, a tender boy,
with his twelve playmates, one of whom was my only
son, Athulf. Dearly he loved Horn, and was beloved
by him. Could I but see them both once more, I
should feel that I could die in peace."

"Then rejoice," they told him, "for Horn and
Athulf are here!"

Joyfully did the old man greet the youths; he embraced his son and bent the knee to Horn, and all three
rejoiced together.

"Where is your company?" asked the old knight.
"I suppose you two have come to explore the land.
Well, your mother still lives, and if she knew you to
be living would be beside herself with joy."

"Blessed be the day that I and my men landed here,"
said Horn. "We will catch these heathen dogs, or
else tame them. We will speak to them in our own
language."

Then Horn blew his horn, so that all on board the
ship heard it and came on shore. As the young birds
long for the dawn, so Horn longed for the fight that
should free his country from her enemies. From morning to night the battle raged, till all the heathen, young
and old, were slain, and young King Horn himself slew
the pirate King. Then he went to church, with all his
people, and an anthem was sung to the glory of God,
and Horn gave thanks aloud for the restoration of his
kingdom, after which he sought the place where his
mother dwelt. How his heart wept for joy when he
saw her! He placed a crown on her head, and arrayed
her in rich robes, and brought her up to the palace.

"Thou art glad to have thy child again," he said to her in the joy of his heart, "but I will make thee gladder still by bringing thee home a daughter, one who will please thee well." And he thought of his love, Riminild, with whom, however, things were just then going very much amiss.

For as soon as Horn had departed, the treacherous Figold had collected a great army of workmen and made them build him a tower in the sea, which could only be reached when the tide was out. Now about this time Horn had a dream, in which he saw Riminild on board a ship at sea, which presently went to pieces, and she tried to swim ashore, steering with her lily white hand, while Figold, the traitor, sought to stop her with the point of his sword. Then he awoke and cried, "Athulf, true friend, we must away across the sea. Unless we make all speed some evil will befall us." And in the midst of a storm they set sail.

In the meantime Figold had left his tower and appeared in the presence of King Aylmer. Cunningly, out of his false heart spoke the traitor, "King Aylmer, Horn has sent me word that he would have his bride handed over to my care. He has regained his crown and realm and would fain have her there to be his Queen."

"Very well," said the King, "let her go with thee."

But Riminild was much displeased at the thought of being put into the hands of Figold, whom in her soul she would not trust.

"Why comes not Horn for me himself?" she asked. "I know not the way to his kingdom either by land or by sea."

"But I know it," said Figold, "and I will soon bring thee thither, most beauteous queen." But his wicked smile made her uneasy at heart.

"If Horn could not come himself," she said, "why did he not send Athulf, his faithful friend?" But this question pleased the traitor so little that he gave her no answer.

Her father blessed her, and she set forth, wringing her white hands.

Meanwhile, Horn, sailing from the south, was driven in shore by a storm, and he beheld Figold's high tower, and asked who had built such an ugly thing. He thought he heard a low murmuring as his ship flew past it before the wind, but knew not what it might be. Soon he saw the battlements of King Aylmer's palace rising in the distance; there Riminild should be, looking out for him, but all was bare and empty. It seemed to him as though a star were missing from heaven; and as he crossed the threshold the ill news was told him how Figold had carried off Riminild. Horn had no mind to linger with the King. "Come, Athulf, true friend," said he, "and help me to search for her." So they searched far and near, in vain, till at last Horn remembered that strange tower in the sea, and set sail for the lonely fortress where Figold had the fair princess in his evil keeping. "Now, my eleven companions, and you, too, Athulf," said he, "abide here while I go up alone with my horn. God hath shown me how to order this attempt."

He left his sword on the ship, and took only a fishing line with a long hook. Then round and round the tower he walked, and he blew a loud blast out into the raging storm, until a head appeared out of a hole in the wall of the tower — it was that wicked knave Figold's; and Horn cast his line, and hauled the writhing traitor clean out of the tower. He whirled round the sea-wolf at the end of the line, and swung him over the water by the sheer force of his arm, so that he was cast over to Athulf in the ship; and sore afraid was the traitor when the true men on board seized him.

Then Horn took up his bugle once more and sounded it so loudly that at the first blast the door was uncovered; at the second he could enter the tower; the third was heard as he led Riminild forth. Lightly did he clasp her round the waist and swing her into his boat, and then pulled for the ship.

He brought Riminild on board his ship, and called to his band, " Ho there, my trusty eleven! Our voyage is ended, and we will now go merrily home. And you, Athulf, my chosen and tried friend, shall now have your guerdon; I will bring you to your bride Swanhild, and Riminild and I will be wedded at the same time — the same wedding feast shall serve us both."

" And Riminild, my sweet pearl, whom I have rescued from the deep, not all that I have suffered on your account grieves me like the perfidy this false one wrought on you, my loving heart. Through him the goodly tale of my twelve followers is broken; now when they gather round the table, one seat will ever be empty. Must it ever be that no dozen of men can be got together but one will prove a traitor? "

Then he bade them " Set the traitor in the boat and let it drift out to sea, as we poor children were made

to do aforetime.   Let the waves bear away treachery
as once they bore innocence — our ship will make better speed : and as for him, let him drift till he find a
land where no traitors are."

THE STORY OF BEOWULF

CHAPTER I.

GRENDEL THE MONSTER.

OLD KING HROTHGAR built for himself a great palace, covered with gold, with benches all round outside, and a terrace leading up to it. It was bigger than any hall men had ever heard of, and there Hrothgar sat on his throne to share with men the good things God had given him. A band of brave knights gathered round him, all living together in peace and joy.

But there came a wicked monster, Grendel, out of the moors. He stole across the fens in the thick darkness, and touched the great iron bars of the door of the hall, which immediately sprang open. Then, with his eyes shooting out flame, he spied the knights sleeping after battle. With his steel finger-nails the hideous fiend seized thirty of them in their sleep. He gave yells of joy, and sped as quick as lightning across the moors, to reach his home with his prey.

When the knights awoke, they raised a great cry of sorrow, whilst the aged King himself sat speechless with grief. None could do battle with the monster, he was too strong, too horrible for any one to conquer. For twelve long years Grendel warred against Hrothgar; like a dark shadow of death he prowled round about the hall, and lay in wait for his men on the misty moors. One thing he could not touch, and that was the King's sacred throne.

Now there lived in a far-off land a youngster called Beowulf, who had the strength of thirty men. He heard of the wicked deeds of Grendel, and the sorrow of the good King Hrothgar. So he had made ready a strong ship, and with fourteen friends set sail to visit Hrothgar, as he was in need of help. The good ship flew over the swelling ocean like a bird, till in due time the voyagers saw shining white cliffs before them. Then they knew their journey was at an end; they made fast their ship, grasped their weapons, and thanked God that they had had an easy voyage.

Now the coastguard spied them from a tower. He set off to the shore, riding on horseback, and brandishing a huge lance.

"Who are you," he cried, "bearing arms and openly landing here? I am bound to know from whence you come before you make a step forward. Listen to my plain words, and hasten to answer me." Beowulf made answer that they came as friends, to rid Hrothgar of his wicked enemy Grendel, and at that the coastguard led them on to guide them to the King's palace. Downhill they ran together, with a rushing sound of voices and armed tread, until they saw the hall shining like gold against the sky. The guard bade them go straight to it, then, wheeling round on his horse, he said, "It is time for me to go. May the Father of all keep you in safety. For myself, I must guard the coast."

The street was paved with stone, and Beowulf's men marched along, following it to the hall, their armor shining in the sun and clanging as they went. They reached the terrace, where they set down their broad shields. Then they seated themselves on the bench, while they stacked their spears together and made themselves known to the herald.

Hrothgar speedily bade them welcome. They entered the great hall with measured tread, Beowulf leading the way. His armor shone like a golden network, and his look was high and noble, as he said, " Hail, O King! To fight against Grendel single-handed have I come. Grant me this, that I may have this task alone, I and my little band of men. I know that the terrible monster despises weapons, and therefore I shall bear neither sword, nor shield, nor buckler. Hand to hand I will fight the foe, and death shall come to whomsoever God wills. If death overtakes me, then will the monster carry away my body to the swamps, so care not for my body, but send my armor to my King. My fate is in God's hands."

Hrothgar loved the youth for his noble words, and bade him and his men sit down to the table and merrily share the feast, if they had a mind to do so. As they feasted, a minstrel sang with a clear voice. The Queen, in cloth of gold, moved down the hall and handed the jewelled cup of mead to the King and all the warriors, old and young. At the right moment, with gracious words, she brought it to Beowulf. Full of pride and high purpose, the youth drank from the splendid cup, and vowed that he would conquer the enemy or die.

When the sun sank in the west, all the guests arose.

The King bade Beowulf guard the house, and watch
for the foe. " Have courage," he said, " be watchful,
resolve on success. Not a wish of yours shall be left
unfulfilled, if you perform this mighty deed."

Then Beowulf lay down to rest in the hall, putting
off from him his coat of mail, helmet, and sword.

Through the dim night Grendel came stealing. All
slept in the darkness, all but one! The door sprang
open at the first touch that the monster gave it. He
trod quickly over the paved floor of the hall; his eyes
gleamed as he saw a troop of kinsmen lying together
asleep. He laughed as he reckoned on sucking the life
of each one before day broke. He seized a sleeping
warrior, and in a trice had crunched his bones. Then
he stretched out his hand to seize Beowulf on his bed.
Quickly did Beowulf grip his arm; he stood up full
length and grappled with him with all his might, till
his fingers cracked as though they would burst. Never
had Grendel felt such a grip; he had a mind to go, but
could not. He roared, and the hall resounded with his
yells, as up and down he raged, with Beowulf holding
him in a fast embrace. The benches were overturned,
the timbers of the hall cracked, the beautiful hall was
all but wrecked. Beowulf's men had seized their
weapons and thought to hack Grendel on every side,
but no blade could touch him. Still Beowulf held him
by the arm; his shoulder cracked, and he fled, wounded
to death, leaving hand, arm, and shoulder in Beowulf's
grasp. Over the moors, into the darkness, he sped as
best he might, and to Beowulf was the victory.

Then, in the morning, many a warrior came from far
and near. Riding in troops, they tracked the monster's

path, where he had fled stricken to death.   In a dismal
pool he had yielded up his life.

Racing their horses over the green turf, they reached
again the paved street.   The golden roof of the palace
glittered in the sunlight.   The King stood on the terrace and gave thanks to God.   " I have had much
woe," he said, " but this lad, through God's might, has
done the deed that we, with all our wisdom, could not
do.   Now I will heartily love you, Beowulf, as if you
were my son.   You shall want for nothing in this
world, and your fame shall live forever."

The palace was cleansed, the walls hung anew with
cloth of gold, the whole place was made fair and
straight, for only the roof had been left altogether
unhurt after the fight.

A merry feast was held.   The King brought forth
out of his treasures a banner, helmet, and mail coat.
These he gave to Beowulf; but more wonderful than
all was a famous sword handed down to him through
the ages.   Then eight horses with golden cheekplates
were brought within the court; one of them was
saddled with King Hrothgar's own saddle, decorated
with silver.   Hrothgar gave all to Beowulf, bidding
him enjoy them well.   To each of Beowulf's men he
gave rich gifts.   The minstrels sang; the Queen, beautiful and gracious, bore the cup to the King and
Beowulf.   To Beowulf she, too, gave gifts: mantle and
bracelets and collar of gold.   " Use these gifts," she
said, " and prosper well!   As far as the sea rolls your
name shall be known."

Great was the joy of all till evening came.   Then
the hall was cleared of benches and strewn with beds.

Beowulf, like the King, had his own bower this night to sleep in. The nobles lay down in the hall, at their heads they set their shields and placed ready their helmets and their mail coats. Each slept, ready in an instant to do battle for his lord.

So they sank to rest, little dreaming what deep sorrow was to fall on them.

CHAPTER II.

THE WATER-WITCH.

HROTHGAR'S men sank to rest, but death was to be the portion of one. Grendel the monster was dead, but Grendel's mother still lived. Furious at the death of her son, she crept to the great hall, and made her way in, clutched an earl, the King's dearest friend, and crushed him in his sleep. Great was the uproar, though the terror was less than when Grendel came. The knights leapt up, sword in hand; the witch hurried to escape, she wanted to get out with her life.

The aged King felt bitter grief when he heard that his dearest friend was slain. He sent for Beowulf, who, like the King, had had his own sleeping bower that night. The youth stood before Hrothgar and hoped that all was well.

"Do not ask if things go well," said the sorrowing King, "we have fresh grief this morning. My dearest friend and noblest knight is slain. Grendel you yourself destroyed through the strength given you by God, but another monster has come to avenge his death. I have heard the country folk say that there were two huge fiends to be seen stalking over the moors, one like

a woman, as near as they could make out, the other
had the form of a man, but was huger far.   It was he
they called Grendel.   These two haunt a fearful spot,
a land of untrodden bogs and windy cliffs.   A waterfall
plunges into the blackness below, and twisted trees
with gnarled roots overhang it.   An unearthly fire is
seen gleaming there night after night.   None can tell
the depth of the stream.   Even a stag, hunted to death,
will face his foes on the bank rather than plunge into
those waters.   It is a fearful spot.   You are our only
help, dare you enter this horrible haunt?"

Quick was Beowulf's answer: "Sorrow not, O King!
Rouse yourself quickly, and let us track the monster.
Each of us must look for death, and he who has the
chance should do mighty deeds before it comes.   I
promise you Grendel's kin shall not escape me, if he
hide in the depths of the earth or of the ocean."

The King sprang up gladly, and Beowulf and his
friends set out.   They passed stony banks and narrow
gullies, the haunts of goblins.

Suddenly they saw a clump of gloomy trees, over-
hanging a dreary pool.   A shudder ran through them,
for the pool was blood-red.

All sat down by the edge of the pool, while the horn
sounded a cheerful blast.   In the water were monstrous
sea-snakes, and on jutting points of land were dragons
and strange beasts: they tumbled away, full of rage, at
the sound of the horn.

One of Beowulf's men took aim at a monster with
his arrow, and pierced him through, so that he swam
no more.

Beowulf was making ready for the fight.   He covered

his body with armor lest the fiend should clutch him. On his head was a white helmet, decorated with figures of boars worked in silver. No weapon could hurt it. His sword was a wonderful treasure, with an edge of iron; it had never failed any one who had needed it in battle.

"Be like a father to my men, if I perish," said Beowulf to Hrothgar, "and send the rich gifts you have given me to my King. He will see that I had good fortune while life lasted. Either I will win fame, or death shall take me."

He dashed away, plunging headlong into the pool. It took nearly the whole day before he reached the bottom, and while he was still on his way the water-witch met him. For a hundred years she had lived in those depths. She made a grab at him, and caught him in her talons, but his coat of mail saved him from her loathsome fingers. Still she clutched him tight, and bore him in her arms to the bottom of the lake: he had no power to use his weapons, though he had courage enough. Water-beasts swam after him and battered him with their tusks.

Then he saw that he was in a vast hall, where there was no water, but a strange, unearthly glow of firelight. At once the fight began; but the sword would not bite — it failed its master in his need; for the first time its fame broke down. Away Beowulf threw it in anger, trusting to the strength of his hands. He cared nothing for his own life, for he thought but of honor.

He seized the witch by the shoulder and swayed her so that she sank on the pavement. Quickly she recovered, and closed in on him; he staggered and fell, worn

out. She sat on him, and drew her knife to take his
life, but his good mail coat turned the point. He stood
up again, and then truly God helped him, for he saw
among the armor on the wall an old sword of huge
size, the handiwork of giants. He seized it, and smote
with all his might, so that the witch gave up her life.

His heart was full of gladness, and light, calm and
beautiful as that of the sun, filled the hall. He scanned
the vast chamber, and saw Grendel lying there dead.
He cut off his head as a trophy for King Hrothgar,
whose men the fiend had killed and devoured.

Now those men who were seated on the banks of the
pool watching with Hrothgar saw that the water was
tinged with blood. Then the old men spoke together
of the brave Beowulf, saying they feared they would
never see him again. The day was waning fast, sc
they and the King went homeward. Beowulf's men
stayed on, sick at heart, gazing at the pool. They
longed, but did not expect, to see their lord and master.

Under the depths, Beowulf was making his way to
them. The magic sword melted in his hand, like snow
in sunshine; only the hilt remained, so venomous was
the fiend that had been slain therewith. He brought
nothing more with him than the hilt and Grendel's
head. Up he rose through the waters where the furious sea-beasts before had chased him. Now not one
was to be seen; the depths were purified when the
witch lost her life. So he came to land, bravely swim-
ming, bearing his spoils. His men saw him, they
thanked God, and ran to free him of his armor. They
rejoiced to get sight of him, sound and whole.

Now they marched gladly through the highways to

the town. It took four of them to carry Grendel's head. On they went, all fourteen, their captain glorious in their midst. They entered the great hall, startling the King and Queen, as they sat at meat, with the fearful sight of Grendel's head.

Beowulf handed the magic hilt to Hrothgar, who saw that it was the work of giants of old. He spake to Beowulf, while all held their peace, praised him for his courage, said that he would love him as his son, and bade him be a help to mankind, remembering not to glory in his own strength, for he held it from God, and death without more ado might subdue it altogether. " Many, many treasures," he said, " must pass from me to you to-morrow, but now rest and feast."

Gladly Beowulf sat down to the banquet, and well he liked the thought of the rest.

When day dawned, he bade the King farewell with noble words, promising to help him in time of need. Hrothgar with tears and embraces let him go, giving him fresh gifts of hoarded jewels. He wept, for he loved Beowulf well, and knew he would never see him any more.

The coastguard saw the gallant warriors coming, bade them welcome, and led them to their ship. The wind whistled in the sails, and a pleasant humming sound was heard as the good ship sped on her way. So Beowulf returned home, having done mighty deeds and gained great honor.

CHAPTER III.

THE DRAGON'S HOARD.

IN due time Beowulf himself became King, and well he governed the land for fifty years. Then trouble came.

A slave, fleeing from his master, stumbled by an evil chance into the den of a dragon. There he saw a dazzling hoard of gold, guarded by the dragon for three hundred winters. The treasure tempted him, and he carried off a tankard of gold to give to his master, to make peace with him.

The dragon had been sleeping, now he awoke, and sniffed the scent of an enemy along the rock. He hunted diligently over the ground; he wanted to find the man who had done the mischief in his sleep. In his rage he swung around the treasure mound, dashing into it now and again to seek the jewelled tankard. He found it hard to wait till evening came, when he meant to avenge with fire the loss of his treasure.

Presently the sun sank, and the dragon had his will. He set forth, burning all the cheerful homes of men: his rage was felt far and wide. Before dawn he shot back again to his dark home, trusting in his mound and in his craft to defend himself.

Now Beowulf heard that his own home had been

burnt to the ground. It was a great grief to him, almost making him break out in a rage against Providence. His breast heaved with anger.

He meant to rid his country of the plague, and to fight the dragon single handed. He would have thought it shame to seek him with a large band, he who, as a lad, had killed Grendel and his kin. As he armed for the. fray, many thoughts filled his mind; he remembered the days of his youth and manhood. " I fought many wars in my youth," said he, " and now that I am aged, and the keeper of my people, I will yet again seek the enemy and do famously."

He bade his men await him on the mountain-side. They were to see which of the two would come alive out of the tussle.

There the aged King beheld where a rocky archway stood, with a stream of fire gushing from it; no one could stand there and not be scorched. He gave a great shout, and the dragon answered with a hot breath of flame. Beowulf, with drawn sword, stood well up to his shield, when the burning dragon, curved like an arch, came headlong upon him. The shield saved him but little; he swung up the sword to smite the horrible monster, but its edge did not bite. Sparks flew around him on every side; he saw that the end of his days had come.

His men crept away to the woods to save their lives. One, and one only, Wiglaf by name, sped through the smoke and flame to help his lord.

" My Lord Beowulf!" he cried, "with all your might defend life, I will support you to the utmost."

The dragon came on in fury; in a trice the flames

consumed Wiglaf's shield, but, nothing daunted, he
stepped under the shelter of Beowulf's, as his own fell
in ashes about him. The King remembered his
strength of old, and he smote with his sword with such
force that it stuck in the monster's head, while splinters flew all around. His hand was so strong that, as
men used to say, he broke any sword in using it, and
was none the worse for it.

Now, for the third time, the dragon rushed upon
him, and seized him by the neck with his poisonous
fangs. Wiglaf, with no thought for himself, rushed
forward, though he was scorched with the flames, and
smote the dragon lower down than Beowulf had done.
With such effect the sword entered the dragon's body
that from that moment the fire began to cease.

The King, recovering his senses, drew his knife and
ended the monster's life. So these two together destroyed the enemy of the people. To Beowulf that
was the greatest moment of his life, when he saw his
work completed.

The wound that the dragon had given him began to
burn and swell, for the poison had entered it. He
knew that the tale of his days was told. As he rested
on a stone by the mound, he pondered thoughtfully,
looking on the cunning work of the dwarfs of old, the
stone arches on their rocky pillars. Wiglaf, with
tender care, unloosed his helmet and brought him
water, Beowulf discoursing the while: "Now I would
gladly have given my armor to my son, had God
granted me one. I have ruled this people fifty years,
and no King has dared attack them. I have held my
own with justice, and no friend has lost his life through

me. Though I am sick with deadly wounds, I have comfort in this. Now go quickly, beloved Wiglaf, show me the ancient wealth that I have won for my people, the gold and brilliant gems, that I may then contentedly give up my life."

Quickly did Wiglaf enter the mound at the bidding of his master. On every side he saw gold and jewels and choice vases, helmets and bracelets, and over head a marvellous banner, all golden, gleaming with light, so that he could scan the surface of the floor and see the curious treasured hoards. He filled his lap full of golden cups and platters, and also took the brilliant banner.

He hastened to return with his spoils, wondering, with pain, if he should find his King still alive. He bore his treasures to him, laid them on the ground, and again sprinkled him with water. "I thank God," said the dying King, "that I have been permitted to win this treasure for my people; now they will have all that they need. But I cannot be any longer here. Bid my men make a lofty mound on the headland overlooking the sea, and there place my ashes. In time to come men shall call it Beowulf's Barrow, it shall tower aloft to guide sailors over the stormy seas."

The brave King took from his neck his golden collar, took his helmet and his coronet, and gave them to his true knight, Wiglaf. "Fate has swept all my kinsmen away," said he, "and now I must follow them."

That was his last word, as his soul departed from his bosom, to join the company of the just.

Of all Kings in the world, he was, said his men, the gentlest to his knights and the most desirous of honor.

RIP VAN WINKLE

By WASHINGTON IRVING.

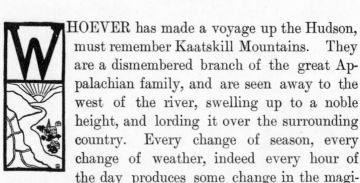

HOEVER has made a voyage up the Hudson, must remember Kaatskill Mountains. They are a dismembered branch of the great Appalachian family, and are seen away to the west of the river, swelling up to a noble height, and lording it over the surrounding country. Every change of season, every change of weather, indeed every hour of the day produces some change in the magical hues and shapes of these mountains; and they are regarded by all the good wives, far and near, as perfect barometers. When the weather is fair and settled, they are clothed in blue and purple, and print their bold outlines on the clear evening sky; but sometimes, when the rest of the landscape is cloudless, they will gather a hood of gray vapors about their summits, which in the last rays of the setting sun, will glow and light up like a crown of glory.

At the foot of these fairy mountains, the voyager may have descried the light smoke curling up from a village, whose shingle roofs gleam among the trees

just where the blue tints of the upland melt away into
the fresh green of the nearer landscape. It is a little
village of great antiquity, having been founded by some
of the Dutch colonists, in the early times of the province, just about the beginning of the government of
the good Peter Stuyvesant (may he rest in peace!), and
there were some of the houses of the original settlers
standing within a few years, built of small yellow
bricks, brought from Holland, having latticed windows and gable fronts, surmounted with weathercocks.

In that same village, and in one of these very houses
(which, to tell the precise truth, was sadly time-worn
and weather-beaten), there lived many years since,
while the country was yet a province of Great Britain,
a simple, good-natured fellow, of the name of Rip Van
Winkle. He was a descendant of the Van Winkles
who figured so gallantly in the chivalrous days of Peter
Stuyvesant, and accompanied him to the siege of Fort
Christina. He inherited, however, but little of the
martial character of his ancestors. I have observed
that he was a simple, good-natured man; he was moreover a kind neighbor, and an obedient henpecked husband. Indeed, to the latter circumstance might be
owing that meekness of spirit which gained him such
universal popularity; for those men are most apt to be
obsequious and conciliating abroad, who are under the
discipline of shrews at home. Their tempers, doubtless, are rendered pliant and malleable in the fiery
furnace of domestic tribulation, and a curtain lecture is
worth all the sermons in the world for teaching the
virtues of patience and long-suffering. A termagant
wife may, therefore, in some respects, be considered a

tolerable blessing; and if so, Rip Van Winkle was thrice blessed.

Certain it is, that he was a great favorite among all the good wives of the village, who, as usual with the amiable sex, took his part in all family squabbles, and never failed, whenever they talked those matters over in their evening gossipings, to lay all the blame on Dame Van Winkle. The children of the village, too, would shout with joy whenever he approached. He assisted at their sports, made their playthings, taught them to fly kites and shoot marbles, and told them long stories of ghosts, witches, and Indians. Whenever he went dodging about the village, he was surrounded by a troop of them hanging on his skirts, clambering on his back, and playing a thousand tricks on him with impunity; and not a dog would bark at him throughout the neighborhood.

The great error in Rip's composition was an insuperable aversion to all kinds of profitable labor. It could not be from the want of assiduity or perseverance; for he would sit on a wet rock, with a rod as long and heavy as a Tartar's lance, and fish all day without a murmur, even though he should not be encouraged by a single nibble. He would carry a fowling-piece on his shoulder for hours together, trudging through woods and swamps, and up hill and down dale, to shoot a few squirrels or wild pigeons. He would never refuse to assist a neighbor even in the roughest toil, and was a foremost man at all country frolics for husking Indian corn, or building stone fences. The women of the village, too, used to employ him to run their errands, and to do such little odd jobs as their less obliging husbands would not do for them; — in a word, Rip was ready to attend to anybody's business but his own; but as to doing family duty, and keeping his farm in order, he found it impossible.

In fact, he declared it was of no use to work on his farm; it was the most pestilent little piece of ground in the whole country; everything about it went wrong, and would go wrong in spite of him. His fences were continually falling to pieces; his cow would either go astray, or get among the cabbages; weeds were sure to grow quicker in his fields than anywhere else; the rain always made a point of setting in just as he had some out-door work to do; so that though his patrimonial estate had dwindled away under his management, acre by acre, until there was little more left than a mere patch of Indian corn and potatoes, yet it was the worst conditioned farm in the neighborhood.

His children, too, were as ragged and wild as if they belonged to nobody. His son Rip, an urchin begotten in his own likeness, promised to inherit the habits, with the old clothes of his father. He was generally seen trooping like a colt at his mother's heels, equipped in a pair of his father's cast-off galligaskins, which he had much ado to hold up with one hand, as a fine lady does her train in bad weather.

Rip Van Winkle, however, was one of those happy mortals, of foolish, well-oiled dispositions, who take the world easy, eat white bread or brown, whichever can be got with least thought or trouble, and would rather starve on a penny than work for a pound. If left to himself, he would have whistled life away, in perfect contentment; but his wife kept continually dinning in his ears about his idleness, his carelessness, and the ruin he was bringing on his family.

Morning, noon, and night, her tongue was incessantly going, and everything he said or did was sure to produce a torrent of household eloquence. Rip had but one way of replying to all lectures of the kind, and that, by frequent use, had grown into a habit. He shrugged his shoulders, shook his head, cast up his eyes, but said nothing. This, however, always provoked a fresh volley from his wife, so that he was fain to draw off his forces, and take to the outside of the house — the only side which, in truth, belongs to a henpecked husband.

Rip's sole domestic adherent was his dog Wolf, who was as much henpecked as his master; for Dame Van Winkle regarded them as companions in idleness, and even looked upon Wolf with an evil eye, as the cause of his master's going so often astray. True it is, in all points of spirit befitting an honorable dog, he was as courageous an animal as ever scoured the woods — but what courage can withstand the ever-enduring and all-besetting terrors of a woman's tongue? The moment Wolf entered the house, his crest fell, his tail drooped to the ground, or curled between his legs, he sneaked about with a gallows air, casting many a sidelong glance at Dame Van Winkle, and at the least flourish of a broomstick or ladle, he would fly to the door with yelping precipitation.

Time grew worse and worse with Rip Van Winkle, as years of matrimony rolled on: a sharp temper never mellows with age, and a sharp tongue is the only edge tool that grows keener with constant use. For a long while he used to console himself, when driven from home, by frequenting a kind of perpetual club of the sages, philosophers, and other idle personages of the village, which held its sessions on a bench before a small inn, designated by a rubicund portrait of his majesty George the Third. Here they used to sit in the shade of a long lazy summer's day, talking listlessly over village gossip, or telling endless sleepy stories about nothing. But it would have been worth any statesman's money to have heard the profound discussions which sometimes took place, when by chance an old newspaper fell into their hands, from some passing traveller. How solemnly they would listen to the contents, as drawled out by Derrick Van Bummel, the schoolmaster, a dapper, learned little man, who was not to be daunted by the most gigantic word in the dictionary; and how sagely they would deliberate upon public events some months after they had taken place.

The opinions of this junto were completely controlled by Nicholas Vedder, a patriarch of the village, and landlord of the inn, at the door of which he took his seat from morning till night, just moving sufficiently to avoid the sun, and keep in the shade of a large tree; so that the neighbors could tell the hour by his movements as accurately as by a sun-dial. It is true, he was rarely heard to speak, but smoked his pipe incessantly. His adherents, however, (for every great man has his adherents,) perfectly understood him, and knew how to gather his opinions. When anything that was read or related displeased him, he was observed to smoke his pipe vehemently, and to send forth short, frequent, and angry puffs; but when pleased, he would inhale the smoke slowly and tranquilly, and emit it in light and placid clouds, and sometimes taking the pipe from his mouth, and letting the fragrant vapor curl about his nose, would gravely nod his head in token of perfect approbation.

From even this stronghold the unlucky Rip was at length routed by his termagant wife, who would suddenly break in upon the tranquillity of the assemblage, and call the members all to nought; nor was that august personage, Nicholas Vedder himself, sacred from the daring tongue of this terrible virago, who charged him outright with encouraging her husband in habits of idleness.

Poor Rip was at last reduced almost to despair, and his only alternative to escape from the labor of the farm and the clamor of his wife, was to take gun in hand, and stroll away into the woods. Here he would sometimes seat himself at the foot of a tree, and share the contents of his wallet with Wolf, with whom he sympathized as a fellow-sufferer in persecution. "Poor Wolf," he would say, "thy mistress leads thee a dog's life of it; but never mind, my lad, whilst I live thou shalt never want a friend to stand by thee!" Wolf would wag his tail, look wistfully in his master's face, and if dogs can feel pity, I verily believe he reciprocated the sentiment with all his heart.

In a long ramble of the kind, on a fine autumnal day, Rip had unconsciously scrambled to one of the highest parts of the Kaatskill Mountains. He was after his favorite sport of squirrel-shooting, and the still solitudes had echoed and re-echoed with the reports of his gun. Panting and fatigued, he threw himself, late in

the afternoon, on a green knoll covered with mountain
herbage, that crowned the brow of a precipice. From
an opening between the trees, he could overlook all the
lower country for many a mile of rich woodland. He
saw at a distance the lordly Hudson, far, far below
him, moving on its silent but majestic course, with the
reflection of a purple cloud, or the sail of a lagging
bark, here and there sleeping on its glassy bosom, and
at last losing itself in the blue highlands.

On the other side he looked down into a deep mountain glen, wild, lonely, and shagged, the bottom filled
with fragments from the impending cliffs, and scarcely
lighted by the reflected rays of the setting sun. For
some time Rip lay musing on this scene; evening was
gradually advancing; the mountains began to throw
their long blue shadows over the valleys; he saw that
it would be dark long before he could reach the village;
and he heaved a heavy sigh when he thought of en-
countering the terrors of Dame Van Winkle.

As he was about to descend he heard a voice from
a distance hallooing, "Rip Van Winkle! Rip Van Winkle!" He looked around, but could see nothing but a
crow winging its solitary flight across the mountain.
He thought his fancy must have deceived him, and
turned again to descend, when he heard the same cry
ring through the still evening air, "Rip Van Winkle!
Rip Van Winkle!"— at the same time Wolf bristled
up his back, and giving a low growl, skulked to his
master's side, looking fearfully down into the glen.
Rip now felt a vague apprehension stealing over him;
he looked anxiously in the same direction, and perceived
a strange figure slowly toiling up the rocks, and bend-

ing under the weight of something he carried on his back. He was surprised to see any human being in this lonely and unfrequented place, but supposing it to be some one of the neighborhood in need of his assistance, he hastened down to yield it

On nearer approach, he was still more surprised at the singularity of the stranger's appearance. He was a short square-built old fellow, with thick bushy hair, and a grizzled beard. His dress was of the antique Dutch fashion — a cloth jerkin strapped round the waist — several pair of breeches, the outer one of ample volume, decorated with rows of buttons down the sides, and bunches at the knees. He bore on his shoulders a stout keg, that seemed full of liquor, and made signs for Rip to approach and assist him with the load. Though rather shy and distrustful of this new acquaintance, Rip complied with his usual alacrity, and mutually relieving each other, they clambered up a narrow gully, apparently the dry bed of a mountain torrent. As they ascended, Rip every now and then heard long rolling peals, like distant thunder, that seemed to issue out of a deep ravine, or rather cleft between lofty rocks, toward which their rugged path conducted. He paused for an instant, but supposing it to be the muttering of one of those transient thunder-showers which often take place in the mountain heights, he proceeded. Passing through the ravine, they came to a hollow, like a small amphitheatre, surrounded by perpendicular precipices, over the brinks of which, impending trees shot their branches, so that you only caught glimpses of the azure sky, and the bright evening cloud. During the whole time, Rip and his companion had labored on in silence;

for though the former marvelled greatly what could be
the object of carrying a keg of liquor up this wild
mountain, yet there was something strange and incomprehensible about the unknown, that inspired awe, and
checked familiarity.

On entering the amphitheatre, new objects of wonder
presented themselves. On a level spot in the centre
was a company of odd-looking personages playing at
nine-pins. They were dressed in a quaint outlandish
fashion : some wore short doublets, others jerkins, with
long knives in their belts, and most of them had enormous breeches, of similar style with that of the guide's.
Their visages too, were peculiar : one had a large head,
broad face, and small piggish eyes ; the face of another
seemed to consist entirely of nose, and was surmounted
by a white sugar-loaf hat, set off with a little red cock's
tail. They all had beards, of various shapes and colors.
There was one who seemed to be the commander. He
was a stout old gentleman, with a weather-beaten countenance ; he wore a laced doublet, broad belt and
hanger, high-crowned hat and feather, red stockings,
and high-heeled shoes, with roses in them. The whole
group reminded Rip of the figures in an old Flemish
painting, in the parlor of Dominie Van Schaick, the
village parson, and which had been brought over from
Holland at the time of the settlement.

What seemed particularly odd to Rip was, that
though these folks were evidently amusing themselves,
yet they maintained the gravest faces, the most mysterious silence, and were, withal, the most melancholy
party of pleasure he had ever witnessed. Nothing in-
terrupted the stillness of the scene but the noise of the

balls, which, whenever they were rolled, echoed along the mountains like rumbling peals of thunder.

As Rip and his companion approached them, they suddenly desisted from their play, and stared at him with such a fixed statue-like gaze, and such strange, uncouth, lack-lustre countenances, that his heart turned within him, and his knees smote together. His companion now emptied the contents of the keg into large flagons, and made signs to him to wait upon the company. He obeyed with fear and trembling; they quaffed the liquor in profound silence, and then returned to their game.

By degrees, Rip's awe and apprehension subsided. He even ventured, when no eye was fixed upon him, to taste the beverage, which he found had much of the flavor of excellent Hollands. He was naturally a thirsty soul, and was soon tempted to repeat the draught. One taste provoked another, and he reiterated his visits to the flagon so often, that at length his senses were overpowered, his eyes swam in his head, his head gradually declined, and he fell into a deep sleep.

On waking, he found himself on the green knoll from whence he had first seen the old man of the glen. He rubbed his eyes — it was a bright sunny morning. The birds were hopping and twittering among the bushes, and the eagle was wheeling aloft, and breasting the pure mountain breeze. "Surely," thought Rip, "I have not slept here all night." He recalled the occurrences before he fell asleep. The strange man with the keg of liquor — the mountain ravine — the wild retreat among the rocks — the woe-begone party at nine-pins —

the flagon — "Oh! that wicked flagon!" thought Rip; "what excuse shall I make to Dame Van Winkle?"

He looked round for his gun, but in place of the clean, well-oiled fowling-piece, he found an old firelock lying by him, the barrel encrusted with rust, the lock falling off, and the stock worm-eaten. He now suspected that the grave roysterers of the mountain had put a trick up on him, and having dosed him with liquor, had robbed him of his gun. Wolf, too, had disappeared, but he might have strayed away after a squirrel or partridge. He whistled after him and shouted his name, but all in vain; the echoes repeated his whistle and shout, but no dog was to be seen.

He determined to revisit the scene of the last evening's gambol, and if he met with any of the party, to demand his dog and gun. As he rose to walk, he found himself stiff in the joints, and wanting in his usual activity. "These mountain beds do not agree with me," thought Rip, "and if this frolic should lay me up with a fit of the rheumatism, I shall have a blessed time with Dame Van Winkle." With some difficulty he got down into the glen; he found the gully up which he and his companion had ascended the preceding evening; but to his astonishment a mountain stream was now foaming down it, leaping from rock to rock, and filling the glen with babbling murmurs. He, however, made shift to scramble up its sides, working his toilsome way through thickets of birch, sassafras, and witch-hazel; and sometimes tripped up or entangled by the wild grape vines that twisted their coils and tendrils from tree to tree, and spread a kind of network in his path.

At length he reached to where the ravine had opened through the cliffs to the amphitheatre; but no traces of such opening remained. The rocks presented a high impenetrable wall, over which the torrent came tumbling in a sheet of feathery foam, and fell into a broad deep basin, black from the shadows of the surrounding forest. Here, then, poor Rip was brought to a stand. He again called and whistled after his dog; he was only answered by the cawing of a flock of idle crows, sporting high in the air about a dry tree that overhung a sunny precipice; and who, secure in their elevation, seemed to look down and scoff at the poor man's perplexities. What was to be done? The morning was passing away, and Rip felt famished for want of his breakfast. He grieved to give up his dog and gun; he dreaded to meet his wife; but it would not do to starve among the mountains. He shook his head, shouldered the rusty firelock, and, with a heart full of trouble and anxiety, turned his steps homeward.

As he approached the village, he met a number of people, but none whom he knew, which somewhat surprised him, for he had thought himself acquainted with every one in the country round. Their dress, too, was of a different fashion from that to which he was accustomed. They all stared at him with equal marks of surprise, and whenever they cast eyes upon him, invariably stroked their chins. The constant recurrence of this gesture, induced Rip, involuntarily, to do the same, when, to his astonishment, he found his beard had grown a foot long.

He had now entered the skirts of the village. A troop of strange children ran at his heels, hooting after him, and pointing at his gray beard. The dogs, too, not one of which he recognized for an old acquaintance, barked at him as he passed. The very village was altered: it was larger and more populous. There were rows of houses which he had never seen before, and those which had been his familiar haunts had disappeared. Strange names were over the doors — strange faces at the windows — everything was strange. His mind now misgave him; he began to doubt whether both he and the world around him were not bewitched. Surely this was his native village, which he had left but a day before. There stood the Kaatskill Mountains — there ran the silver Hudson at a distance — there was every hill and dale precisely as it had always been — Rip was sorely perplexed — "That flagon last night," thought he, " has addled my poor head sadly! "

It was with some difficulty that he found the way to his own house, which he approached with silent awe, expecting every moment to hear the shrill voice of Dame Van Winkle. He found the house gone to decay — the roof fallen in, the windows shattered, and the doors off the hinges. A half-starved dog, that looked like Wolf, was skulking about it. Rip called him by name, but the cur snarled, showed his teeth, and passed on. This was an unkind cut indeed. — "My very dog," sighed poor Rip, " has forgotten me! "

He entered the house, which, to tell the truth, Dame Van Winkle had always kept in neat order. It was empty, forlorn, and apparently abandoned. This desolateness overcame all his connubial fears — he called loudly for his wife and children — the lonely chambers rang for a moment with his voice, and then all again was silence.

He now hurried forth, and hastened to his old resort, the village inn — but it too was gone. A large rickety wooden building stood in its place, with great gaping windows, some of them broken, and mended with old hats and petticoats, and over the door was painted, "The Union Hotel, by Jonathan Doolittle." Instead of the great tree that used to shelter the quiet little Dutch inn of yore, there now was reared a tall naked pole, with something on the top that looked like a red night-cap, and from it was fluttering a flag, on which was a singular assemblage of stars and strips — all this was strange and incomprehensible. He recognized on the sign, however, the ruby face of King George, under which he had smoked so many a peaceful pipe, but even this was singularly metamorphosed. The red coat was changed for one of blue and buff, a sword was held in the hand instead of a sceptre, the head was decorated with a cocked hat, and underneath was painted in large characters, GENERAL WASHINGTON.

There was, as usual, a crowd of folk about the door, but none that Rip recollected. The very character of the people seemed changed. There was a busy, bustling, disputatious tone about it, instead of the accustomed phlegm and drowsy tranquillity. He looked in vain for the sage Nicholas Vedder, with his broad face, double chin, and fair long pipe, uttering clouds of tobacco smoke, instead of idle speeches; or Van Bummel, the schoolmaster, doling forth the contents of an ancient newspaper. In place of these, a lean bilious-looking fellow, with his pockets full of handbills, was haranguing vehemently about rights of citizens — election — members of Congress—liberty—Bunker's Hill—heroes of seventy-six — and other words, that were a perfect Babylonish jargon to the bewildered Van Winkle.

The appearance of Rip, with his long, grizzled beard, his rusty fowling-piece, his uncouth dress, and the army of women and children that had gathered at his heels, soon attracted the attention of the tavern politicians. They crowded round him, eying him from head to foot, with great curiosity. The orator bustled up to him, and drawing him partly aside, inquired " On which side he voted?" Rip stared in vacant stupidity. Another short but busy little fellow pulled him by the arm, and rising on tiptoe, inquired in his ear, " Whether he was Federal or Democrat." Rip was equally at a loss to comprehend the question; when a knowing, self-important old gentleman, in a sharp cocked hat, made his way through the crowd, putting them to the right and left with his elbows as he passed, and planting himself before Van Winkle, with one arm a-kimbo, the other resting on his cane, his keen eyes and sharp hat penetrating, as it were, into his very soul, demanded in an austere tone, " What brought him to the election with a gun on his shoulder, and a mob at his heels, and whether he meant to breed a riot in the village?"

" Alas! gentlemen," cried Rip, somewhat dismayed, " I am a poor, quiet man, a native of the place, and a loyal subject of the King, God bless him!"

Here a general shout burst from the bystanders — " a tory! a tory! a spy! a refugee! hustle him! away with him!"

It was with great difficulty that the self-important man in the cocked hat restored order; and having assumed a tenfold austerity of brow, demanded again of the unknown culprit, what he came there for, and whom he was seeking. The poor man humbly assured him that he meant no harm, but merely came there in search of some of his neighbors, who used to keep about the tavern.

"Well — who are they? — name them."

Rip bethought himself a moment, and inquired, "Where's Nicholas Vedder?"

There was a silence for a little while, when an old man replied, in a thin, piping voice, "Nicholas Vedder? why, he is dead and gone these eighteen years! There was a wooden tomb-stone in the church-yard that used to tell all about him, but that's rotten and gone too."

"Where's Brom Dutcher?"

"Oh, he went off to the army in the beginning of the war; some say he was killed at the storming of Stony Point — others say he was drowned in the squall, at the foot of Antony's Nose. I don't know — he never came back again."

"Where's Van Bummel, the schoolmaster?"

"He went off to the wars, too; was a great militia general, and is now in Congress."

Rip's heart died away, at hearing of these sad changes in his home and friends, and finding himself thus alone in the world. Every answer puzzled him, too, by treating of such enormous lapses of time, and of matters which he could not understand: war — Congress — Stony Point! — he had no courage to ask after any more friends, but cried out in despair, "Does nobody here know Rip Van Winkle?"

"Oh, Rip Van Winkle!" exclaimed two or three. "Oh, to be sure! that's Rip Van Winkle yonder, leaning against the tree."

Rip looked, and beheld a precise counterpart of himself as he went up the mountain; apparently as lazy, and certainly as ragged. The poor fellow was now completely confounded. He doubted his own identity, and whether he was himself or another man. In the midst of his bewilderment, the man in the cocked hat demanded who he was, and what was his name.

"God knows," exclaimed he at his wit's end; "I'm not myself — I'm somebody else — that's me yonder — no — that's somebody else, got into my shoes — I was myself last night, but I fell asleep on the mountain, and they've changed my gun, and everything's changed, and I'm changed, and I can't tell what's my name, or who I am!"

The bystanders began now to look at each other, nod, wink significantly, and tap their fingers against their foreheads. There was a whisper, also, about securing the gun, and keeping the old fellow from doing mischief; at the very suggestion of which, the self-important man with the cocked hat retired with some precipitation. At this critical moment a fresh comely woman passed through the throng to get a peep at the gray-bearded man. She had a chubby child in her arms, which, frightened at his looks, began to cry, "Hush, Rip," cried she, "hush, you little fool; the old man won't hurt you." The name of the child, the air of the mother, the tone of her voice, all awakened a train of recollections in his mind.

"What is your name, my good woman?" asked he.

"Judith Gardener."

"And your father's name?"

"Ah, poor man, his name was Rip Van Winkle; it's

twenty years since he went away from home with his gun, and never has been heard of since — his dog came home without him; but whether he shot himself, or was carried away by the Indians, nobody can tell. I was then but a little girl."

Rip had but one more question to ask; but he put it with a faltering voice :

" Where's your mother ? "

Oh, she too had died but a short time since : she broke a blood-vessel in a fit of passion at a New-England pedler.

There was a drop of comfort, at least, in this intelligence. The honest man could contain himself no longer. He caught his daughter and her child in his arms. " I am your father ! " cried he — " Young Rip Van Winkle once — old Rip Van Winkle now — Does nobody know poor Rip Van Winkle ! "

All stood amazed, until an old woman, tottering out from among the crowd, put her hand to her brow, and peering under it in his face for a moment, exclaimed, " Sure enough ! it is Rip Van Winkle — it is himself. Welcome home again, old neighbor — Why, where have you been these twenty long years ? "

Rip's story was soon told, for the whole twenty years had been to him but as one night. The neighbors stared when they heard it ; some were seen to wink at each other, and put their tongues in their cheeks ; and the self-important man in the cocked hat, who, when the alarm was over, had returned to the field, screwed down the corners of his mouth, and shook his head — upon which there was a general shaking of the head throughout the assemblage.

It was determined, however, to take the opinion of old Peter Vanderdonk, who was seen slowly advancing up the road. He was a descendant of the historian of that name, who wrote one of the earliest accounts of the province. Peter was the most ancient inhabitant of the village, and well versed in all the wonderful events and traditions of the neighborhood. He recollected Rip at once, and corroborated his story in the most satisfactory manner. He assured the company that it was a fact, handed down from his ancestor the historian, that the Kaatskill Mountains had always been haunted by strange beings. That it was affirmed that the great Hendrick Hudson, the first discoverer of the river and country, kept a kind of vigil there every twenty years, with his crew of the Half-moon, being permitted in this way to revisit the scenes of his enterprise, and keep a guardian eye upon the river and the great city called by his name. That his father had once seen them in their old Dutch dresses playing at nine-pins in the hollow of the mountain; and that he himself had heard, one summer afternoon, the sound of their balls, like distant peals of thunder.

To make a long story short, the company broke up, and returned to the more important concerns of the election. Rip's daughter took him home to live with her; she had a snug, well-furnished house, and a stout cheery farmer for a husband, whom Rip recollected for one of the urchins that used to climb upon his back. As to Rip's son and heir, who was the ditto of himself, seen leaning against the tree, he was employed to work on the farm; but evinced a hereditary disposition to attend to anything else but his business.

Rip now resumed his old walks and habits; he soon
found many of his former cronies, though all rather the
worse for the wear and tear of time; and preferred
making friends among the rising generation, with
whom he soon grew into great favor.

Having nothing to do at home, and being arrived at
that happy age when a man can do nothing with impunity, he took his place once more on the bench, at
the inn door, and was reverenced as one of the patri-
archs of the village, and a chronicle of the old times
"before the war." It was some time before he could
get into the regular track of gossip, or could be made
to comprehend the strange events that had taken place
during his torpor. How that there had been a revolu-
tionary war — that the country had thrown off the
yoke of old England — and that, instead of being a
subject of his majesty George the Third, he was now a
free citizen of the United States. Rip, in fact, was no
politician; the changes of states and empires made but
little impression on him; but there was one species of
despotism under which he had long groaned, and that
was — petticoat government. Happily, that was at an
end; he had got his neck out of the yoke of matrimony, and could go in and out whenever he pleased,
without dreading the tryanny of Dame Van Winkle.
Whenever her name was mentioned, however, he shook
his head, shrugged his shoulders, and cast up his eyes;
which might pass either for an expression of resignation
to his fate, or joy at his deliverance.

He used to tell his story to every stranger that arrived at Mr. Doolittle's hotel. He was observed, at
first, to vary on some points every time he told it,

which was doubtless owing to his having so recently awaked. It at last settled down precisely to the tale I have related, and not a man, woman, or child in the neighborhood, but knew it by heart. Some always pretended to doubt the reality of it, and insisted that Rip had been out of his head, and that this was one point on which he always remained flighty. The old Dutch inhabitants, however, almost universally gave it full credit. Even to this day, they never hear a thunder-storm of a summer afternoon about the Kaatskill, but they say Hendrick Hudson and his crew are at their game of nine-pins; and it is a common wish of all henpecked husbands in the neighborhood when life hangs heavy on their hands, that they might have a quieting draught out of Rip Van Winkle's flagon.

SELECTIONS FROM OSSIAN

CATH–LODA

A TALE OF THE TIMES OF OLD.

WHENCE is the stream of years? Whither do they roll along? Where have they hid, in mist, their many-colored sides?

I look into the times of old, but they seem dim to Ossian's eyes, like reflected moon-beams, on a distant lake. Here rise the red beams of war! There, silent, dwells a feeble race! They mark no years with their deeds, as slow they pass along. Dweller between the shields! thou that awakest the failing soul! descend from thy wall, harp of Cona, with thy voices three! Come with that which kindles the past: rear the forms of old, on their own dark-brown years!

U-thorno, hill of storms, I behold my race on thy side. Fingal is bending, in night, over Duth-maruno's tomb. Near him are the steps of his heroes, hunters of the boar. By Turthor's stream the host of Lochlin is deep in shades. The wrathful kings stood on two hills; they looked forward from their bossy shields. They

looked forward to the stars of night, red-wandering in
the west. Cruth-loda bends from high, like a formless
meteor in clouds. He sends abroad the winds, and
marks them with his signs. Starno foresaw that Morven's king was not to yield in war.

He twice struck the tree in wrath. He rushed before
his son. He hummed a surly song; and heard his hair
in wind. Turned from one another, they stood, like
two oaks, which different winds had bent; each hangs
over its own loud rill, and shakes its boughs in the
course of blasts.

"Annir," said Starno of lakes, "was a fire that consumed of old. He poured death from his eyes, along
the striving fields. His joy was in the fall of men.
Blood to him was a summer stream, that brings joy to
withered vales, from his own mossy rock. He came
forth to the lake Luth-cormo, to meet the tall Corman-
trunar, he from Urlor of streams, dweller of battle's
wing."

The chief of Urlor had come to Gormal, with his
dark-bosomed ships. He saw the daughter of Annir,
white-armed Foina-brâgal. He saw her! Nor careless
rolled her eyes, on the rider of stormy waves. She fled
to his ship in darkness, like a moon-beam through a
nightly vale. Annir pursued along the deep; he called
the winds of heaven. Nor alone was the king! Starno
was by his side. Like U-thorno's young eagle, I turned
my eyes on my father.

We rushed into roaring Urlor. With his people
came tall Corman-trunar. We fought; but the foe
prevailed. In his wrath my father stood. He lopped
the young trees with his sword. His eyes rolled red

in his rage. I marked the soul of the king, and I retired in night. From the field I took a broken helmet:
a shield that was pierced with steel: pointless was the
spear in my hand. I went to find the foe.

On a rock sat tall Corman-trunar, beside his burning
oak; and near him, beneath a tree, sat deep-bosomed
Foina-brâgal. I threw my broken shield before her. I
spoke the words of peace. " Beside his rolling sea, lies
Annir of many lakes. The king was pierced in battle;
and Starno is to raise his tomb. Me, a son of Loda, he
sends to white-handed Foina, to bid her send a lock
from her hair, to rest with her father, in earth. And
thou king of roaring Urlor, let the battle cease, till
Annir receive the shell, from fiery-eyed Cruth-loda."

Bursting into tears, she rose, and tore a lock from
her hair; a lock, which wandered, in the blast, along
her heaving breast. Corman-trunar gave the shell;
and bade me rejoice before him. I rested in the
shade of night; and hid my face in my helmet deep.
Sleep descended on the foe. I rose, like a stalking
ghost. I pierced the side of Corman-trunar. Nor did
Foina-brâgal escape. She rolled her white bosom in
blood.

Why then, daughter of heroes, didst thou wake my
rage?

Morning rose. The foe were fled, like the departure
of mist. Annir struck his bossy shield. He called his
dark-haired son. I came, streaked with wandering
blood: thrice rose the shout of the king, like a bursting
forth of a squall of wind from a cloud, by night. We
rejoiced, three days, above the dead, and called the
hawks of heaven. They came, from all their winds, to

feast on Annir's foes. Swaran! Fingal is alone,[1] on
his hill of night. Let thy spear pierce the king in
secret; like Annir, my soul shall rejoice.

"Son of Annir," said Swaran, "I shall not slay in
shades. I move forth in light: the hawks rush from
all their winds. They are wont to trace my course: it
is not harmless through war."

Burning rose the rage of the king. He thrice raised
his gleaming spear. But, starting, he spared his son;
and rushed into the night. By Turthor's stream a cave
is dark, the dwelling of Conban-carglas. There he laid
the helmet of kings, and called the maid of Lulan; but
she was distant far, in Loda's resounding hall.

Swelling in his rage, he strode, to where Fingal lay
alone. The king was laid on his shield, on his own
secret hill.

Stern hunter of shaggy boars! no feeble maid is laid
before thee. No boy, on his ferny bed, by Turthor's
murmuring stream. Here is spread the couch of the
mighty, from which they rise to deeds of death! Hunter
of shaggy boars, awaken not the terrible!

Starno came murmuring on. Fingal arose in arms.
"Who art thou, son of night?" Silent he threw the
spear. They mixed their gloomy strife. The shield of
Starno fell, cleft in twain. He is bound to an oak.
The early beam arose. It was then Fingal beheld the
king. He rolled awhile his silent eyes. He thought of
other days, when white-bosomed Agandecca moved like
the music of songs. He loosed the thong from his

---

[1] Fingal, according to the custom of the Caledonian kings, had retired
to a hill alone, as he himself was to resume the command of the army the
next day.

hands. "Son of Annir," he said, "retire. Retire to Gormal of shells; a beam that was set returns. I remember thy "white-bosomed daughter; dreadful king away! Go to thy troubled dwelling, cloudy foe of the lovely! Let the stranger shun thee, thou gloomy in the hall!"

A tale of the times of old!

THE WAR OF INIS-THONA

A POEM.

OUR youth is like the dream of the hunter on the hill of health. He sleeps in the mild beams of the sun; he awakes amidst a storm; the red lightning flies around: trees shake their heads to the wind! He looks back with joy, on the day of the sun; and the pleasant dreams of his rest! When shall Ossian's youth return? When his ear delight in the sound of arms? When shall I, like Oscar, travel in the light of my steel? Come, with your streams, ye hills of Cona! listen to the voice of Ossian. The song rises, like the sun, in my soul. I feel the joys of other times!

I behold thy towers, O Selma! the oaks of thy shaded wall: thy streams sound in my ear; thy heroes gather around. Fingal sits in the midst. He leans on the shield of Trenmor: his spear stands against the wall; he listens to the song of his bards. The deeds of his arm are heard; the actions of the king in his youth! Oscar had returned from the chase, and heard the hero's praise. He took the shield of Branno[1] from the wall; his eyes were filled with tears. Red was the cheek of youth. His voice was trembling low. My

[1] Grandfather to Oscar.

spear shook its bright head in his hand : he spoke to
Morven's king.

"Fingal! thou king of heroes! Ossian, next to him
in war! ye have fought in your youth; your names are
renowned in song. Oscar is like the mist of Cona; I
appear and I vanish away. The bard will not know my
name. The hunter will not search in the heath for my
tomb. Let me fight, O heroes, in the battles of Inis-
thona. Distant is the land of my war! ye shall not
hear of Oscar's fall! Some bard may find me there;
some bard may give my name to song. The daughter
of the stranger shall see my tomb, and weep over the
youth, that came from afar. The bard shall say, at
the feast, 'Hear the song of Oscar from the distant
land!'"

"Oscar," replied the king of Morven; "thou shalt
fight, son of my fame! Prepare my dark-bosomed
ship to carry my hero to Inis-thona. Son of my son,
regard our fame; thou art of the race of renown! Let
not the children of strangers say, feeble are the sons of
Morven! Be thou, in battle, a roaring storm : mild as
the evening sun in peace! Tell, Oscar, to Inis-thona's
king, that Fingal remembers his youth; when we strove
in the combat together, in the days of Agandecca."

They lifted up the sounding sail: the wind whistled
through the thongs [1] of their masts. Waves lash the
oozy rocks : the strength of ocean roars. My son beheld, from the wave, the land of groves. He rushed
into Runa's sounding bay, and sent his sword to Annir
of spears. The gray-haired hero rose, when he saw
the sword of Fingal. His eyes were full of tears; he

---

[1] Leather thongs were used among the Celtic nations instead of ropes.

remembered his battles in youth. Twice had they
lifted the spear, before the lovely Agandecca; heroes
stood far distant, as if two spirits were striving in
winds.

"But now," began the king, "I am old; the sword
lies useless in my hall. Thou, who art of Morven's
race! Annir has seen the battle of spears; but now
he is pale and withered, like the oak of Lano. I have
no son to meet thee, with joy, to bring thee to the halls
of his fathers. Argon is pale in the tomb, and Ruro is
no more. My daughter is in the hall of strangers: she
longs to behold my tomb. Her spouse shakes ten thousand spears; he comes a cloud of death from Lano.
Come, to share the feast of Annir, son of echoing
Morven!"

Three days they feasted together; on the fourth,
Annir heard the name of Oscar. They rejoiced in the
shell.[1] They pursued the boars of Runa. Beside the
fount of mossy stones, the weary heroes rest. The tear
steals in secret from Annir: he broke the rising sigh.
"Here darkly rest," the hero said, "the children of my
youth. This stone is the tomb of Ruro; that tree
sounds over the grave of Argon. Do ye hear my voice,
O my sons, within your narrow house? Or do ye speak
in these rustling leaves, when the winds of the desert
rise?"

"King of Inis-thona," said Oscar, "how fell the
children of youth? The wild boar rushes over their
tombs, but he does not disturb their repose. They
pursue deer formed of clouds, and bend their airy bow.

---

[1] *To rejoice in the shell*, is a phrase for feasting sumptuously and drinking freely.

They still love the sport of their youth; and mount
the wind with joy."

"Cormalo," replied the king, "is a chief of ten thousand spears.   He dwells at the waters of Lano,[1] which
sends forth the vapor of death.   He came to Runa's
echoing halls, and sought the honor of the spear.[2]   The
youth was lovely as the first beam of the sun; few
were they who could meet him in fight!   My heroes
yielded to Cormalo: my daughter was seized in his
love.   Argon and Ruro returned from the chase; the
tears of their pride descend; they roll their silent eyes
on Runa's heroes, who had yielded to a stranger.
Three days they feasted with Cormalo: on the fourth
young Argon fought.   But who could fight with Argon!
Cormalo is overcome.   His heart swelled with the grief
of pride; he resolved, in secret, to behold the death of
my sons.   They went to the hills of Runa: they pursued the dark-brown hinds.   The arrow of Cormalo
flew in secret; my children fell in blood.   He came to
the maid of his love; to Inis-thona's long-haired maid.
They fled over the desert.   Annir remained alone.
Night came on, and day appeared: nor Argon's voice,
nor Ruro's came.   At length their much-loved dog was
seen; the fleet and bounding Runar.   He came into
the hall and howled; and seemed to look towards the
place of their fall.   We followed him: we found them
here: we laid them by this mossy stream.   This is the
haunt of Annir, when the chase of the hinds is past.

[1] A lake of Scandinavia, remarkable, in the days of Ossian, for emitting
a pestilential vapor in autumn. *And thou, O valiant Duchomar! like the
mist of marshy Lano; when it sails over the plains of autumn, and brings
death to the host.* — Fingal, B. i.

[2] The tournament practised among the ancient northern nations.

I bend like the trunk of an aged oak; my tears for
ever flow!"

"O Ronnan!" said the rising Oscar, "Ogar king of
spears! call my heroes to my side, the sons of streamy
Morven. To-day we go to Lano's water, that sends
forth the vapor of death. Cormalo will not long rejoice: death is often at the point of our swords!"

They came over the desert like stormy clouds, when
the winds roll them along the heath: their edges are
tinged with lightning; the echoing groves foresee the
storm! The horn of Oscar's battle is heard; Lano
shook over all its waves. The children of the lake
convened around the sounding shield of Cormalo.
Oscar fought, as he was wont in war. Cormalo fell
beneath his sword: the sons of dismal Lano fled to
their secret vales! Oscar brought the daughter of
Inis-thona to Annir's echoing halls. The face of age
is bright with joy; he blest the king of swords!

How great was the joy of Ossian, when he beheld
the distant sail of his son! it was like a cloud of light
that rises in the east, when the traveller is sad in a land
unknown; and dismal night, with her ghosts, is sitting
around in shades! We brought him with songs to
Selma's halls. Fingal spread the feast of shells. A
thousand bards raised the name of Oscar: Morven
answered to the sound. The daughter of Toscar was
there; her voice was like the harp; when the distant
sound comes, in the evening, on the soft-rustling breeze
of the vale!

O lay me, ye that see the light, near some rock of
my hills! let the thick hazels be around, let the rustling oak be near. Green be the place of my rest; let

the sound of the distant torrent be heard.   Daughter
of Toscar, take the harp, and raise the lovely song of
Selma; that sleep may overtake my soul in the midst
of joy; that the dreams of my youth may return, and
the days of the mighty Fingal.   Selma! I behold thy
towers, thy trees, thy shaded wall!   I see the heroes
of Morven; I hear the song of bards; Oscar lifts the
sword of Cormalo; a thousand youths admire its
studded thongs.   They look with wonder on my son:
They admire the strength of his arm.   They mark the
joy of his father's eyes; they long for an equal fame.
And ye shall have your fame, O sons of streamy Morven!   My soul is often brightened with song; I remember the friends of my youth.   But sleep descends
in the sound of the harp! pleasant dreams begin to
rise!   Ye sons of the chase stand far distant, nor disturb my rest.   The bard of other times holds discourse
with his fathers, the chiefs of the days of old!   Sons
of the chase, stand far distant! disturb not the dreams
of Ossian!